Neoliberalism and After?

GLOBAL
STUDIES IN
EDUCATION

A.C. (Tina) Besley, Michael A. Peters,
Cameron McCarthy, Fazal Rizvi
General Editors

Vol. 4

PETER LANG
New York • Washington, D.C./Baltimore • Bern
Frankfurt • Berlin • Brussels • Vienna • Oxford

Neoliberalism and After?

"In this crisp, elegant volume Michael A. Peters dissects the fascinating history of neoliberalism from its roots in the Mont Pelerin Society and German ordoliberalism, and the Chicago and Public Choice schools, to its irradiation through obscure think tanks into the world of public policy....Peters' style is urbane, his tenor is summative, and his analysis is crystal sharp. ...[He] sums up the experiences of a generation that critiqued the neoliberals without ever conquering them. He does this with pithy erudition and a terse command of the intellectual ardours of the past forty years."

—*Peter Murphy, Associate Professor of Communications, Monash University*

"Bringing together findings from several decades of observation and analysis, Michael A. Peters' cosmopolitan survey draws on the recent experience of his own country, Aotearoa/New Zealand, to sharply illuminate the impacts in several countries of neoliberal governmentality on public education policies, and their corrosive implications for public culture and social justice."

—*Colin Gordon, Royal Brompton & Harefield NHS Trust*

"World recessions are always turning points. In *Neoliberalism and After?* Michael A. Peters opens to clear-minded scrutiny the main political-economic ideas that evolved after the last world recession, that of the 1930s. Those ideas reached a dead end in 2008–2009. Critical scrutiny is vital if we are to clear away the rubble on the road—left by the wreckage of neoliberalism as both a guide to action and a system of rule—and move forward. This brilliant book demonstrates that in uncertain times, we have continuing resources with which to illuminate the next phase—the critique of liberal political philosophy, Foucault's demolition of control systems, creative cultures in universities and civil society, education as a universal welfare right and a condition of democratic advance."

—*Simon Marginson, Centre for the Study of Higher Education,*
University of Melbourne, Australia

"One of our leading contemporary social philosophers and educational theorists takes us on a journey across the complex and uneven contours of neoliberalism—a concept that is much used but rarely defined and exemplified so clearly as it is in this book. Peters examines neoliberalism's roots in the foundational ideologies and practices of modernity, tracing multiple lines of development through to its spectacular collapse in the financial contagion of 2008, and its subsequent virulent return. This book is an indispensable context-setting guide for all those with an interest in, and concern for, contemporary social and educational policy."

—*William Cope, Research Professor, Department of Educational Policy Studies,*
College of Education, University of Illinois, Urbana-Champaign

"There have been many efforts over many decades to promote (or defend) 'neoliberal' institutions and practices as the best basis for economic, legal, political, social, and moral order in complex social formations. Neoliberalism began life as an intellectual-cum-political project in 1938; enjoyed growing acceptance as an economic and political strategy in the 1970s; witnessed panic-stricken meetings in New York and Washington in 2008 at the height of the global financial crisis; and, currently, seems to be a key element in 'the new normal.' It has been applied across many fields of social life with significant effects in most of them. Michael A. Peters' excellent new book illustrates many of these general points and details their impact in the educational field."

—*Bob Jessop, Sociology Department, Lancaster University*

Michael A. Peters

Neoliberalism and After?

Education, Social Policy, and the Crisis of Western Capitalism

PETER LANG
New York • Washington, D.C./Baltimore • Bern
Frankfurt • Berlin • Brussels • Vienna • Oxford

Library of Congress Cataloging-in-Publication Data

Peters, Michael A.
Neoliberalism and after?: education, social policy,
and the crisis of Western capitalism / Michael A. Peters.
p. cm. — (Global studies in education; v. 4)
Includes bibliographical references.
1. Education and state—United States.
2. Educational change—Social aspects—United States.
3. Education and globalization—United States. 4. Capitalism.
5. Socialism. 6. Social conflict. I. Title.
LC191.4.P48 379.73—dc22 2011003400
ISBN 978-1-4331-1206-5 (hardcover)
ISBN 978-1-4331-1205-8 (paperback)
ISSN 2153-330X

Bibliographic information published by **Die Deutsche Nationalbibliothek.**
Die Deutsche Nationalbibliothek lists this publication in the "Deutsche
Nationalbibliografie"; detailed bibliographic data is available
on the Internet at http://dnb.d-nb.de/.

Cover image © Michael McGuerty

The paper in this book meets the guidelines for permanence and durability
of the Committee on Production Guidelines for Book Longevity
of the Council of Library Resources.

Contents

Acknowledgments

These essays were written over the course of a career engagement with 'neoliberalism' spanning a period over thirty years from the viewpoint of someone trained in philosophy and education. I first started writing about the political ideology known as neoliberalism in the late 1980s from the perspective of one trained as a philosopher of education. I had completed my PhD in 1984 on 'The Problem of Rationality' a thesis that provided an interpretation of Ludwig Wittgenstein and earlier had majored in philosophy of science at the University of Canterbury and completed an MA in Philosophy at the University of Auckland, New Zealand. New Zealand as it turned out was an important 'experiment' of the internationalization of neoliberalism.

I was fortunate to be born and grow up in New Zealand and was in reality part of the last welfare generation to get an entitlement of free education and health from a well-developed welfare state. My philosophy degrees in some sense also were the result of having the freedom to study what I considered to be my interests and my passion rather than a meal-ticket and while the philosophy degrees, at least the courses that I took, said nothing directly about neoliberalism (or liberalism for that matter—these themes were to be found in politics departments) they did give me the analytical skills to pursue the contours of neoliberalism. Actually, philosophy in New Zealand had been dominated by Karl Popper, who was an original member of the Mount Pelerin Society and who wrote *The Open Society and Its Enemies* while professor of philosophy at the University of Canterbury during the late 1930s and early 1940s, yet philosophers had little to say about the rise of neoliberalism in New Zealand.

I started writing about neoliberalism in the mid 1980s shortly after the Labour Party took the Treasury benches and I worked on the 'politics of choice,' the ideology of individualism and community in political thought, the 'new right' and the crisis of the welfare state. I worked closely with James Marshall who later became the Dean of Education at the University of Auckland and Jim helped me to get clearer about the history of liberalism. He had a capacity to study historical origins that enabled me to see clearly the political continuities between liberalism and neoliberalism; and later, through his work on Foucault he influenced me and a generation of scholars in New Zealand that became his and later our students as they moved through their careers to take up academic positions themselves: Nesta Devine, Patrick Fitzsimons, Janet Mansfield, Peter Fitzsimons, Ruth Irwin, Andrew Gibbons and many others. These people helped to form a community of scholars at Auckland University who along with colleagues such as Colin Lankshear, Roger Dale, Peter Roberts, Graham Smith, Susan Robertson, Alison Jones, Linda Smith, Eve Coxon, Eric Braithwaite and others, developed into a nucleus that provided a constant stream of analysis in the New Zealand context. This grouping also had links with the geographers, anthropologists and those in Maori studies at Auckland, including in particular, Warren Moran (Dean of Arts), Ranganui Walker, and Nick Lewis. There were of course links with their scholars around the country particularly with educationists at Canterbury (Huge Lauder, John Freeman-Moir, Liz Gordon) and Massey University at Palmerston North (John Codd, Richard Harker, Roy Nash, John Clark). A strong friend and colleague was Mark Olssen at Otago University whose career suffered for his socialist beliefs—Otago was a Popper stronghold in New Zealand.

I was also fortunate in that having chosen education over philosophy and in the company of good colleagues I began to get a taste of the practical side of politics especially around educational issues. During the early 1990s Henry Giroux and Peter McLaren reached out across the Pacific to offer publishing opportunities and also to acquaint me with what was happening in the U.S. I have been forever grateful for their generosity. In this context I should also mention the generosity of Ron Barnett at the London Institute of Education. Very few of the philosophers of education in the U.K. at that point seemed interested in the politics of education.

By the early to mid 1990s, after discovering Jean-François Lyotard's work in 1984 I had also discovered the tradition of French philosophy and particularly the work of Michel Foucault. Jim Marshall by that time had also picked up Foucault's books and quickly established himself as a leading commentator, especially in relation to the theme of the 'autonomous chooser.' In this period we wrote together over 30 papers, many in terms of applied policy in relation to the neoliberal reforms of education in New Zealand and written within a Foucauldian perspective. Some of these writings found their way into government through the Royal Commission of Social Policy in 1988 but also through evaluations of Maori education that had become marginalized by neoliberal politics. I was soon absorbed in academic politics, becoming a member of the branch executive of the Association of University teachers (AUT) and then its national vice-president.

It was a strange and heady mix of New Zealand policy and politics, neoliberal internationalism, French philosophy, and educational theory. I continued this line of thinking in new locations first in Scotland (United Kingdom) and then Illinois in the United States. At the University of Glasgow (2000–2005) I was able to study philosophers and political economists of the Scottish Enlightenment like Adam Smith, David Hume and Adam Ferguson. Later at the University of Illinois (2005-) I began by teaching a Masters' course in the political economy of education focusing on neoliberalism and neoconservatism. In courses like these I never strayed too far from the political and historical context within which education has its place, teaching a course in 2010 on the concept of global citizenship and running a PhD reading group on Foucault's (2008) *Birth of Biopolitics*—his lectures on the birth of neoliberalism in Germany and the U.S. My thanks go to Rodrigo Britez, Dan Araya, Hüseyin Esen, James Geary, Margaret Fitzpatrick, James Thayer, and Mousumi Mukherjee in this class and to Global Studies PhD students— Ergin Bulut, Viviana Pitton, Garret Gietzen, Melvin Armstrong, Gabriela Walker, Dave Ondercin, and Tze-Chang Liu—who have helped me work through my ideas either directly through collaborative writing or indirectly through discussion and conversation. In this context also I should mention my great colleagues at the University of Illinois Fazal Rizvi, Cameron McCarthy and Tina Besley, all of whom have written extensively on neoliberalism in relation to policy and theory. McCarthy and Besley, in addition, have both written on Foucault in relation to Foucault. I am fortunate indeed to have such great colleagues.

This collection is a result of a long-term engagement with neoliberalism as a intellectual system, ideology and set of policies. Finally, I would like to thank Chris Myers, Bernadette Shade and the production team at Peter Lang whose combined support, enthusiasm and professionalism make the task of writing and publishing a real pleasure.

Chapter 3. Neoliberalism and the Emergence of Knowledge as Intellectual Capital appears in Roberts, P. & Peters, M.A. *Neoliberalism, Scholarship and Intellectual Life* Rotterdam, Sense Publishers, 2008; Chapter 4. Neoliberalism, Higher Education and the Knowledge Economy: From the Free Market to

Knowledge Capitalism (with Mark Olssen) first appeared in *Journal of Education Policy 20,* (3): 313–345, 2005; Chapter 5. Neoliberalism, the Market and Performativity first appeared in *International Encyclopedia of Education,* 3rd Edition. Penny Enslin (Section editor). Editors-in-Chief: Barry McGaw, Eva Baker and Penelope P Peterson. Oxford: Elsevier; 2010; Chapter 6. Neoliberal Governmentality: Foucault on the Birth of Biopolitics first appeared in S. Weber & S. Maurer (Eds.): *Gouvernementalität und Erziehungswissenschaft* (Governmentality and educational science), VS Verlag (Publisher for Social Sciences VS), Wiesbaden, Germany, pp.37–50, 2006; Chapter 7. The Politics of Postmodernity and the Promise of Education, first appeared in *Access: Critical Perspectives on Communication, Cultural & Policy Studies,* 21 (1) 2002: 33–52; Chapter 8, Governmentality, Education and the End of Neoliberalism? first appeared in Peters, M.A., Besley, T., Olssen, M., Maurer, S. Weber, S. (Eds.) *Governmentality Studies in Education,* Rotterdam, Sense Publishers, 2009; Chapter 9. The Global Failure of Neoliberalism: Privatize Profits; Socialize Losses, first appeared in *Global–e, A Global Studies Journal,* 2008: http://global-ejournal.org/2008/11/06/the-global-failure-of-neoliberalism-privatize-profits-social-ize-losses/; Chapter 10, Global Recession, Unemployment and the Changing Economics of the Self, first appeared in *Policy Futures in Education,* 7 (1): 129-133, 2009.

Michael A. Peters,
University of Illinois
1st September 2010

Introduction

NEOLIBERALISM REPRESENTS A STRUGGLE between two forms of welfare or social policy discourse based on opposing and highly charged ideological metaphors of 'individualism' and 'community.' One form posits the sovereign individual or family emphasizing the primacy over community and State; the other, what might be called a rejuvenated social democratic model, inverts the hierarchy of value to emphasize community or 'the social' over the individual. As such it is an intellectual struggle that runs through twentieth century thought and traverses a range of subjects, with roots going back at least to the Enlightenment in different native traditions. It is therefore complex, subtle and dynamic, changing its historical and disciplinary forms as it matured as a political doctrine, international movement, and set of political and policy practices.

Since the early 1980s the terms 'individual' and 'community'—and their associated ideologies, individualism and communitarianism—have defined the ideological space within which competing conceptions of the state, of welfare, and of education have been articulated. In countries around the world, the reform of the core public sector, the massive privatisation program involving state assets sales, the restructuring of health and education, the welfare benefit cuts in the 1990s, and the historically high levels of unemployment bear witness to the triumph of an ideology of individualism over one of community. Indeed, since the mid-1980s many countries have experienced the effects of an experiment modeled on a neoliberal view of community: broadly speaking, that of 'a society in which free individuals pursue their own interests in the marketplace according to agreed rules of conduct, and thereby maximise the use of information and resources to the benefit of the community as a whole' (Upton, 1987:21). This view of community as 'the free society' implies a restricted role for government with clear limitations in providing certain common goods by way of taxation—the nightwatchman state. In short, this neoliberal view rests on an ideology of individualism as the most fundamental and unifying premise which emphasizes individual responsibility within a free-market economy and, thereby, defends the notion of the minimal state on moral as well as efficiency grounds.

New Zealand, while a paradigm example and neoliberal experiment, is only one place where neoliberalism became a set of policies that changed the political landscape. Neoliberalism is often seen in terms of doctrine as beginning in Chile with the 'Chicago boys'—a group of Chilean economists influenced by the Chicago School—and Pinochet's deposing of Allende in 1973. But things have changed, or so it seems.

The era of market fundamentalism came to an abrupt end when in 2008 the American financial system underwent internal bleeding wreaking havoc on economies around the world with spread effects that imperiled Iceland, the Eurozone and economies of East Asia. It is no longer fashionable to hold that the market can provide for the public good. The ideology had begun to unravel and it began to unravel quickly in Latin America which as the hothouse for neoliberalism since the international debt crisis of the early 1980s had suffered large and uneven increases of inequality alongside slow growth rates. Then beginning with Hugo Chavez's victory at the polls in Venezuela in 1998, a succession of progressive populist governments came to power across the Latin America, each advertising itself against the neoliberalism that ruled the previous era.

Laura Macdonald and Arne Ruckert (2009) argue that Latin America's turn to the Left reflected popular disenchantment with the performance of neoliberalism as well as the political desire to rescue the principle that governments have a central role to play in ensuring social justice. At the same time neo-Keynesian redistributive policies of the Obama administration also became increasingly apparent with an unparalleled stimulus that followed the equally large bail-out of American banks initiated by Henry Paulson under George W. Bush.

Laura Macdonald and Arne Ruckert (2009) point out that 'post-neoliberalism' does not mean the complete rejection of all that came before. Latin American governments maintained low inflation rates, tried to balance budgets, kept free-floating exchange rates and attempted to attract foreign direct investment. They did not try to restore protectionist barriers that had fallen with the region-wide shift toward liberalised trade, although significantly they began to experiment with innovative approaches to social policy and modest initiatives to boost employment, alongside the commitment to land reforms and the nationalisation of industry such as oil in Venezuela.

Just as the timing and scope of neoliberal waves of reform took place unevenly so too the unraveling of neoliberalism has taken place differentially with Latin America taking the lead in social policy and poverty alleviation in a post-neoliberal settlement while North America remained firmly neoliberal, at least until Obama's ascendency.

In a strong sense the essays in this collection also record the tension between Marxism or neo-Marxism and forms of postmodernism or, more properly speaking, poststructuralism, especially the work of Jean-François Lyotard, Michel Foucault and Jacques Derrida. There was great suspicion about postmodernism by the traditional Left even though they didn't really understand what it meant. On more than one occasion while I was leading the union of university teachers, members would come up to me and ask how was it possible for me to be a 'postmodernist' and at the same time work for solidarity. In the field of education the split between the neo-Marxist sociologists and the (few) educational philosophers drawing on modes of poststructuralist thought was more than apparent. In some quarters it is still the case that these groups look furtively at each other while huddling together in separate groups. Yet the postmodern attack on mainstream economics had already begun even if the Chicago hegemony has persisted beyond its own shelf-life.

Luther Tweeten and Carl Zulauf (1999) were among the first to note the challenge of postmodernism to applied economics arguing that analytic philosophy has dominated economics at least since Adam Smith and that postmodernism, springing from Continental philosophy, has the potential 'to influence how applied economists choose problems worthy of research, how they analyze those problems, and how they interpret results.' They trace the three grandfathers of postmodernism—Marx, Freud and Nietzsche—before analyzing the influence of 'three fathers of postmodernism'—Lyotard, Foucault, and Derrida. While they claim that postmodernism is replacing Marxism as the ideology of protest movements but has nihilistic impulses, they also acknowledge that 'applied economists who see a brighter future through science, technology, sound economics, and rational processes of democratic-capitalism can learn much from postmodernists.'

Tweeten and Zulauf's (1999) call has been taken up by others. As Matthias Klaes (2008) writes in the *New Palgrave Dictionary of Economics* postmodernism is a recent concept for economics and yet one that implies a certain stance on history and world views especially inherent in notions of the modern and modernization and their equivalents in the concept of postmodern and postmodernization; and, of course, the concept of postmodernity itself that has engendered much discussion in the literature by neo-Marxists like Fredric Jameson and David Harvey, as well as poststructuralist thinkers. Klaes also notes that both John Maynard Keynes and Gary Becker have been interpreted in postmodern terms, especially in relation to questions of methodology. The rationalist basis of much modern economics, including rational actor paradigm and mathematical modeling has been subject to postmodern epistemological critique. In particular, readings of the economic subject and decentered economic selves have followed the de-psychologization of *homo economicus* (e.g. Cullenberg et al., 2001; Davis, 2003; Mirowski, 2003).

Phillip Mirowski and Dieter Plehwe (2009) in *The Road from Mont Pèlerin: the Making of the Neoliberal Thought Collective* have begun critical historiographies of neoliberalism encouraged by the work of Foucault and Harvey focusing on the Colloque Walter Lippmann and including chapters on French neoliberalism (François Denord), liberalism and neoliberalism in Britain in the period (1930–80) (Kenneth Tribe), neoliberalism in Germany and the ordoliberal foundations of the social market economy (Ralf Ptak), the rise of the Chicago School of Economics and the birth of neoliberalism (Philip Mirowski and Rob van Horn), the origins of neoliberal economic development discourse (Dieter Plehwe), the Mont Pelerin Society (Kim Phillips-Fein), the influence of neoliberals in Chile (Karin Fischer), among other topics. Mirowski (2009) suggests that fundamentally neoliberalism is a doctrine that is held together by a set of epistemic commitments (p. 417) that focuses on a constructivism which not only denies objectivism but also substitutes the market as a knowledge discovery mechanism.

My approach to neoliberalism in the chapters that follow is in terms of critical historiographies that emphasize different eras, transitions, mutations, and histories. It is strongly influenced by Foucault's work as is clearly evident from the chapters that follow. At the same time I am sympathetic to neo-marxist critique of the capitalist system as a whole. It seems more relevant than ever especially in the age of the system and the system-event where one change can affect other parts of the system and can trigger system-events leading to collapse, that it is necessary to have some understanding of systems theory and second-order cybernetics. The understanding of the capitalist *system* can be enhanced by the best models of systems theory in mathematics and the new biology in order to promote analysis of the delicate intricacies not only of social systems but also their interface with natural systems of all kinds. In my view this is where future research needs to be directed. We need to look to knowledge and learning systems that provide the basis for forms of economy that are green and sustainable in the long term (Peters, 2010; Peters et al., 2010).

1

Neoliberalism and After?

Education, Social Policy and the Crisis of Western Capitalism

SINCE THE EARLY 1980S, WITH THE ELECTION of the Reagan and Thatcher Governments, the current era has been dominated by contemporary forms of neoliberalism that have colonized the future with a view of the market and globalization as the political project of world economic integration based on the cosmopolitan ideology of 'free trade.' Neoliberalism has its immediate roots in debates that took place in the 1920s and 1930s over the efficiency of the market and the role of the state and government failure. It received its ideological starting point in the setting up of the Mt Pelerin Society by Hayek in 1947 and it is undeniably still the ruling ideology even though it has transmuted in form a number of times since its rearticulation by the Austrian school, the Freiburg 'law and economics' school (*ordoliberlen*), and the Chicago School in the early 1960s. The Mont Pelerin Society comprised some thirty-six scholars mostly economists who used the forum 'to facilitate an exchange of ideas between like-minded scholars in the hope of strengthening the principles and practice of a free society and to study the workings, virtues, and defects of market-oriented economic systems.'[1] The Society included eight Nobel Prize-winning economists (Hayek, Friedman, Stigler, Buchanan, Allias, Coarse, Becker and Smith) as well as members of the Austrian school and the philosopher Karl Popper. A flavor of the organisation and its liberal causes immediately after WWII with the defeat of Nazi Germany, the rise of Soviet Russia and the beginning of the Cold War can be gained from the Statement of Aims which begins:

The central values of civilization are in danger. Over large stretches of the earth's surface the essential conditions of human dignity and freedom have already disappeared. In others they are under constant menace from the development of current tendencies of policy. The position of the individual and the voluntary group are progressively undermined by extensions of arbitrary power. Even that most precious possession of Western Man, freedom of thought and expression, is threatened by the spread of creeds which, claiming the privilege of tolerance when in the position of a minority, seek only to establish a position of power in which they can suppress and obliterate all views but their own (http://www.montpelerin.org/mpsGoals.cfm).

The Statement went on to develop an agenda based around the moral and economic origins of 'crisis,' the redefinition of the functions of the state and the differences between the totalitarian and the liberal order, methods of re-establishing the rule of law, means for upholding the freedom and rights of the individual, the smooth functioning of the market, ways of dealing with creeds hostile to liberalism, and 'the creation of an international order conducive to the safeguarding of peace and liberty and permitting the establishment of harmonious international economic relations.' The context of the immediate postwar period provides a useful lens when the world was still reeling from State phobia and concerned with reconstruction of West Germany and Japan as bulwarks against the spread of Soviet influence. In writing the history of neoliberalism it is important to emphasize the continuities with classical liberalism and also the difference between 'theory' and the actual historical experience of different countries.

During the 1980s a distinctive strand of neoliberalism emerged as the dominant paradigm of public policy in the West and continues to exert influence: citizens were redefined as individual consumers of newly competitive public services with the consequence that 'welfare rights' have become commodified as consumer rights; the public sector itself underwent considerable 'downsizing' as governments pursued an agenda of commercialization, corporatization and incremental privatization; often management of public services, following principles of 'new public management' and emulating private sector styles, was delegated rather than genuinely devolved, while executive power became concentrated even more at the centre. Nowhere was this shift more evident than in the related areas of education and social policy. In many OECD countries there has been a clear shift away from universality to a 'modest safety net.' The old welfare goals of participation and belonging in countries committed to principles of social democracy were abolished. User-charges for social services and education were introduced across the board. Sometimes these changes were accompanied, especially at the height of the New

Right ascendancy, by substantial cuts in benefits and other forms of income support and eligibility criteria for all forms of welfare have been tightened up under the guise of 'accountability.' Targeting of social assistance became the new ethos of social philosophy and there was, in addition, a greater policing of the welfare economy aimed at reducing benefit fraud. The stated goal of neoliberals has been to free people from the dependence on state welfare and some commentators have talked of the shift from welfare to workfare, where stable employment is now taken as the basis for participation in society. The old welfare policies, allegedly, discouraged effort and self-reliance and, in the eyes of neoliberals can be held responsible for *producing* young illiterates, juvenile delinquents, alcoholics, substance abusers, school truants, 'dysfunctional families' and drug addicts.

This particular variant of neoliberalism, which revitalizes the master discourse of neoclassical economic liberalism, has been remarkably successful in advancing a *foundationalist* and *universalist* reason as a basis for a radical global reconstruction of all aspects of society and economy. A form of economic reason encapsulated in the notion of *homo economicus*, with its abstract and universalist assumptions of individuality, rationality and self-interest, has captured the policy agendas of most Western countries and also been the basis for structural adjustment policies imposed in other parts of the world. Part of its innovation has been the way in which the neoliberal master narrative has successfully extended the principle of self-interest into the status of a paradigm for understanding politics itself, and, in fact, not merely market but *all* behavior and human action. Consequently, in the realm of education policy, especially in the U.S. and OECD countries but also in developing countries, at every opportunity the market has been substituted for the state: citizens are now 'customers' and state agencies are 'providers.' In education the notion of vouchers and creeping privatization is suggested as a universal panacea to problems of funding and quality, and the teaching/learning relation has been reduced to an implicit contract between buyer and seller.

Two Liberalisms: 'Individual' and 'Community'

In the West today there is an ongoing struggle between two forms of liberty and society that originates in two forms of liberalism—on the one hand, classical liberalism that developed in nineteenth century England based on the ideals of individual liberty, rational self-interest, property rights, limited government, free markets and laissez-faire capitalism, and, on the other, social or welfare liberalism arising out of the critique of classical liberalism and criticisms of the performance of capitalism, especially during the Great Depression and more recently in the global economic recession of the mid-2000s. Welfare liberalism, by contrast with classical liberalism, is committed to a social market economy based upon equality of opportunity, social rights, multi-party and sometimes also social democracy, social justice and government intervention to provide full employment. Economic and social policy discourse over the last century has been based on opposing and highly charged ideological metaphors of 'individual' and 'community' and the associated political ideologies and methodologies of individualism and communitarianism. One form posits the sovereign individual as logically prior and separate from society, emphasizing the primacy of the individual over community and State; the other, emphasizing a concept of positive rights and universal welfare within a social democratic model, inverts the hierarchy of value to emphasize community and 'the social' over the individual. These two views representing both ends of the spectrum of liberalism clearly differ over the metaphysics of the nature of the self and society. Classical liberals like Mill and Bentham maintained that individuals are ontologically prior, while Hegelian and idealist philosophers in the nineteenth century and after, strongly influenced by Darwin, criticized radical individualism and emphasised society as an organism and the individual as part of a larger social whole. This debate has erupted again and again in the twentieth century over that nature of radical individualism, methodological individualism, the agent of choice, the purely rational autonomous chooser, forms of collectivism, 'organicism,' the communitarian critique, relational and historical ontology, group, minority and cultural rights, and most recently, the nature of 'networks.'

The fundamental liberal principle accords liberty the prime political value (Gaus, 1996: 162–166) and any law or form of authority must be justified in so far as they limit the freedom of citizens. The onus of justification is on anyone who departs from individual liberty. While liberals may be able to agree on the fundament political value of freedom they disagree about the content or description of liberty and therefore also differ on the tasks and basic functions of government. Those who embrace a negative view of liberty such as Isaiah Berlin (1969) maintain that the individual is free to the extent that no one interferes with his actions—freedom is understood as the absence of coercion; those that embrace a positive view of liberty such as the British philosopher Thomas Green argue that a person is free only if she is self-directed or autonomous. This view of the ideal of the free person based on the concept of autonomy has its roots in Rousseau and Kant.

Liberal political theory thus splinters over the concept of freedom and also its relationship to the concept of property and market-based society. Classical liberals see liberty and private property as conceptually related, if not the same thing ('my rights are my property'), and suggest that market society based on private property is the embodiment of freedom. Welfare liberals challenge the connection between personal liberty and private property as the market basis of a free society questioning the stability of the market and its power to distribute wealth and generate economic and social equality such that no group advances at the expense of another. One side blames 'government failure'; the other emphasizes 'market failure.'

The modern Kantian John Rawls (2001) in his classic *Political Liberalism* introduces the concept of pluralism and suggests the main problem today is:

> How is it possible that there may exist over time a stable and just society of free and equal citizens profoundly divided by reasonable though incompatible religious, philosophical, and moral doctrines? Put another way: How is it possible that deeply opposed though reasonable comprehensive doctrines may live together and all affirm the political conception of a constitutional regime? What is the structure and content of a political conception that can gain the support of such an overlapping consensus? (p. xviii).

He explains further that 'the aim of political liberalism is to uncover the conditions of the possibility of a reasonable public basis of justification on fundamental political questions' (p. xix). For Rawls this conception rests on a form of political and moral constructivism that argues for a version of 'justice as fairness.' In one sense Rawls is concerned with the basic fact and problem of pluralism, tolerance and fairness especially as it developed historically through and over religious conflicts from the Reformation onwards. This is not the place to entertain criticisms of Rawls' conception except to say that it is not clear how Rawls' overlapping consensus settles the disputes between classical and social or welfare liberals. Rawls is concerned with similar matters—problems about the grounds of basic civil liberties, the limits of political obligation, and the justice of economic and other inequalities—but he bypasses the utilitarian thought of Hume, Mill and Sidgwick, to rehabilitate the tradition of Locke, Rousseau and, above all, Kant, based on the idea of social contract. In other words, basic civil and political rights are sacrosanct and the state's first duty is to respect this capacity for autonomy among its citizens. He gives first priority to the right over the good, that is, to claims based on the rights of individuals over all other claims including those that result from claims for the good life and he reconciles basic freedoms through the artifice of the 'original position'—a 'veil of ignorance' that operates to screen out any prior knowledge of race, gender, social class, talents and abilities, religious beliefs or conception of the good life when a group of individuals come together to agree on the basic constitution of a society (Rawls, 1971). Later Rawls (2001) relinquished his earlier view expressed in a *Theory of Justice* that liberal principles might be realized in a 'capitalist welfare state' to hold they could only be achieved in either 'a property-owning democracy' characterized by universally high levels of education and 'the widespread ownership of productive assets,' or in a market-socialist regime.

The Emergence of Neoliberalism

The narrative of classical liberalism and its holy trinity of individual liberty, property rights and the free market is the story of the twentieth century—of decline and rise of liberalism in the post-war period, the defeat of Fascism, the reconstruction of the German and Japanese economies, the spread of liberal democracy, the fall of the Soviet system, and the globalization of the free market. Central to this historical story—essentially European and Anglo-American in origin—is first the decline of liberalism in the late nineteenth century and its rise in the post-war period, and alongside this development, the organized revival of classical liberalism beginning with members of the Austrian school at the turn of the century and particularly with Ludwig von Mises who wrote his tract *Liberalism* in 1927. His *Socialism: An Economic and Sociological Analysis* (orig. 1922) is a critique of the economics of socialism and a refutation of collectivist methodology. In the Preface to the English edition of 1950 there is no mistaking his original intentions, when he writes:

> The world is split today into two hostile camps, fighting each other with the utmost vehemence, Communists and anti-Communists. They both aim at the abolition of private enterprise and private ownership of the means of production and at the establishment of socialism. They want to substitute totalitarian government control for the market economy....The great ideological conflict of our age must not be confused with the mutual rivalries among the various totalitarian movements. The real issue is not who should run the totalitarian apparatus. The real problem is whether or not socialism should supplant the market economy (http://mises.org.books/socialism/contents.aspx).

In the Epilogue to this work added in 1947 and originally titled 'Planned Chaos' von Mises comments on the failure of interventionism and questions the alleged inevitability of socialism. Von Mises was a highly influential economist and member of the Austrian school who recruited Friedrich von Hayek and significantly influenced the likes of Wilhelm Röpke and Alfred Müller-Armack, both advisors to Ludwig Erhard, who was Minister of Economics under Chancellor Konrad Adenauer after 1949 and responsible for Germany's economic recovery after

WWII. Von Mises also knew well Jacques Rueff, economic advisor to Charles de Gaulle as well as Lionel Robbins, Director of the London School of Economics and Luigi Einaudi, the President of Italy. He became a founding member of the Mont Pelerin Society.

The Austrian school was one of four main geographical schools of economic liberalism that was responsible for the revival of classical liberalism especially after WWII, along with German ordoliberalism, so called after ORDO the title of the German periodical established by the Law and Economics movement at the University of Freiburg in the 1930s. American neoliberalism based on the Chicago school established by Frank Knight who with Jacob Viner presided over the school from the 1920s to the 1960s, became increasingly important once Milton Friedman and his friend George Stigler provided a restatement of a free market political philosophy that determined the research agenda for the discipline of economics for at least a generation. Friedman became economic advisor to Ronald Reagan and trained the group of young Chilean economists known as the 'Chicago boys' who were responsible for carrying out economic liberalization, privatization of state owned companies, and stabilization of inflation under the ruling military junta headed by General Augusto Pinochet, after the coup in 1973. While economic liberalism took many other distinctive forms public choice theory (PCT) associated with James Buchanan and Gordon Tullock at University of Virginia and Virginia Polytechnic Institute and State University, and later associated with George Mason University, deserves special mention. While PCT is ostensibly concerned with the theory of political organisation its method and form of conceptual analysis derives from economics. Buchanan and Tullock's (1962) *The Calculus of Consent: Logical Foundations of Constitutional Democracy* was a founding text for an academic society that developed quickly after 1965 and became a major tool of analysis and methodology that regarded politics as market based on an economic theory of democracy beginning from the 'individualist postulate' and treating the citizen as a consumer of state services.

These schools of economic liberalism geographically located in Austria, Germany, France, the United Kingdom and the U.S. provided the basis for the internationalist orientation it took on with learned societies, journals, university departments and international symposia, colloquia and the establishment of liberal think-tanks like the Mont Pelerin Society, predating the huge growth of some 1200 U.S. think-tanks in the postwar era, many international, most offering 'independent' economic advice and analysis.[2] Two historical moments prefigure the shape, direction and influence of neoliberalism, especially as embedded economic policy both within the national administrations of the Thatcher and Reagan governments in the 1980s and as the basis for neoliberal globalization under the flag of the 'Washington consensus' in the 1990s and administrated by the World Bank (WB) and International Monetary Fund (IMF): the Walter Lippmann Colloque in 1938 and the establishment of the Mont Pelerin Society in 1947.

Colloque Walter Lippmann, 1938

Louis Rougier was a French philosopher—the only French member of the Vienna Circle and friend of both Hans Reichenbach and Moritz Schlick—strongly influenced by Poincaré and Wittgenstein who made an original contribution on the status of logical systems called 'conventionalism' that closely resembled the main articles of logical empiricism. He argued that logical propositions are neither necessarily true and therefore not deducible nor to be discovered empirically through induction. Rougier was also a political philosopher who belonged to the liberal tradition of Montesquieu and Tocqueville basing his account of liberal politics on the same notion of 'conventionalism' arguing as there are no eternal truths political systems must be chosen on pragmatic grounds of how well they work. On this basis in the early 1930s after a visit to the Soviet Union he became convinced that planned economies do not function as well as market economies.

Rougier, the author of over twenty-four books, has largely disappeared from history except as a footnote to the origin of the term 'neoliberalism.' Louis Rougier used the term 'neoliberalism' in reference to a meeting of a group of twenty-five prominent intellectuals committed to the revitalization of liberalism in Paris in 1938 that he organized under the title 'La Colloque Walter Lippmann' based around a discussion of Lippmann's (1937) *The Good Society*. The group included Friedrich Hayek, Ludwig von Mises, both Austrian School economists, the Hungarian philosopher of science, Michel Polyani, Raymond Aron, the French political philosopher, Jacques Rueff, the French conservative economist, Wihelm Röpke and Alexander Rüstow, German ordoliberals responsible for developing the 'social market economy' in the postwar period, Ernest Mercier, the French entrepreneur, as well as Lippmann and Rougier himself. The meeting acted as a prototype and inspired Hayek to set up the Mont Pelerin Society in 1947, almost a decade later. What was interesting about this group was that it was decidedly internationalist and that it included philosophers, economists and entrepreneurs. This implies that the birth of neoliberalism is not to be conflated with neoclassicial economics as Harvey (2005) does or even with a broad reductive economicism popularized by Pierre Bourdieu. From the beginning it is in part at least a broad political project that aimed at the revival of a form of liberalism especially in the light of the growth of the overweening Nazi state and the rise of state power associated with totalitarianism.

Rougier's connection to the Vienna Circle is not just an accident of history but speaks to a larger historical engagement with Austrian liberalism and the Austrian mind in fin-de-siècle Vienna (Johnson, 1972; Janik & Toulmin, 1973) that provides the backdrop for concerns of liberalism as a failed project and the need to rejuvenate liberalism. As Carl Schorske (1980) remarks:

> Austrian liberalism, like that of most other European nations, had its heroic age in the struggle against aristocracy and baroque absolutism. This ended in the stunning defeat of 1848. The chastened liberals came to power and established a constitutional regime in the 1860s almost by default. Not their own internal strength, but the defeats of the old order at the hands of foreign enemies brought the liberals to the helm of the state. From the first they had to share their power with the aristocracy and the imperial bureaucracy. Even during their two decades of rule, the liberals' social base remained weak, confined to the middle-class Germans and German Jews of the urban centers. Increasingly identified with capitalism, they maintained parliamentary power by the undemocratic device of the restricted franchise (p. 45).

The aims of Austrian liberalism at this point were to develop a form of constitutional monarchy; to encourage entrepreneurs to replace nobility as ruling class and the propagation of scientific rationalism to replace superstitious Catholicism. The long depression after the panic in 1873 lead to heavily anti-capitalist and anti-liberal sentiments and the liberal movement in Austria began to decline with pan-German sentiments and support gaining ground. It was against this background that Carl Menger published his *Principles of Economics* in 1871 challenging classical theories of value with his subjective theory of value. He founded the Austrian school in 1883 in opposition to the historical school of German economics led by Gustav von Schmoller. The Austrian school became firmly established after Menger's *Investigations into the Method of the Social Sciences with Special Reference to Economics* and *The Errors of Historicism in German Economics* lead to the famous *Methodenstreit,* or methodological debate with the historicists over the epistemological status of economics.

Walter Lippmann, the American intellectual journalist, was the co-founder of the Socialist Club at Harvard University who rejected his earlier socialism to become a supporter of Woodrow Wilson and the Democratic Party in 1916. In *The Good Society* Lippmann begins with 'The Providential State' to cast aspersions on the then current 'dogma' of central planning and control of economic activity. Against all forms of collectivism Lippmann pits the reconstruction of liberalism, outlining the basic differences between Adam Smith and Karl Marx, and suggesting that liberalism in the second half of the nineteenth century was 'decadent' leading politicians to abandon it and embrace collectivism. Thereupon he outlines the principles of liberalism and the government of a liberal state ending with the 'testament' and 'pursuit' of liberty. *The Good Society*, influenced by the Austrian School, was an answer to Laski's (1933) *Democracy in Crisis* which focused on the inability of capitalism to provide for the working class. Lippmann's riposte was to argue that collectivism degenerated into totalitarianism, thus identifying himself with the liberalism of Mises, Hayek and Lionel Robbins. Lippmann sent Hayek the proofs of the book. He wanted to start a systematic investigation of the 'Agenda of Liberalism' (the title of one of Lipmann's chapters) which Hayek thought would serve well as the name of a journal. Lippmann made clear that the liberal state was far removed from laissez faire and in line with a progressive taxation system and better distribution and equalization of incomes with public expenditure of health, education and public works. He even applauded Roosevelt's adoption of Keynesian policies for ending the depression. Lippmann's purpose as he states in the Introduction is to 'find out why the development of the liberal doctrine was arrested and why liberalism lost its influence on human affairs' (p.xlvii).

At the 'Colloque Walter Lippmann,' Lippmann thus presented a picture that differed both from European socialism and the laissez-faire Manchester school. His call for a new liberal project, already well supported by Hayek, eventually took the name 'neoliberalism' after the original recommendation by Rüstow who in a seminal 1932 paper had argued for both a free economy *and* a strong state (Hartwich, 2009). Rüstow, as one of the German ordoliberals though not a member of the Freiberg School, emphasized that the state must create the necessary legal environment for the economy if it is to reach it maximum allocative efficiency, to protect against the possibility of the emergence of monopoly and to safeguard healthy competition. The Freiberg School established by Franz Böhm, Walter Eucken, and Hans Großmann-Doerth theorized the legitimate role of government in a democracy arguing that only some forms of competition are good. The term 'Ordoliberalism' was also the title of a journal called ORDO: *Jahrbuch für die Ordnung von Wirtschaft und Gesellschaft* (*The Ordo Yearbook of Economic and Social Order*)[3] established by Eucken and Böhm in 1948 and is still being published after sixty years.

The Freiberg School of Law and Economics contrasted with the Hayekian classical liberal view of the market economy and the state that focused on spontaneous order. Manfred S. Streit and Michael Wohlgemuth (1997) note that while there is not *one* ordoliberal conception of market economy and state—they distinguish between Freiburg and Cologne models—membership between the two groups was shared. The Freiburg School focused on the question of private power within a free society and it tried to define the 'order' (*ordo*) in terms of a set of legal rules for a society ruled by market competition. The Freiburg school sought to establish a set of legal rules that provided an institutional guarantee of open markets not only to promote the goal of economic growth and efficiency but also to limit the power of economic agents and organisations that implies a small though strong state. By contrast, Hayek focused on spontaneous order that emerged out of individuals pursuing their own self-interest. The difference was that Eucken, Böhm and their colleagues, influenced by Husserl's phenomenology, understood the market as a juridical, legal construction that could be changed by changing the rules (anticipating James Buchanan's constitutional economics) while Hayek held to a naturalist thesis arguing that the market, like language and morality, (and in other respects like natural phenomena—crystals, snowflakes, galaxies) were the result of human action but not of human design.

Yet it was Rüstow who first used the term 'neoliberalism' in 1932 which was later adopted by Lippmann and colleagues to describe the revival of a certain kind of liberalism. Hartwich (2009) tells the story this way:

> The year in which Rüstow first formulated the neoliberal program was 1932. Germany's leading economics association, the *Verein für Socialpolitik*, had invited him to its annual conference in Dresden. The *Verein's* long-serving president was Werner Sombart, the leader of the so-called *Kathedersozialisten* ('catheder socialists') from the Historical School of Economics. Sombart, an open supporter of nationalsocialism, lacked any sympathies for liberalism. He had planned to make the Dresden meeting a rallying cry for his cause. But to his dismay, the relatively little known Rüstow delivered the most noticed speech at the conference, which was later published and republished many times. Until the present day, it is widely regarded as the founding document of neoliberalism.

As Hartwich (2009) notes Rüstow's speech was titled '*Freie Wirtschaft, starker Staat*' (Free Economy, Strong State). He argues for a small but strong state that provided the legal framework and rules for economic activity and enforced them. While the state ought not to engage in markets Rüstow saw a limited role for state intervention to ensure competition. Later he defined his approach as the 'third way' between capitalism and communism, between laissez faire and socialism. Hartwich makes the point that Rüstow's neoliberalism was the 'third way,' an odd state of affairs for those supporters of the 'third way' today which pictures itself as fighting against neoliberalism. Rüstow's 1932 speech became the talisman of the Colloque Walter Lippmann defining a 'market economy under the guidance and the rules of the state' (p. 20). There was immediate agreement that the Colloque should become a standing think-tank as the new Centre International d'Études pour la Rénovation du Libéralisme (CIRL) based in Paris and there were plans to reach out to other audiences including trade unions and Catholic corporatists but war intervened and plans were put on hold until after the wa when Hayek established the Mont Pelerin Society in 1947. Yet even in the 1930s and 1940s there were tensions between the ordoliberals like Rüstow and Lippmann—the 'true neoliberals'—and the old-fashioned liberals like Mises, differences that became more pronounced later.

Mont Pelerin Society, 1947

Hayek studied law and political science at the University of Vienna and on graduation was hired by von Mises to work on the legal aspects of the Treaty of Saint Germaine. He began to jettison his socialist ideas after reading Mises' *Socialism* and became drawn in by the liberalism of Carl Menger. He served as the director of a research institute investigating the Austrian business cycle in the late 1920s before joining the London School of Economics in 1931 at the invitation of its director, Lionel Robbins. Bruce Caldwell (2007) recorded the fact that *The Road to Serfdom*, perhaps Hayek's most famous book,

> began as a memo to the director of the London School of Economics, Sir William Beveridge, written by Hayek in the early 1930s and disputing the then-popular claim that fascism represented the dying gasp of a failed capitalist system.

It was published in 1944 by the University of Chicago Press having been turned down by three American publishing houses. Hayek argued that all forms of collectivism tend towards tyranny destroying individual economic and personal freedom. The 'abandoned road' was liberalism and Hayek devoted Chapter 3 to 'Individualism and Collectivism,' arguing in subsequent chapters against planning, how it was at odds with democracy and the rule of law, and developing a strong critique of both 'The Socialist Roots of Nazism' and 'The Totalitarians in Our Midst.' The book was received well by Hayek's contemporaries including Keynes himself and it was read widely selling more than 350,000 copies since its origin publication. The *Reader's Digest* published in abridged version in 1945 reaching over 600,000 readers.[4] Karl Polyani made the exact opposite case concerning unfettered markets and Fabian socialists criticized Hayek's thesis.

The Road to Serfdom, as Milton Friedman (1994) described it 'was a sort of manifesto and a call to arms to prevent the accumulation of a totalitarian state' and he went on to describe the general climate of opinion.

> It's very hard to remember now what the attitude was in 1944–45. Throughout the Western world, the movement was toward centralization, planning, govern-

ment control. That movement had started already before World War II. It started really with the Fabian Society back in the late 19th century—George Bernard Shaw, the Webbs and so on. But the war itself and the fact that in war you do have to have an enormous amount of government control greatly strengthened the idea that after the war what you needed was to have a rational, planned, organized, centralized society and that you had to get rid of the wastes of competition. That was the atmosphere http://www.booknotes.org/Transcript/?ProgramID=1226

Hayek, in the jacket notes to the condensed version wrote:

> The economic freedom which is the prerequisite of any other freedom cannot be the freedom from economic care which the socialists promise us and which can be obtained only by relieving the individual at the same time of the necessity and of the power of choice: it must be the freedom of economic activity which, with the right of choice, inevitably also carries the risk and the responsibility of that right (p. 27).

The Road to Serfdom paved the road also to the establishment of the Mont Pelerin Society (MPS) a few years later. Professor Friedrich von Hayek invited 36 scholars from around the world to meet at Mont Pelerin, near Montreux, Switzerland, 'to discuss the state and the possible fate of liberalism (in its classical sense) in thinking and practice' as the MPS website[5] indicates. In his inaugural address to the Society, Hayek stated:

> The basic conviction which has guided me in my efforts is that, if the ideals which I believe unite us, and for which, in spite of so much abuse of the term, there is still no better name than liberal, are to have any chance of revival, a great intellectual task must be performed. This task involves both purging traditional liberal theory of certain accidental accretions which have become attached to it in the course of time, and also facing up to some real problems which an over-simplified liberalism has shirked or which have become apparent only since it has turned into a somewhat stationary and rigid creed (Hayek, 1992: 237–8).

Some 36 scholars were invited and attended the first meeting, including: Maurice Allais (Paris), Carlo Antoni (Rome), Hans Barth (Zurich), Karl Brandt (Stanford), John Davenport (New York), Stanley Dennison (Cambridge, England), Aaron Director (Chicago), Walter Eucken (Freiburg), Erich Eyck (Oxford), Milton Friedman (Chicago), Harry Gideonse (Brooklyn), Frank Graham (Princeton), F.A. Harper (Irvington-on-Hudson), Henry Hazlitt (New York), T.J.B. Hoff (Oslo), Albert Hunold (Zurich), Carl Iversen (Copenhagen), John Jewkes (Manchester), Bertrand de Jouvenel (Chexbres), Frank Knight (Chicago), Fritz

Machlup (Buffalo), L.B. Miller (Detroit), Ludwig von Mises (New York), Felix Morley (Washington, DC), Michael Polanyi (Manchester), Karl Popper (London), William Rappard (Geneva), Leonard Read (Irvington-on-Hudson), Lionel Robbins (London), Wilhelm Ropke (Geneva), George Stigler (Providence, Rhode Island), Herbert Tingsten (Stockholm), Francois Trevoux (Lyon), V.O. Watts (Irvington-on-Hudson), and C.V. Wedgwood (London).

At the end of the meeting the participants agreed on the following aims:

Believing that what is essentially an ideological movement must be met by intellectual argument and the reassertion of valid ideals, the group, having made a preliminary exploration of the ground, is of the opinion that further study is desirable inter alia in regard to the following matters:

1. The analysis and exploration of the nature of the present crisis so as to bring home to others its essential moral and economic origins.
2. The redefinition of the functions of the state so as to distinguish more clearly between the totalitarian and the liberal order.
3. Methods of re-establishing the rule of law and of assuring its development in such manner that individuals and groups are not in a position to encroach upon the freedom of others and private rights are not allowed to become a basis of predatory power.
4. The possibility of establishing minimum standards by means not inimical to initiative and functioning of the market.
5. Methods of combating the misuse of history for the furtherance of creeds hostile to liberty.
6. The problem of the creation of an international order conducive to the safeguarding of peace and liberty and permitting the establishment of harmonious international economic relations.

The group does not aspire to conduct propaganda. It seeks to establish no meticulous and hampering orthodoxy. It aligns itself with no particular party. Its object is solely, by facilitating the exchange of views among minds inspired by certain ideals and broad conceptions held in common, to contribute to the preservation and improvement of the free society.

Mont Pelerin (Vaud), Switzerland, April 8, 1947

In the preceding remarks the statement of aims suggested that 'The central values of civilization are in danger' and that 'freedom' and 'dignity' had already disappeared in many parts of the world and 'freedom of thought and expression is threatened by the spread of creeds' [totalitarianism and fascism] which are trying to suppress them. The rest of the statement is angled against Marxism and the Hegelian view of history on which it rests:

> The group holds that these developments have been fostered by the growth of a view of history which denies all absolute moral standards and by the growth of theories which question the desirability of the rule of law. It holds further that they have been fostered by a decline of belief in private property and the competitive market; for without the diffused power and initiative associated with these institutions it is difficult to imagine a society in which freedom may be effectively preserved, at http://www.montpelerin.org/mpsGoals.cfm.

Karl Popper, a close friend, fellow Viennese and eventual colleague of Hayek at the London School of Economics (LSE), had already published the two volumes of *The Open Society and Its Enemies* which were written and published while he was a philosophy lecturer at the University of Canterbury in New Zealand during the period 1937–46. Popper referred to the two volumes as his 'war effort.' Popper had been friendly with members of the Vienna Circle but was never invited to become a member, partly because of his hostility to Wittgenstein. Hayek was instrumental in getting Popper a position at the LSE and he left New Zealand for England in 1946. Popper (2008: 408–9) mentions that Hayek read *The Logic of Scientific Discovery* within a week of their first meeting at the LSE in September or October 1935 and Hayek refers to it as the first footnote in his 1936 presidential essay 'Economics and Knowledge' delivered to the London Economic Club on November 10.[6]

The Open Society and Its Enemies published in 1945 was an impassioned defense of democratic liberalism and concerted attack on all forms of totalitarianism. The year previous he had published *The Poverty of Historicism* (1944) in which he fiercely criticized the 'The Historicist Doctrine of the Social Sciences' as theoretically misconceived and socially dangerous because, he maintained, it led to totalitarianism and to centralized governmental control of the individual. Indeed, Hayek as the editor of *Economica* had been in correspondence with Popper and had made cuts to the original essay and commented at length upon what was to become *The Open Society* although Hayek did not like the title (Shearmur, 1998). By contrast, at the heart of Popper's vision of the open society is his critical falsificationism that links his epistemology and social philosophy, encouraging individual scrutiny of any government's piecemeal reform and social engineering. Plato, Hegel and Marx are the villains of the Western tradition as Popper argues that historicism underpins and contaminates their political philosophies. Jan-Werner Müller (2008) identifies a distinct strand of 20th-century liberal thought exemplified by Isaiah Berlin, Raymond Aron and Karl Popper which founded their liberalism, as he says, 'on a "politics of knowledge" that was directed primarily against Marxist philosophies of history and less against the idea of bureaucratic planning, as, in contrast, was the case with Friedrich von Hayek's thought' (p. 45). Popper claims that his conception of the 'open society' has much in common both with Henri Bergson earlier use of the term and with Lippmann's 'good society' (see Vernon, 1976). While there are clearly important differences between Hayek and Popper—Hayek's 'subjectivism' vs, Popper's 'objectivism,' their views on the state's role in reducing inequalities and promoting welfare—at the meta-theoretical level they both held to principles of 'criticism' and 'refutation' and both argued fiercely for a theory of liberal democracy that rejected historicism, collectivism and central planning (Hayes, 2009). They were close friends after 1935 and especially once Popper moved to the LSE. While there was only three years difference in age, Popper regarded Hayek as a father figure, and although Popper remained to the left of Hayek politically, retaining an 'affinity for socialist ideas throughout his life' (Ebenstein, 2003: 182), they shared the main articles of faith of the open and free society.

Keynes and the New Zealand Welfare State

When Margaret Thatcher became leader of the Conservative Party in 1975 and assumed office a mere four years later, she already had some nearly thirty years of political experience including being Secretary of State for Education and Science (1970–74) in Edward Heath's government.[7] As Prime Minister she acknowledged how influenced she was by the monetarist view of Friedman and how she regarded Hayek's *Road to Serfdom* as her bible. In her second government (1983–87) she initiated a program of wholesale privatization. Ronald Reagan became the 40th President of the U.S. in 1981 and served in this capacity until 1989. In his inaugural address he wrote: 'In this present crisis, government is not the solution to our problems; government is the problem.'[8] Reagan implemented supply-side policies, advocating a classical liberal philosophy based on individual freedom and laissez-faire, and initiated massive tax-cuts on the basis of Arthur Laffer's work on tax elasticity (known as the Laffer curve). 'Thatcherism' and 'Reaganomics' signaled the end of Keynesianism and the crisis of the welfare state.

From the end of the Great Depression to the late 1970s Keynesian economic policy had prevailed. Keynes was instrumental in preventing unrealistically high war reparations from Germany when he was appointed financial representative for the Treasury in the Versailles peace conference. During the 1920s he had already advocated fiscal response by government to the rising unemployment. By government spending of public works he argued high unemployment could be averted. He began to develop his theory of the relationship between unemployment, money and prices during the Great Depression publishing his *General Theory of Employment, Interest and Money* in 1936 which challenged the neo-classical economics on the assumption that the market free from state intervention would establish full employment. Keynes argued that demand rather than supply was the key to good macroeconomic policy. His views influenced Franklin D. Roosevelt and his New Deal of relief, recovery and reform. Keynes was the leader of the British delegation in the negotiation and establishment of the Bretton Woods system intended to rebuild the international monetary system after WWII. The negotiations held in 1944 were responsible for setting up rules, institutions, and procedures to regulate the international monetary system, and establishing the IMF and the International Bank for Reconstruction and Development, which became part of the WB. The rules established a system of exchange rate value within a fixed rate in terms of the gold standard.[9]

These policies of reconstruction and development after WWII were marked by a strong interventionist role for government the development of a comprehensive welfare state. As the sociologist T. H. Marshall (1950) suggested in his classic essay 'Citizenship and Social Class' the welfare state is based on a distinctive blend of democracy, welfare and capitalism and development of citizenship as a progressive development of civil, then political, then social rights. A citizen must possess these three sets of rights and they in turn are linked to social class. The welfare state has early expressions in Bismarckian social insurance in Germany and in the Nordic states as well as New Zealand.

In particular, New Zealand was an early leader in welfare reform with the First Liberal Government in 1898 introducing one of the first old age pensions and later widow's pensions. The Liberal Party governed from 1891 until 1912 gaining its support from workers and the socially progressive middle class. It introduced women's suffrage in 1893 and a raft of welfare reforms that some scholars argue emanated from an early social liberalism. These Liberal policies were precursors to fully-fledged social welfare policies introduced by the first Labour Government in the 1930s and subsequent administrations up until the 1970s: state housing, unemployment benefits (relief payments), other forms of social security, family benefit, domestic purposes benefit (support for solo parents) and universal superannuation. From the late 19th century New Zealand had gained a reputation as the 'social laboratory of the world.' Beatrice and Sidney Webb, the British Fabians, spent a month in New Zealand in 1898, and while unenthusiastic about democracy in action, were impressed with social reform. They were the first set of visitors to come to New

Zealand over the next decade to see at first sight the significance of New Zealand's early welfare state. It is an irony to say the least that in the 1980 and '90s New Zealand once again became an experiment, this time a 'new right' experiment that some argue represented a form of Thatcherism sped up and taken to its logical conclusion.

In *Three Worlds of Welfare Capitalism* Esping-Anderson (1990) identifies liberal, conservative, and social democratic welfare regime-types within capitalism in relation to the question of decommodified labor. The types of welfare states are correlated with particular profiles for educational policy—certain types of welfare regimes exhibit a tendency to choose between educational opportunities or social insurance programs as alternative policy strategies (Hega and Hokenmaier, 2002). Francis Castles (1985) distinguishes a fourth welfare type which he calls 'wage-earner's welfare state' model that better fits the historical experience of Australia and New Zealand than the U.S. Entitlement in that the New Zealand welfare state was based upon membership of well defined categories and entitlement was typically statutory, and generous. The commitment to full employment was crucial and as unemployment began to rise, the traditional welfare state system began to get into difficulties and move towards a residual welfare state, where entitlement is based upon narrow and selective criteria of eligibility. Castles & Mitchell (1992) distinguish three 'worlds' of welfare capitalism after Esping-Andersen: liberal, conservative and social democratic, and they go on to suggest the existence of a fourth 'radical' world that has 'characteristics which depart at least somewhat from the expenditure-based orthodoxy that more social spending is the only route to greater income redistribution.' In this fourth world are three countries: New Zealand, Australia and the United Kingdom. They go on to argue that:

> structural impediments to democratic socialist incumbency…are the fundamental determinants of a failure to obtain governmental status to legislate more generous welfare benefits (p. 18).

While the restructuring of the state under the Labour Government was not restricted to the core public sector—education, health and local government underwent major reorganisation—it was with the National Government, which came to power in 1990, that the 'residual' public sector was re-defined in terms of a more limited or minimal state. The National Government embarked on the most significant changes to the welfare state since its establishment in the 1930s. The major initiatives included substantial cuts in benefits and other forms of income support, together with much stricter eligibility criteria, greater targeting of social assistance and changes to the method of targeting, and 'a radical redesign of the means by which the state provides assistance,' particularly in the areas of housing, health care and tertiary education (Boston, 1992, p. 1). While the changes have been justified in terms of the need for fiscal stringency, given the country's high external debt and the failure of the previous policy regime, it is clear that, as Boston (1992: 1) notes, the changes 'also originate from a marked shift in political philosophy' which focused on the question of the nature and scope of the state.

The changes to NZ society and state were not exceptional. They were repeated in Western styled liberal capitalist countries around the globe. What was perhaps different was the way in which the 'politics of reform' were pursued by members of the Fourth Labour Government, in particular Roger Douglas and Richard Prebble, but also by members of the National government such as Ruth Richardson, that would have been better situated in a neoliberal party or government, given that they shared the main article of faith that defined the neoliberal agenda. These politicians on both sides of the House were assisted by state department officials including the, then, Secretary of the Treasury, Graham Scott, and others, during the 1980s who shared and helped prepare for the incoming neoliberal agenda. Young Treasury graduates were sent to the Chicago school in the early 1980s to received training in monetarist economics; politicians and state officials attended the Mont Pelerin meetings in the 1980s and after. The election of Helen Clarke's Fifth Labor Government based in a series of coalitions with minor parties during three terms from 1999 to 2008 slowed the neoliberal onslaught by promoting traditional social democratic policies, before being replaced by the current Prime Minister, John Key, leader of the National Party who previously worked for Merrill Lynch as global head of foreign exchange.

The Crisis of Western Capitalism and the Resurgence of Keynesianism

During 2007–2010 the world suffered a global recession the likes of which we have not experienced since the Great Depression of the 1930s. The recession was sparked by the burst of the housing bubble in the U.S. and a financial crisis related to lending practices associated with the deregulation and securitization of housing mortgages. The decade of the 2000s saw a global explosion in house prices not only in the U.S. but also elsewhere in world. It is now clear that Alan Greenspan and others in the Federal Reserve opposed any regulation of so-called derivatives of mortgage-backed security while at the same time actively undermining the Commodity Futures Trading Commission (CFTC) headed up by Brooksley E. Born who was appointed by President Clinton in 1994. She lobbied the President to give the CFTC oversight of off-exchange markets for derivatives. She was particularly concerned about 'swaps,' financial instruments that are traded over the counter between banks, insurance companies or other funds or companies, and thus have little transparency. Swaps are a form of derivative which is the name for a class of financial instruments that *derive* their value from other financial instruments known as the *underlying*. Derivatives are categorized by the relationship between the underlying and the derivative (e.g. forward, option, swap), the type of underlying which might be equity, foreign exchange interest rate or credit derivatives and the market in which they trade (e.g., exchange traded or over-the-counter [OTC]). The CFTC released its paper in 1998 to develop a comprehensive regulatory reform effort designed to update the agency's oversight of both exchange and off-exchange markets.[10]

There have been 47 recessions in the U.S. since 1790, thirteen since the Great Depression.[11] The most recent economic downturn contributed to a global financial crisis that led to the failure or collapse of many of the United States' largest financial institutions including Bears Sterns, Fannie Mae, Freddie Mac, Lehmann Brothers and the giant insurance company AIG (American International Group). The Bush government responded with an unprecedented $700 billion bank bailout (The Emergency Economic Stabilization Act of 2008) proposed by Henry Paulson named TARP (Troubled Assets Relief Program) and used to purchase failing bank assets. This was an amazing turnaround for a government of the free market that was intended to prevent further erosion of confidence in the U.S. credit markets that could have led to a massive global depression. In a radical move government intervention was suddenly back in favor. Paulson summarized the rationale for the bailout before the U.S. Senate by arguing that it would stabilize markets and improve liquidity and provide time for a comprehensive review of the regulatory framework. The plan was criticized by academic economists as basically unfair, ambiguous and with uncertain long-term effects.

On assuming office President Obama instituted a $787 billion fiscal stimulus package (The American Recovery and Reinvestment Act of 2009). The Act includes federal tax cuts ($288 billion), expansion of unemployment benefits ($82.5 billion) and other social welfare provisions and domestic spending in education ($90.0 billion), health care ($147.7 billion), and infrastructure ($80.9 billion), including the energy sector ($61.3 billion), housing ($12.7 billion), scientific research ($8.9 billion) and other projects ($18.1 billion). Economists are almost equally divided on the stimulus package with Keynesian and neo-Keynesians like Paul Krugman and Joseph Stiglitz favoring the large stimulus package and Austrian and Chicago School economists criticizing the government's plan.

Global free market economics Chicago school style has spelt the end of the monetarist consensus about the self-healing capacity of the market and prominent economists suggested that Keynes is back in fashion. In particular, Paul Krugman[12] has argued the case for government intervention but also Brad Delong, Robert Reich, and Joseph Stiglitz have all advocated Keynesian type policies. Robert Shiller (2008), the behaviorist economist, takes Keynes' *The Economic Consequences of the Peace* as his inspiration when he argues for a new institution modeled on the old Home Owners Loan Corporation of the 1930s as a means of shoring up confidence in the mortgage market. Shiller's (2000) *Irrational Exhuberance* warned of the coming stock market crash and his 'Economic View' column in *The New York Times* has consistently argued for bold thinking and a larger stimulus. Zhou Xiaochuan, the governor of the People's Bank of China recently came out in favor of Keynes's idea of a centrally managed global reserve currency and countries around the world have been following Obama's example with bank bail outs and stimulus packages. The U.S. was in deep recession when Obama took office and the economy was contracting at an annual rate of about six percent. The financial system was on the verge of collapse and the housing market was in free fall. Three quarters of a million Americans were losing their jobs a month and the U.S. faced a deficit of $1.3 trillion dollars and projected deficits that on one estimate would more than double the nation's debt over the next decade.

The costs have been enormous and beyond precise calculation. The International Monetary Fund (IMF) in its *Global Financial Stability Report* indicated that U.S. institutions were about half way through their loss cycle and needed write-downs, while their European counterparts are still lagging. Banks will bear about two-thirds of the write-downs, which are coming on $58 trillion of debt originating in the United States, Europe and Japan.[13] Altman (2009: 5) makes the following estimates:

> Total home equity in the United States, which was valued at $13 trillion at its peak in 2006, had dropped to $8.8 trillion by mid-2008 and was still falling in late 2008. Total retirement assets, Americans' second-largest household asset, dropped by 22 percent, from $10.3 trillion in 2006 to $8 trillion in mid-2008. During the same period, savings and investment assets (apart from retirement savings) lost $1.2 trillion and pension assets lost $1.3 trillion. Taken together, these losses total a staggering $8.3 trillion.

In the period since 2007 over 140 U.S. banks have failed.[14] The aftermath of the banking crisis has been associated with massive declines in unemployment and output. Unemployment has been running over 10% during much of 2008–10.

Reinhart and Rogoff (2008) suggest that 'the present U.S. financial crisis is severe by any metric.' Many have pointed to the systemic nature of the crisis. Gokay (2009) suggests an analysis in terms of 'the explosive growth of the financial system during the last three decades relative to manufacturing and the economy as a whole' with the huge growth of finance capitalism and 'the proliferation of speculative and destabilising financial institutional arrangements and instruments of wealth accumulation.' This has meant 'the rise of new centres and the loss of relative weight of the U.S. as a global hegemonic power' with increasing resource depletion and ecological crisis. He goes on to argue:

> The current financial crisis (and economic downturn) has not come out of blue. It is the outcome of deep-seated contradictions within the structure of global economic system. It is not a 'failure' of the system, but it is central to the mode of functioning of the system itself. It is not the result of some 'mistakes' or 'deviations,' but rather it is inherent to the logic of the system. (http://www.globalresearch.ca/index.php?context=va&and=123)

He asks 'Is this the end of capitalism?' to which he responds 'There is nothing to suggest that the present crisis is paving the way for the collapse of the capitalist system. It signifies the opening of a new epoch in history, in which some of the old structures give way and new forms may develop to radically affect the global structures of power and hegemony.'

Certainly what was a crisis originating in the industrialized countries of the West soon spread to the rest of the world not only to Iceland and Eurozone countries that are in recession but also to Asia and Africa through a 'crisis contagion' around channels of foreign trade and finance, prompting a new political economy of sovereign debt relief. Clearly, we have not yet seen all the policy consequences as this crisis of globalization also severely erodes governments' ability to redistribute wealth and fund social policy developments.[15]

The question is the nature of the systemic crisis: does it mean the end of U.S. style capitalism? Does it mean the end of neoliberalism? Does it mean the end of capitalism itself? Undoubtedly, the financial and economic crisis of 2008 is a major geopolitical setback for the United States and Europe. Altman (2009) argues that governments in the U.S. and Europe will turn inward to focus on domestic recovery especially as their citizens begin to make demands, such as the 'tea-party' phenomenon in the U.S. The international fiscal deficits will discourage the U.S. and Western nations from embarking on any international initiatives in foreign policy and Western capital markets will take several years to recover as the banks insulate themselves by becoming risk-averse. Perhaps, most importantly 'the economic credibility of the West has been undermined by the crisis' (p. 10). As he argues:

This is important because for decades much of the United States' influence and soft power reflected the intellectual strength of the Anglo-Saxon brand of market-based capitalism. But now, the model that helped push back socialism and promoted deregulation over regulation—prompting the remaking of the British Labour Party, economic reforms in eastern Europe, and the opening up of Vietnam in the 1990s—is under a cloud. The U.S. financial system is seen as having failed (p. 10).

All these large-scale nationalist interventions 'will stop the global shift toward economic deregulation' and he quotes Sarkozy and Wang Qishan:

> As President Sarkozy put it, "Le laissez-faire, c'est fini." Or, as Chinese Vice Premier Wang Qishan said more diplomatically, "The teachers now have some problems." This coincides with the natural and very long-term movement away from the U.S.-centric world that started after the fall of the Berlin Wall two decades ago (p. 11).

The decline of a U.S.-centric world, what Fareed Zakaria (2008) calls *The Post-American World*, at the same time signals the rise of China and India, indeed of the BRICs (Brazil, Russia, India and China; now less so Russia). Altman's analysis is that China is not affected much by the financial crisis in the West; its foreign exchange reserves of $2 trillion grew up $700 last year [2008] and it has begun to extend its model of State capitalism to other parts of the globe in the search for raw materials. India too is less harmed by the fallout from the Western financial crisis and less dependent of external capital for development. This prompts Altman to argue that the G-8 framework is obsolete.

Fareed Zakaria's (2008) analysis also indicates the end of 'Pax Americana': 'The world has shifted from anti-Americanism to *post*-Americanism.' Zakaria argues:

> We are living through the third great power shift in modern history. The first was the rise of the Western world, around the 15th century. It produced the world as we know it now—science and technology, commerce and capitalism, the industrial and agricultural revolutions. It also led to the prolonged political dominance of the nations of the Western world. The second shift, which took place in the closing years of the 19th century, was the rise of the United States. Once it industrialized, it soon became the most powerful nation in the world, stronger than any likely combination of other nations. For the last 20 years, America's superpower status in every realm has been largely unchallenged–something that's never happened before in history, at least since the Roman Empire dominated the known world 2,000 years ago. During this Pax Americana, the global economy

has accelerated dramatically. And that expansion is the driver behind the third great power shift of the modern age—the rise of the rest.[16]

According to Zakaria, Americans should not be worried because a post-American world 'will not be a world defined by the decline of America but rather the rise of everyone else. It is the result of a series of positive trends that have been progressing over the last 20 years, trends that have created an international climate of unprecedented peace and prosperity.' Zakaria's polite and optimistic analysis focuses on the economic expansion that allegedly comes with globalization that accounts for the growth in economic power of China, India, Brazil and Russia. But economic growth is not a zero sum game: America benefits from the 'rise of the rest.' And the openness and flexibility of U.S. society means that it will adapt in an ultimately win-win scenario.

Whatever the economic advantages of progress toward the 'knowledge economy,' the 'creative economy' and, even the 'green economy' the fact is that the current financial crisis poses a fundamental challenge to globalization and to the finance capitalism of the Anglo-American neoliberal model of the free market. As Harold James (2009: 168) reminds us 'The response to the Asian crisis of 1997–98 was the reinforcement of the American model of financial capitalism, the so-called Washington consensus' and he goes on to argue 'The response to the contagion caused by the U.S. subprime crisis of 2007–8 will be the elaboration of the Chinese model.' Yet is not clear what the Chinese model means, what its effects will be on U.S.-Chinese relations, or indeed whether China has started to move away from its market based reforms back to forms of state control (Economy & Segal, 2009; Scissors, 2009), especially with its four-trillion-yuan ($586 billion) stimulus plan. And China faces its own problems: is growth sustainable and to what extent do socio-political concerns weigh on the future of China? As Scissors (2009) explains 'China's ascendance is neither inevitable nor impossible, and it will depend on policy choices.'[17]

Notes

1. From the Society's website at http://www.montpelerin.org/mpsAbout.cfm
2. See the World Press index of international think tanks and research organisations at http://www.worldpress.org/library/ngo.cfm.
3. See the journal's website at http://www.ordo-journal.com/en/.
4. See the condensed version at http://www.iea.org.uk/files/upld-publication43pdf?.pdf.
5. See http://www.montpelerin.org/mpsAbout.cfm.

6. See the online version reprinted from *Economica IV* (new ser., 1937), 33–54, at http://www.virtualschool.edu/mon/Economics/HayekEconomicsAndKnowledge.hml.

7. As Education Secretary she abolished free milk and Labour's commitment to comprehensive schooling.

8. The full text of his speech can be found at http://www.americanrhetoric.com/speeches/ronaldreagandfirstinaugural.html.

9. In 1971 the U.S. unilaterally terminated the convertibility of the dollar to gold making the dollar the reserve currency.

10. See http://www.cftc.gov/opa/press98/opamntn.htm; see also the frontline interview with Born at http://www.pbs.org/wgbh/pages/frontline/warning/interviews/born.html.

11. See http://recession.org/history.

12. See for instance Krugman's column in *The New York Times*, for example, 'Fighting off Depression' at http://www.nytimes.com/2009/01/05/opinion/05krugman.html?_r=1.

13. See http://www.imf.org/external/pubs/ft/GFSR/index.htm.

14. See the FDIC website at http://www.fdic.gov/bank/individual/failed/banklist.html.

15. For a collection of essays that discuss the global financial crisis see Carmen Reinhart and Andrew Felton (2009) (Eds.) *The First Global Financial crisis of the 21st Century: Part II, June-December, 2008*, at http://mpra.ub.uni-muenchen.de/13604/2/MPRA_paper_13604.pdf and for a list of papers see '2008–2009 Global Financial Crisis' at http://wtfaculty.wtamu.edu/~sanwar.bus/otherlinks.htm#GlobalFinCrisis.

16. This excerpt is taken from Zakaria's (2008) 'The Rise of the Rest' appearing in *Newsweek* at http://www.newsweek.com/id/135380/page/2.

17. See the discussion at http://www.foreignaffairs.com/discussions/interviews/qa-with-derek-scissors-on-chinas-economy.

2

'Individual' and 'Community' as Political and Policy Metaphors

THIS CHAPTER REPRESENTS AN ATTEMPT TO REFLECT on the themes of individualism and community both as they have defined the space of argument within which competing ideologies have sought to develop alternative conceptions of society in Western states in the post-war period. The first metaphor expresses neoliberal values and is committed firmly to the market, the second works as a metaphor for social democracy, signalling the welfare state and the value of public participation in policy formulation and delivery.

The metaphors individual and community function as ideologies. By metaphors I mean that whenever we use these words to make a statement about a society, we are setting up, implicitly or explicitly, a series of allusions to past usage that resonate in a theory-laden and contestable fashion. Within the western sociological tradition these terms have served as the major signs dividing both field and method between them and generating a whole host of oppositional concepts, together with their normative orientations. For example, the notion of community has a prehistory in the conception of the Greek polis and in the early Christian concept where people were held to be brothers and sisters in Christ. It has a set of historical reference points in present day usage to the utopias that emerged during the Renaissance and Enlightenment. The term is rediscovered as an important ideal in the late eighteenth and early nineteenth centuries in the writings of Herder, Schiller and Hegel. By the nineteenth century with the emergence of sociology as an academic discipline the concept had acquired new content and a new urgency; increasingly it came to be contrasted with the individualism and the alienation characteristic of industrial society (Kamenka, 1982). By the twentieth century 'community' had become a central value in the sociological tradition taking on a strong evaluative force. Tönnies' distinction between *Gemeinschaft* and *Gesellschaft* came to express the preoccupation of successive generations of modern sociologists concerned with the loss of community.

The New Right and Neoliberal Individualism

The neoliberal view rests on an ideology of individualism as the most fundamental and unifying premise that emphasises individual responsibility within a free-market economy and, thereby, defends the notion of the minimal state on moral as well as efficiency grounds.

The New Right has been characterised in a variety of ways. Some commentators emphasise the diversity of political groupings: free-marketeers, libertarians, religious fundamentalists, and moral conservatives. Yet most, at the same time, recognise the primacy of a belief in a form of individualism as the unifying and underlying premise. Sawyer (1982:viii), for instance, writing in the context of Australian politics, while drawing attention to the diversity, emphasises that the New Right:

> are united in the belief that state intervention to promote egalitarian social goals has been responsible for the present economic malaise, and has represented an intolerable invasion of individuals' rights. Equality and freedom are incompatible and the latter is indispensable for both economic health and moral well-being.

King (1987:8) distinguishes between two elements of the New Right: an economic and political liberalism where liberal economic arguments for the free market are joined with political arguments about individualism, and a conservatism which arises from the pursuit of liberal economic policy. Abercrombie et al. (1986:3) write:

> Modern liberals of the New Right postulate that capitalism and individualism are intimately connected. They suggest that capitalism promotes the economic and political freedom of persons, and so defends the individual against the state. They claim as their prerogative the championing of the individual against all forces of collectivism.

Even those theorists who are favourably disposed to the ideology of the New Right detect the common theme of those various standpoints critical of statism as a form of individualism. In the words of Green (1987:210): 'that individuals should be able to direct their lives to a far greater extent than now is possible, and that one of the chief obstacles to greater self-direction is the over-mighty state.' This is not to argue that individualism is an undifferentiated phenomenon for there are at least four strands to be identified. There is the strand which can be traced to Hobbes and his view of human nature in a form of pre-social life where human beings were seen as essentially egoistic, concerned only with their own self-preservation. There is the form of individualism identified by Hayek, which descends from Locke, Hume, Smith and Burke. This form on Hayek's (1947) account is to be distinguished from the strand of individualism descended from Rousseau and Marx. In the former societal order is established not by design (the result of human reason) but by the unforseen results of and the spontaneous order by individual human actions exemplified in the institution of exchange (the market). The latter, what Hayek calls 'collective individualism' is explained by Marx in the following terms:

> the individual *is* the *social* being…is equally the *whole*, the ideal *whole*, the subjective existence of society as thought and experience…the representation and real mind of social existence…(cited in O'Connor, 1984:14).

The fourth strand, again descended from Locke, is seen in the work of Nozick (1974) where individualism is defined in terms of property rights (see Marshall et al., 1991:86–90). The New Right most often represents the kind of individualism found in Hayek and Nozick, although both the roots and the dilemma of liberal democratic theory has been traced by Macpherson (1962: 3) to both Hobbes' and Locke's theory of political obligation which is powerfully shaped a 'possessive' individualism: 'The individual, it was thought, is free inasmuch as he is proprietor of his person and capacities.'

Hayek on 'True Individualism'

Hayek (1949) distinguishes between what he calls true and false individualism. 'True' individualism, Hayek informs us, begins its modern development with Locke, Mandeville and Hume, and reaches its full stature for the first time in the work of Josiah Tucker, Adam Ferguson, Adam Smith and Edmund Burke. By contrast, 'false' individualism is presented in the work of French and other Continental writers. Hayek mentions the Encyclopaedists, Rousseau, and the physiocrats. 'False' individualism, in Hayek's (1949: 4) formulation, is wedded to a Cartesian rationalism and 'always tends to develop into the opposite of individualism, namely, socialism or collectivism.'

'True' individualism, for Hayek, is primarily a theory of society and only secondly a set of political maxims derived from this theory. The basic contention is 'that there is no other way toward an understanding of social phenomena but through our understanding of individual actions directed toward other people and guided by their expected behaviour' (Hayek, 1949: 6). The next step for Hayek is to emphasise in an antirational approach that many of the institutions which characterise society have arisen and function without design: 'the spontaneous collaboration of free men often creates things which are the greater than their individual minds can ever fully comprehend' (Hayek, 1949:70). This is Hayek's celebrated conception of 'spontaneous order,' a reinterpretation of the 'invisible hand' hypothesis, which is used to explain and legitimise the market as the paradigm social institution—allegedly, 'a system under which bad men can do least harm.'

It is from this basic perspective on what Hayek calls true individualism that he derives both his defence of 'private property' and the notion of the minimal state. The general principle of private property is to be understood as the endeavour 'to make man by the pursuit of his interests contribute as much as possible to the needs of other men.' The minimal state is a consequence of the 'demand for a strict limitation of all coercive or exclusive power' (Hayek, 1949:16). Hayek (1949: 22) effectively summarises his view of the state thus:

> the state, the embodiment of deliberately organized and consciously directed power, ought to be only a small part of the much richer organism which we call 'society,' and…the former ought to provide merely a framework within which free…collaboration of men has the maximum of scope.

The market, according to Hayek, establishes a workable individualist order because it ensures that the individual's remunerations correspond to the objective results of his or her efforts, and of their value to others. The individual, therefore, must be free to choose and it is 'inevitable' that he or she must bear the risk attached to their choice-making for in consequence he or she is rewarded not according to the goodness or badness of their intentions but solely on the basis of the value of the results to others. The preservation of individual freedom therefore in Hayek's view, is incompatible with the notion of distributive justice and, in general, with the notion of equality as it has been progressively interpreted over the period of the development of the welfare state. In other words, the notion of individual freedom subscribed to by Hayek and those who follow him, is at odds with the twentieth-century notion of social rights, involving the gradual expansion of citizenship, which served as the basis of the development of the welfare state.

Public Choice Theory

The central tenet of the theories underlying public sector restructuring is a philosophy of individualism that represents a renewal of the main article of faith underlying classical economic liberalism. It asserts that all human behaviour is dominated by self-interest. Its major innovation in contemporary terms is to extend this principle to the status of a paradigm for understanding politics itself, and, in fact, to understanding all behaviour.

The economic theory of politics maintains that people should be treated, *tout court*, as rational utility maximisers. For example, James Buchanan (1980:19–27), as one of the main spokesmen of Public Choice theory, identifies its two major elements as the catallactic approach to economics and the classical *homo economicus* postulate of individual behaviour. Catallactics is the term given to the study of institutions of exchange which Buchanan deems the proper object of study of inquiry in economics. It allegedly rests on the principle of spontaneous order developed most thoroughly in the work of Hayek: order in society is seen to be a spontaneous formation which is given by the economic theory of market exchanges. Buchanan's innovation is to apply this spontaneous order conception beyond simple exchange (two persons/two commodities) to complex exchange and finally to all processes of voluntary agreement among persons. Buchanan (1986:20) writes:

> By a more or less natural extension of the catallactic approach, economists can look on politics and on political processes in terms of the exchange paradigm.

This is the case so long as collective action is modelled with individual decision makers as the basic units. Politics then becomes confined to the realm of non-voluntary relationships among persons—that is, those relationships involving power or coercion. Normative implications are derived from this theory, which carry with them an approach to institutional reform. To the extent that voluntary exchange is valued positively while coercion is valued negatively, such theorists favour market-like arrangements. The constitutional perspective is said to emerge naturally from the politics-as-exchange paradigm. Buchanan (1986:22) writes:

> To improve politics it is necessary to improve or reform the rules, the framework within which the game is played…A game is described by its rules, and a better game is produced only by changing the rules.

The second element identified by Buchanan is the behavioural postulate known as *homo economicus* that is the modern rediscovery of the main tenet of classical liberal economics that people should be treated as rational utility maximisers in all of their behaviour. In other words, individuals are modelled as seeking to further their own interests, defined in terms of measured net wealth positions, in politics as in other aspects of behaviour.

Individualism has become the prevailing ideology behind New Right reforms. The individual, in Lockean fashion, is seen as standing separate from and prior to society. The so-called 'free' individual is regarded as the basic unit of political order and the safeguarding of the individual's life, liberty and property as the state's fundamental purpose. There is a bias towards a *minimal state* for any extension of the role of the state over and above these ends is regarded as both unnecessary and dangerous. Moreover, the bureaucratic welfare state is seen as having created a 'culture of dependency' in that it has discouraged self-reliance and thereby evaded investment and work incentives. The combined effects of policies which in the past have focused on social goals have strengthened organised labour *vis a vis* capital, augmented wages as against capital goods, and increased state borrowings from itself, leading to declining levels of profitability and productivity. The individual is seen as the most important element in promoting welfare and the well being of individuals is regarded as the logical starting point for an analysis of social and education policy.

Critiques of Neoliberal Individualism

Jameson (1985:115) distinguishes two clear positions in the critique of neoliberal individualism. The first argues that in the classical age of competitive capitalism there was such a thing as individualism but that today, in the age of corporate or multinational capitalism the older bourgeois individual subject simply does not exist. The second argues that not only is the bourgeois individual subject a feature of a past classical capitalism, it is also a myth in the sense that it never really existed in the first place. Rather the notion of the autonomous, 'free,' choice-making individual is merely 'a philosophical and cultural mystification.'

The first position is given expression by O'Connor (1984) and Abercrombie et al. (1986). O'Connor who studied the crisis of American capitalism as part of the global pattern of capitalist accumulation, maintained that conditions of economic and social reproduction are inexplicable outside the context of the dominant national ideology of individualism. He argues that while capitalist accumulation created the basis for the development of modern ideologies of individualism—anti-statism, privatisation, autonomy, self-development, and laissez-faire—American individualism became self-contradictory and illusory as corporate capitalism developed. Centralised state activity and corporate capitalism replaced privacy and freedom from interference with passivity, dependence, the colonisation of individual wills. Standardisation became substituted for self-development. 'Corporatism' and sectionalism in politics replaced a society based on the interests of free individuals. Forced collectivisation of the capitalist division of industrial labour replaced economic individualism. In other words, as O'Connor (1984:18) maintains:

> modern ideologies of individualism became mere shadows of that traditional American individuality which flowered in the old subsistence economy, small-town life, the frontier, and later, small-scale capitalism.

The New Right advocated an ideology of individualism, privatisation, consumer sovereignty, user-pays, self-reliance and individual enterprise as the solution to all economic and social ills. While for some purposes we might want to recognise that society is comprised of individuals freely expressing their preferences and their right of voluntary association, it must also be recognised that some 'associations' such as multinational corporations are much more powerful than others and do not compete in the political market place on equal terms. Further, New Right arguments of individualism are inconsistent with arguments concerning 'middle class' or bureaucratic capture, which are ascribed on the basis of criteria over and above that of the individual.

Foucault's analysis operates on the basis of a radical decentering that denies an epistemic or historic privilege to either the traditional Cartesian notion of a centered subjectivity or the humanist ideal of a rational autonomous and responsible self. In one sense Foucault stands in a tradition of French twentieth-century thought that has sought to specify the subject in terms of its finitude, its historical and temporal boundaries, its physical embodiment.

Foucault's work—his investigations into the humanist practices and institutions by which we have constituted ourselves as individuals—has seriously challenged the assumptions with which liberalism, in its various forms, represents itself as the theoretical basis for a progressive politics and social criticism. It is interesting to note that at his seminar at the Collège de France in the early 1980s Foucault began to deal with the work of Hayek and Von Mises (the Austrian School of economics which in many of its developments underlies New Right thinking). Questioned about this and the status of the 'sovereign' subject in an interview the year of his death, Foucault (1989:313) responded:

I don't think there is actually a sovereign, founding subject, a universal form that one could find everywhere. I am very sceptical and very hostile toward this conception of the subject. I think on the contrary that the subject is constituted through practices of subjection, or, in a more anonymous way through practices of liberation, of freedom . . .

According to Foucault there are two types of techniques that human beings use to understand and control themselves. Technologies of domination are concerned with defining and controlling the conduct of individuals, submitting them through the exercise of power to certain ends so as to lead useful, docile and practical lives. Technologies of the self, by contrast, permit individuals 'to effect certain operations on their own bodies, souls, thoughts, conduct and way of being' (Foucault, 1982:18), so as to reconstruct and transform themselves to attain certain states of wisdom, perfection, purity and even happiness. His interest in techniques, technologies and practices arises from his approach that bypasses questions about the nature and legitimacy of power, to focus on questions about *how* individuals have come to be significant elements of the state. He is not interested in the role of the state, its institutions and forms of decision-making, or in theories or ideologies that have been developed in order to justify the state. Rather his interest is with *how*, in the emergence of the modern state, individuals become utilised by this 'new' state to live, to work, to produce and to consume. His interest, then, is in what he calls *disciplinary power* and the way in which this power is invested in modern forms of governance by the state to utilise individuals to augment and reinforce the state. Governance in this sense requires a political knowledge of individuals, of their propensities, abilities, preferences and capacities. On this view individuals become instrumental to the ends of the state through investments in justice, welfare, health and education. Power is to be understood at the micro-level as a series of institutional strategies for individualising and normalising human beings. To recognise with Foucault the existence of different forms of power is to recognise empirically the historical modes of subjection of individuals, which relate directly to questions of government in the widest sense. To accept this kind of analysis achieves two objectives: first, Foucault's analysis of power challenges a uniform and monolithic construction of power which motivates the traditional liberal conception; second, it provides a framework for understanding how the institution of exchange (the market) as the neoliberal paradigm for all institutional reform is related to questions of governance and at one and the same time relieves administrations of their wider social responsibilities while setting up strategies so that we come to constitute ourselves as market individuals (or rational utility maximisers) exercising 'free' choice in the 'free' market. As Gruber (1989:615) comments:

If Foucault's insights are valid, liberalism's flaw is not that it has been inefficacious in pressing its agenda on behalf of individuals against modern tendencies that repress individuality and obstruct its potential, but that its rhetoric and its practices are themselves tragically and completely implicated in the burdensome network within which we find ourselves. His observations on the intertwinement of liberalism's individuality with its apparent opposite suggest that the current task for thinking and for action is not yet another attempted revivification and return to the individual, but instead is the rejection of, and resistance to, the individualities that we are, one critical component of which is liberalism's programs and rhetoric.

The Critique of Community

The individualism/community dichotomy is reflected in a series of binary oppositions which have been crucial in setting the terms of debate for recent reforms: private/public, separated self/shared self, male/female, self/other, market/state. Yet the terms individualism and community, as Iris Young (1990: 228) has forcefully argued, share a common logic that permits them to define each other negatively:

> Each entails a denial of difference and a desire to bring multiplicity and heterogeneity into unity, though in opposing ways. Liberal individualism denies difference by positing the self as a solid, self-sufficient unity, not defined by anything or anyone other than itself. Its formalistic ethic of rights also denies difference by bringing all such separated individuals under a common measure of rights. Proponents of community, on the other hand, deny difference by positing fusion rather than separation as the social ideal. They conceive the social subject as a relation of unity or mutuality composed by identification and symmetry among individuals within a totality. Communitarianism represents an urge to see persons in unity with one another in a shared whole.

The notion of community has been appealed to in order to sanction some very dubious practices, for instance, in the notion of community as advanced by neo-conservatives to reconstruct and venerate cultural traditions—a modern 'one culture, one nation' interpretation. The notion of community here is central to the ideal of assimilation at the heart of liberal ideology: it expresses the vision of a common national culture in which all individuals, freed from their ethnic origins, their tribal histories, and their traditional cultural beliefs, can participate in a modern democratic society. On this view, cultural pluralism and ethnic diversity is seen as a threat to the demands of modern society because such pluralism promotes the idea of group identity, group loyalties and group rights. It is, therefore, not surprising that modern liberal discourse in its conception of citizenship has systematically excluded groups historically defined as Other. It has effectively pursued this end by promoting an idea of civic community that is both homogeneous and monocultural. Such a view of civic community which originates in a shared order of being as the foundation of one group with a bounded and coherent identity is completely at odds with the contemporary politics of voice and representation.

The communitarian critique of liberalism has taught us to be suspicious of the universalist and rationalist pretensions underlying an individualism which both abstracts the individual from their social and cultural contexts and disregards the role of social relationships in constituting the nature and identity of people. It has also helped us to realise that the individuals of neoliberalism, posited as rational utility maximisers and theorised to form communities based fundamentally on competition, covertly screens out different cultural and gender values. Yet at the same time communitarian philosophy, in substituting one universalist notion for another, privileges unity over difference, the social self over the individual self. This republican discourse sets up a vision of a substantive civic community based on the regulative ideal of a participatory and dialogical reason, which is, however, monocultural and intolerant of a plurality of differences. The communitarian ideal postulates a public that comes into being through reason; a rational consensus that assimilates substantive cultural differences and denies the heterogeneity of social life.

Not only is the communitarian ideal intolerant of cultural differences, it also often disregards gender related problems. It is clear that traditional communities have been highly oppressive for women, ascribing them subservient roles on the basis of a primitive division of labour. It is easy, in face of the individualisation and privatisation of society, to falsely romanticise the notion of community not recognising the way in which arguments based on its appeal can be undesirably utopian and politically problematic. For instance, as Young (1990) argues, alienation and violence are as much a function of face-to-face relationships than they are of mediated social relations. Contemporary studies of rape and child abuse make this point very strongly.

The starting point for a politics of difference is the combined critique of liberalism and republicanism, of individualism and community, to show that all homogeneous constructions of individual or community identity are, in fact, historical and contingent constructions which depend on deliberate and systematic exclusions. Social groups conceived in these terms are, therefore, non-interrelational and mutually exclusive. A politics of difference, by contrast, unfreezes fixed and essential identities. It treats difference as variation rather than exclusive opposition. It sees identities as both relational and contextual, often a matter of political choice. To this extent, a politics of difference understands that the identity of the subject is constructed at the point of intersection of a multiplicity of subject-positions 'between which there exists no a priori or necessary relation and whose articulation is the result of hegemonic practices' (Mouffe, 1988:35).

Marxism and Freudianism led to a profound decentering of the subject as the fount of all reason, signification and action. Both individuals and groups are always inserted in existing social practices and can never be the sole origin or authors of those practices. The social movements of the 1960s and 70s established some refinements, questioning the priority of class as the leading collective emancipatory subject. There was a greater recognition of ethnicity and gender as specifying in non-reductive ways, lines of oppression. Yet these social movements still subscribed to the old logic of identity as stable, essential and homogeneous categories:

> which could be spoken about almost as if they were singular actors in their own right but which, indeed, placed, positioned, stabilized, and allowed us to understand and read, almost as a code, the imperatives of the individual self: the great collective social identities of class, of race, of nation, of gender, and of the West (Hall, 1991:14).

Elsewhere Stuart Hall (1992: 254) addresses himself to the question of a significant shift that has taken place in black politics in terms of a 'politics of representation' that he characterises as 'the end of the essential black subject.' By this he means that the category 'black' is a politically and culturally constructed category that is never fixed but is historically articulated, and contains within it a tremendous diversity of experience. A politics of representation recognises racism as the play of identity and difference that positions the black subject not only in relation to the dimensions of class, gender, nation but also in relation to sexuality and desire. Hall (1992: 256) explains as follows:

> Just as masculinity always constructs femininity as double—simultaneously Madonna and Whore—so racism constructs the black subject: noble savage and violent avenger...This double fracturing entails a different kind of politics because...black radical politics has frequently been stabilized around particular conceptions of black masculinity, which are only now being put into question by black women and black gay men.

The critique of individualism and community—the metaphors and their associated political ideologies—has to a large extent been invigorated by debates concerning the politics of identity. It can be taken another step forward with the emergence of Third Way politics. As Sarah Hale (200) notes the Scottish philosopher John Macmurray is purported to have had a significant influence upon Tony Blair's thinking and she cites Blair's biographer, John Rentoul:'Blair's idea of community, which is perhaps his most distinctive theme as a politician, derives directly from Macmurray.' The distinctiveness of Blair New Labour policies is allegedly derived from Blair's reinvention of community by reference to Macmurray. Hale disputes both the relation between Blair and Macmurray, or at least that Blair's philosophy is modelled on Macmurray and also that Macmurray can be seen as a modern communitarian. Yet the point remains how Third Way politics sees itself as articulating a notion of community as part of its distinctiveness. Third Way politics had much more to do with the embrace of a form of neoliberal individualism at least at the level of economic policy, that is a commitment broadly to principles of neoliberalism and to globalisation, with the attempt to 'socialise' the market by guaranteeing consumer rights, providing public consumer watchdog institutions, and by regulating the market. Clearly, whether one agrees that Third Way concerns a philosophy of community or not, or whether Third Way policies can be seen as issuing from such a philosophy, it is the case that the terms of the debate concerning Third Way politics and policies, still fits squarely within the political metaphors of individualism and community.

3

Neoliberalism, Higher Education and Knowledge Capitalism

with Mark Olssen

THE ASCENDANCY OF NEOLIBERALISM and the associated discourses of 'new public management,' over the last thirty years, has produced a fundamental shift in the way universities and other institutions of higher education have defined and justified their institutional existence. The traditional professional culture of open intellectual enquiry and debate has been replaced with an institutional stress on performativity, as evidenced by the emergence of an emphasis on measured outputs: on strategic planning, performance indicators, quality assurance measures, and academic audits. This chapter traces the links between neoliberalism and globalisation on the one hand, and neoliberalism and the knowledge economy on the other. It maintains that in a global neoliberal environment, the role of higher education for the economy is seen by governments as having greater importance to the extent that higher education has become the new star ship in the policy fleet for governments around the world. Universities are seen as a key driver in the knowledge economy, and as a consequence higher education institutions have been encouraged to develop links with industry and business in a series of new venture partnerships. The recognition of economic importance of higher education and the neccessity for economic viability has seen initiatives to promote greater entrepreneurial skills as well as the development of new performative measures to enhance output and to establish and achieve targets. This chapter attempts to document these trends at the level of both political philosophy and economic theory.

Neoliberalism As a Dimension of Globalisation

At an economic level, neoliberalism is linked to globalisation, especially as it relates to the 'freedom of commerce,' or to 'free trade.' In this sense, neoliberalism is a particular element of globalisation in that it constitutes the form through which domestic and global economic relations are structured. Yet, neoliberalism is only one dimension of globalisation, which is to say, it is not to be seen as identical to the phenomenon of globalisation as such. Globalisation is a much broader phenomenon in that should neoliberalism not have replaced Keynesianism as the dominant economic discourse of western nations, it would still constitute a significant process. This is the sense that it has partly occurred as a consequence of changes in technology and science which have brought many parts of the world closer together through developments in forms of technology as they have influenced information, communications, and travel.

The advent of neoliberalism would not have prevented this process from occurring, and thus, it must not be confused with globalisation as such. Rather it must be seen as a specific economic discourse or philosophy which has become dominant and effective in world economic relations as a consequence of superpower sponsorship. neoliberalism is a politically imposed discourse, which is to say that it constitutes the hegemonic discourse of western nation states. As such it is quite independent of the forms of globalisation that we have spoken of above, based as they are on changes in technology and science, nor can it be seen as part of their effects, although this is not to say that there is no relationship at all. Its major characteristics emerged in the USA in the 1970s as a forced response to stagflation and the collapse of the Bretton Woods system of international trade and exchange, leading to the abolition of capital controls in 1974 in America and 1979 in Britain (Mishra, 1999; Stiglitz, 2002). This made it extremely difficult to sustain Keynesian demand management. Financial globalisation made giant strides. Exchange rates were floated and capital controls abolished, giving money and capital the freedom to move across national boundaries. The changes in technology did certainly facilitate these changes, for developments in microelectronics and computers made it possible to shift financial reserves within seconds.

Neoliberalism and Higher Education Policy

Within higher education neoliberalism has introduced a new mode of regulation or form of governmentality. In order to understand this it is necessary to understand that the welfare liberal mode it replaced maintained fundamentally different premises at the level of political and economic theory, as well as at the level of philosophical assumption. The central defining characteristic of this new brand of neoliberalism can be understood at one level as a revival of many of the central tenets of classical liberalism, particularly classical economic liberalism. The central presuppositions shared include:

1. the self-interested individual: a view of individuals as economically self-interested subjects. In this perspective the individual was represented as a rational optimiser and the best judge of his/her own interests and needs.
2. free market economics: the best way to allocate resources and opportunities is through the market. The market is both a more efficient mechanism and a morally superior mechanism.
3. a commitment to laissez-faire: because the free market is a self-regulating order it regulates itself better than the government or any other outside force. In this, neoliberals show a distinct distrust of governmental power and seek to limit state power within a negative conception, limiting its role to the protection of individual rights.
4. a commitment to free trade: involving the abolition of tariffs or subsidies, or any form of state-imposed protection or support, as well as the maintenance of floating exchange rates and 'open' economies.

Notwithstanding a clear similarity between neo and classical liberal discourse, the two cannot be seen as identical, and an understanding of the differences between them provides an important key to understanding the distinctive nature of the neoliberal revolution as it has impacted on OECD countries over the last 30 years. Whereas classical liberalism represents a negative conception of state power in that the individual was taken as an object to be freed from the interventions of the state, neoliberalism has come to represent a positive conception of the state's role in creating the appropriate market by providing the conditions, laws and institutions necessary for its operation. In classical liberalism the individual is characterised as having an autonomous human nature and can practise freedom. In neoliberalism the state seeks to create an individual that is an enterprising and competitive entrepreneur. As Graham Burchell (1996: 23–24) puts this point, while for classical liberalism the basis of government conduct is in terms of "natural, private-interest-motivated conduct of free, market exchanging individuals," for neoliberalism "the rational principle for regulating and limiting governmental activity must be determined by reference to *artificially* arranged or contrived forms of free, *entrepreneurial* and *competitive* conduct of economic-rational individuals." This means that for neoliberal perspectives, the end goals of freedom, choice, consumer sovereignty, competition and individual initiative, as well as those of compliance and obedience, must be constructions of the state acting now in its positive role through the development of the techniques of *auditing, accounting* and *management*. It is these techniques, as Barry, Osborne and Rose (1996: 14) put it:

> [that] enable the marketplace for services to be established as 'autonomous' from central control. neoliberalism, in these terms, involves less a retreat from governmental "intervention" than a re-inscription of the techniques and forms of expertise required for the exercise of government.

In his own analysis, Burchell is commenting on and articulating Foucault's perspective on liberalism as a form of state reason or 'governmentality.' For Foucault (1991a), neoliberalism represents an art of government or form of political reason. A political rationality is not simply an ideology but a worked-out discourse containing theories and ideas that emerge in response to concrete problems within a determinate historical period. For Foucault, like Weber, political reason constituted a form of disciplinary power containing forms and systems of expertise and technology utilisable for the purposes of political control. Liberalism, rather than being the discovery of freedom as a natural condition, is thus a prescription for rule, which becomes both the *ethos* and *techne* of government. In this sense, as Barry, Osborne and Rose (1996: 8) put it:

> Liberalism is understood not so much as a substantive doctrine or practice of government in itself, but as a restless and dissatisfied ethos of recurrent critique of State reason and politics. Hence, the advent of liberalism coincides with discovering that political government could be its own undoing, that by governing over-much, rulers thwarted the very ends of government.

For Foucault (1991a), liberalism represented a constructed political space, or a political reconstruction of the spaces in terms of which market exchanges could take place and in terms of which a domain of individual freedom could be secure. As such a constructed space, liberalism, says Foucault, enabled the domain of "society" to emerge in that it stood opposed to the *polizeiwissenschaft* of the *ancien regime* which constituted a formula of rule that sought total control. In this sense liberalism is a form of permanent critique of state reason, a form of rationality which is, as Thomas Osborne (1993: 346) puts it, "always suspicious of governing over-much, a form of government always critical of itself."

Markets As a New Disciplinary Technology in the Public Sector

Ron Barnett (2000) utilises Lyotard's concept of 'performativity' to argue that marketisation has become a new universal theme manifested in the trends towards the commodification of teaching and research and the various ways in which universities meet the new performative criteria, both locally and globally in the emphasis upon measurable outputs.

Markets were of course traditionally important in classical economics, and formed an essential part of the welfare state, for regulating private entrepreneurial conduct in the public sphere of society. Under neoliberalism, markets have become a new technology by which control can be effected and performance enhanced, in the public sector. As a technique by which government can effect control, its development for non-private institutional contexts depended upon developments in knowledge and research from the 1930s. These included the writings of Frederick A. Hayek; the development of monetarist economics by Milton Friedman; the development of Public Choice theory by James Buchanan and his collaborators at Chicago, as well as the later development of institutional theories of internal organisational functioning, such as Agency Theory and Cost-Transaction Economics.

Although Frederich Hayek (1899–1992) must in many senses be considered a classical liberal, his writings from the 1930s onwards contributed to neoliberalism in that he shared many of the themes of neoliberalism and, in addition, he deeply influenced later forms of the doctrine. Hayek can be considered a part of, and having major debts to, the Austrian School of Economics founded by Menger (1840–1921) and carried on by von Wieser (1851–1926) and von Mises (1881–1973). One of the major ways that Hayek departs from classical economic theory relates to his acceptance of the Austrian School's subjective theory of value, the theory that value is conferred on resources by the subjective preferences of agents. As John Gray (1984: 16) puts it, it was this "profound insight which spelt the end of the tradition of classical economic theory," marking a departure from economic theorists such as Adam Smith, David Ricardo, J. S. Mill and Karl Marx who had all analysed value in objective terms as deriving from the labour content of the asset or resource under consideration. Like von Mises, Hayek defends subjectivism in economic theory regarding value, but goes further, noting that the data of the social sciences are themselves subjective phenomena and that social objects like money or tools are constituted by human beliefs.[1]

Amongst the major themes of his economic and social philosophy are his argument that 'local knowledge,' as is found in markets, is always more valid and effective than the forms of codified text-book-type knowledge that it is possible to introduce through planning. For this reason, markets have distinct advantages over state regulation or planning. The laws of supply and demand operate, via the price mechanism, as indicators of under- and over-supply as well as incentives for producers to produce high-quality, competitively priced goods for which there is an established demand. In a multitude of ways, markets provide fast and efficient methods of supplying information on consumer demand, and a sure way of making sure that producers and providers will respond (see Hayek 1945 especially).

Consequently, Hayek (1944, 1948, 1952, 1960, 1976) maintains that the proper functioning of markets is incompatible with state planning of any sort, either full-scale socialism or the more limited conception of the welfare state. A full-scale rational socialism is impossible because it would have no markets to guide resource allocation. In addition, central planning of any form, he claims, is not practical because of the scale of centralised calculation any effective attempt at allocation would require. On this basis Hayek contends that all forms of state action beyond the *minimal* functions of the defence of the realm and the protection of basic rights to life and property are dangerous threats to liberty which are likely to lead down the 'road to serfdom.'

His main arguments against central planning are based on two claims: (1) on its inefficiency, and (2) on the threat to freedom of the individual. It would be inefficient, in Hayek's view, because real knowledge is gained and true economic progress made as a consequence of locally generated knowledge derived from "particular circumstances of time and place" and the state is not privy to such knowledge (Hayek, 1944: 521). The market then is the mechanism which best allocates resources in society. Planning ignores this localistic character of knowledge and interferes with the self-regulating mechanism of the market.

Buchanan and Public Choice Theory

While Hayek argued for the importance of markets for the regulation of private-business conduct, it was James Buchanan and his collaborators that argued for an extension of the market as a mechanism for the institutional regulation of public sector organisational contexts. In this, Buchanan introduced a major shift from liberal to neoliberal governmentality. For markets, rather than being seen, as they were for Hayek, and for classical political economy, as a natural, self-regulating reserve, where the hand of nature will produce an optimal social and economic equilibrium, would now become a technique of government's 'positive' power, acting deliberately through the vehicle of the state to engineer the conditions for efficient economic production.

The difference between Hayek and Buchanan on this point has not been sufficiently stressed in the literature on markets. For Hayek, in the classical tradition, economies are the outcome of spontaneous evolution which demonstrate the superiority of unregulated markets for creativity and progress. A spontaneous societal order such as a market order can utilise practical fragmented knowledge in a way which a holistically planned order cannot. Hayek states his theory of spontaneous order first in relation to a comment on Bernard Mandeville when he says:

> For the first time [he] developed all the classical paradigmata of the spontaneous growth of orderly social structures: of law and morals, of language, the market and money, and also the growth of technological knowledge. (Hayek, 1978: 253)

A spontaneous order emerges for Hayek as a natural process. It can be observed in population biology of animal species, in the formation of crystals, and even in galaxies (Hayek, 1952: 180; 1967: 76; 1973: 39; 1976: 39–40). It is this idea that self-organising and self-replicating structures emerge without design, and that knowledge about some parts of the structure permit the formation of correct understanding about the behaviour of the structure as a whole, that Hayek is most keen to emphasise. It underpins his rejection of Cartesian rationalism, his historicism, his anti-foundationalism, his theory of the evolution of mind (1978: 250). In that the market is a spontaneous order, it displays a tendency to equilibrium, although an actual perfect equilibrium is never achieved but must be viewed as a constantly changing process of tending towards orderliness. This is not only with reference to economic life and the spontaneous emergence of markets, but also in social life in relation to the growth of language where we find the spontaneous formation of self-regulating structures, as well as in relation to the development of moral norms. Hence, as Gray points out, the emergence of spontaneous systems is "somewhat akin to the generalisations of Darwinian evolution" (Gray, 1984: 31) in that Hayek maintains that "selective evolution is the source of all order" (Gray, 1984: 32). Thus, in a market economy there is a real analogy to Darwinian natural selection in that the "profit-loss system provides a mechanism for the elimination of unfit systems" (Gray, 1984: 32) with the proviso that, in contradistinction to Herbert Spencer or W. G. Sumner, natural selection is not solely about individuals but about groups and populations. Such a thesis incorporates Hayek's arguments that social institutions arise as a result of human action but not human design (the 'invisible hand' thesis); that knowledge embodied in practices and skills that is practical, tacit and local is primary in terms of its epistemological status; and that there is a natural selection of competitive traditions whereby rules and practices that confer success come to replace those unsuited to the human environment. Following closely in the footsteps of von Mises, Hayek argues that any attempt to supplant market relations by public planning cannot avoid calculational calamities and is therefore doomed to failure.

In Buchanan's view, markets are a useful technology for use by the state. Partly aided by developments in national incomes accounting after World War II, partly by the perceived difficulties of Keynesianism, and also by the general context of the Cold War, Buchanan and the Public Choice theorists were concerned with the marketisation of the public sector by the deliberate actions of the state. This is to say that Buchanan had little faith in the 'spontaneous' ordering of the market or in the efficacy of the social evolutionary process. For him, evolution may produce social chaos and dysfunctional patterns as readily as it may social harmony and equilibrium. Significantly, it is on this point that Buchanan (1975: p. 194n) criticises Hayek:

> My basic criticism of F. A. Hayek's profound interpretation of modern history and his diagnosis for improvement is directed at his apparent belief or faith that social evolution will, in fact, ensure the survival of efficient institutional forms. Hayek is so distrustful of man's explicit attempts of reforming institutions that he accepts uncritically the evolutionary alternative. (Buchanan, 1975: 194n)

Rejecting all talk of *automaticity* and *evolution*, Buchanan expresses a much greater faith in *conscious action* to legitimate the "long over-due task of institutional overhaul" that many commentators were calling for (Reisman, 1990: 74). It is on these grounds that he makes the distinction between the 'protective state' and the 'productive state.' While the former is concerned with the basic constitutional framework of rights enforced by law and with national defence, the latter is both 'policeman' and 'participant' (Reisman, 1990: 81). These two levels of state relate to, as Buchanan (1975: x) says, two stages of social interaction: one which involves the selection of rules and one which involves action within these rules as selected. While the distinction between 'protective' and 'productive' is the distinction between law and politics (Buchanan and Tullock, 1962: 69), importantly in terms of the political theory of neoliberalism, it is also a distinction between 'negative' and 'positive' freedom, and of the 'negative' and 'positive' role of the state. Importantly in this context, Buchanan's state has a *positive arm*. Hence, while the stringent constitutional safeguards on the protective state make any change in the status quo or redistribution of property almost impossible, the positive arm of the productive state effectively extracts compliance from individuals in order to engineer a market order. In doing so it cuts across the traditional guarantees of classical liberalism regarding the spaces it sought to protect—a domain of personal freedom, the rights of privacy involving freedom from scrutiny and surveillance, as well as professional autonomy and discretion in one's work. PCT effectively undermines and re-organises the protected domains of their classical liberal forebears. The shift, I will claim shortly, is both theoretically and practically important for understanding the changes in higher education in Britain and other OECD countries in the last two decades.

Neoliberal Theories of Institutional Redesign: Agency Theory and Cost-Transaction Economics

It is with PCT that market techniques were systematically developed and first became a technology for institutional governance. Centrally PCTconstituted a supply-side process of 'governing without governing,' a process by which compliance is extracted through systems that measure performance according to both externally imposed levers, and internally reinforced targets. Influenced and building upon PCT, a number of internal theories of organisation through which efficiency and effectiveness are rendered operative in public sector institutions became prominent from the 1950s. Foremost amongst these were Agency Theory and Transaction Cost Economics.

Agency theory (AT) has been widely used in the economic and social restructuring programmes in OECD countries, including Britain, America, Australia and New Zealand[2]. As a theoretical orientation, it represents work relations hierarchically as a series of contracts between one party referred to as the principal and another referred to as the agent. The theory is concerned with problems of compliance and control in the division of labour between work relationships. Although initially developed in relation to business firms, it became adapted and extended to public sector work relationships as a means of exacting the accountability and performance of employees where market incentives and sanctions did not operate. AT theorises work relations hierarchically in terms of chains of authority and command which can be used to characterise authority relations at all levels of the management hierarchy. Hence, a single person will be principal to those further down the chain of command and agent to those further up. Central to its focus is how one gets an agent to act in accordance with the interests of the principal. Rather than specify a broad job specification based on a conception of professional autonomy and responsibility, it specifies chains of principal-agent relationships as a series of contracts as a means of rendering the management function clear and accountable. AT theorises hierarchical work relationships as contracts where a principal becomes a commissioning party to specify or delegate work to an agent to perform in return for some specified sanction or reward. As such, it is concerned with how to extract compliance from a voluntary exchange relationship based on dependency. Hence, it speaks to the relationship between employer and employee in all types of work contexts—schools, government agencies, universities and businesses.

In order to minimise risks and enable control in the employment situation, AT specifies a range of monitoring, information eliciting, and performance appraisal techniques which include the following:

- determining the best form of contract
- determining the best way of motivating agents
- determining the best way of spurring performance (via targets, rewards and sanctions)
- finding the best way of monitoring and specifying contracts to guard against excesses and dangers produced by opportunism on part of agent, due to 'shirkin,g' deception, cheating, or collusion.

Agency costs are effectively the subject of Transaction Cost Economics (TCE), which is another form of economic theory linked closely to AT, PCT and Property Rights Theory[3]. Principally espoused in the work of Oliver Williamson (1975, 1983, 1985, 1991, 1992, 1994), it seeks to analyse and account for the efficiency costs of transacting business and the effect these have on organisational form. In this respect, as Charles Perrow (1986a: 18) puts it, TCE is "relentlessly and explicitly an efficiency argument." In this sense TCE is used to evaluate the efficiency of alternative governance structures or sets of institutional arrangements for various kinds of transactions, especially those generated by the market. Like other neoliberal theories, it assumes a social-ontological context of 'uncertainty,' 'bounded rationality,' 'limited' and 'asymmetrical' information, and of the 'opportunism' of the 'self-interested' subject. Using theory-specific concepts such as 'small numbers bargaining' and 'asset specificity,' TCE endeavours to show why various sorts of organisational forms (involving mergers or takeovers or various forms of organisational integration) may be preferred to a pure market form. In accounting for the increasing size of business organisations over the century, Williamson (1983: 125) argues "that efficiency is the main and only systematic factor responsible for the organisational changes that have occurred." In essence, then, TCE is about the most efficient method of organisation given a particular market context.

TCE has a number of central theory-specific concepts. These are 'uncertainty,' 'small numbers bargaining,' 'bounded rationality,' 'opportunism,' and 'asset specificity.' While opportunism expresses the 'self-interested' nature of individual actions, bounded rationality attests to the absence of perfect information, or to the asymmetrical nature of information between two or more parties in any exchange relation. It is due to the absence of perfect information that the market equilibrium becomes unstable, introducing 'uncertainty,' which in turn allows agents to act 'opportunistically.' For instance, where it is possible, a party to a contract may exhibit dishonest or unreliable behaviour in order to secure a market advantage. However, the ability to do so will depend upon the nature of the context, the degree of uncertainty in the environment and the extent to which information between the parties is 'asymmetrical.'

Williamson introduces several other concepts which attest to the bilateral nature of exchange and the distortions that are introduced and which need to be overcome when real-life interactions fail to match the precise model of the classical market. 'Small numbers bargaining' gives the parties to an initial contract an advantage over parties not so included in the contract and tends to constitute a conservative pressure for firms not to change or not to be responsive to actual market signals. In this sense, the convenience of preserving an existing arrangement, or of continuing to hire existing staff, may override the fact that more competitive tenders exist, or that 'better' or less disruptive staff could be employed. The concept of 'asset specificity' is related, for long term parties to a contract tend to have specific assets which become a form of bargaining power and, again, militate against change in line with the expectations generated by the classical model of the market order.

In the context of these potentially disruptive influences, TCE proposes that forms of administrative and governance structures can be instituted which counteract these adverse effects and which render transaction costs efficient relative to a specific form of market competition. Hence, while opportunism and bounded rationality produce different kinds of costs, these must be in turn offset by the types of governance structures in place. AT becomes relevant here in specifying a formalised structure of contracts between principals and agents to counter the possible distortions or costs associated with opportunism and bounded rationality. Forms of monitoring and performance appraisal also operate in this regard. In his later works, Williamson (1991, 1992, 1994) focuses attention on public-sector governance issues and specifically with the problem of selecting governance structures which are most efficient i.e., which minimise the costs of the different organisational transactions involved.

Both AT and TCE, as well as the other neoliberal theories (such as PCT, Property Rights Theory), are relevant to understanding the unprecedented disaggregation of the public sector that has occurred in Britain and other OECD countries since the late 1980s. As Catherine Althaus (1997: 138) observes, AT has been central to the dramatic scale of the restructuring that has occurred in these countries. It has underpinned funder/provider and policy/delivery splits (the 'decoupling' strategies) both within the public-sector bureaucracy as well as between the bureaucracy and the state, and resulted in policies of deregulation, corporatisation, and privatisation. In addition, notes Althaus (1997: 137), "New Zealand and the United Kingdom have engaged in a unique application of agency theory which places them at the forefront of its application to the public sector." Indeed, "the striking aspect of an analysis of [the neoliberal]reform programme is its use of theory" notwithstanding the fact that "the agency model has serious deficiencies if applied uncritically to public sector management" (1997: 138). Such a model increases accountability and efficiency, rendering pubic non-private institutions analogous to private companies. As such:

> AT is a means of conceptualising and rationalising human behaviour and organ-isational forms…[i]t is a scrutiny of the interaction between a distinct relation-ship between two parties—the principal and agent—within a context assuming individual self-interest maximisation, bounded rationality, risk-aversion, goal conflict among members and the treatment of information as a commodity which can be purchased. (Althaus, 1997: 141)

Underpinning TCE as well as AT is Property Rights Theory (PRT), which is the fundamental grounding theory for the conception of self-interested human behaviour assumed in neoliberal theories. As such, the incentives structure of agents and principals in AT is assumed using PRT which is essentially a theory of 'ownership' of property as it inheres in the individual. Hence, central to PRT is the entitlement to scarce commodities and a conception of the system of exchange rules in terms of which such commodities may be transferred. As McKean (1974: 175) states, property rights are essentially "one's effective rights to do things and effec-tive claims to reward (positive or negative) as a result of one's action." Such a the-ory assists in conceptualising the structuring of incentives in relation to the management of institutions.

TCE with AT, PRT, and PCT are collectively represented as part and parcel of the New Institutional Economics (NIE) or of New Public Management (NPM). The common language of such approaches stresses concepts such as 'outputs,' 'out-comes,' 'accountability,' 'purchase,' 'ownership,' 'specification,' 'contracts,' 'purchase agreements,' etc. Central to such an approach is an emphasis on contract which ostensibly replaces central regulation by a new system of public administration which introduces such concepts as clarification of purpose, role clarification, task specification, reliable reporting procedures and the freedom to manage. According to Matheson (1997), contractualism includes relations where (1) parties have some autonomy to their role, (2) where there are distinctions between roles and therefore where a clarification of roles is obtainable, (3) where the specific role com-ponents are specifiable and where as a consequence individuals can be held account-able, (4) where responsibility flows downwards, rather than upwards, i.e., responsibility can be identified as fixed in terms of a specific role, (5) where the assignment of work is by agreement, (6) where there is an objective basis for judg-ing performance, (7) where transparency is a feature of the agreement process, and (8) where there are explicit consequences (sanctions or rewards) for fulfillment or non-fulfillment.

The consequence of such a contractualism was to view all work relations as principal-agent hierarchies, thereby redefining the appropriate process in terms of outputs, and where services are viewed in terms of cost and quality. Such a system gave rise to new patterns of employment (fixed-term contracts) and new forms of accountability whereby relationships were more directly clarified and services more clearly described. Such an approach has low transaction costs, few legal fees, and few direct compliance costs.

The New Institutional Economics, especially AT, constituted a strategy that appeared promising in terms of its commitments to (1) strategic management, (2) divestment of non-core activities, (3) re-engineering to create customer focus, (4) delayering/de-coupling, (5) total quality management, (6) use of modern information technology for management information systems, (7) improved accountability systems, and (8) establishing appropriate cultural values, teamwork and leadership. Not only was the NIE important for the selection and modification of governance structures, but it enabled a much tighter and clearer specification of roles, as well as greatly increased accountability. The key concerns of the NIE were a concern with transaction costs, concepts and principles for analysing them through enhanced specification of tasks and goals, increased transparency, clear allocation of responsibilities and duties, the imposition of a heightened incentive structure, a greater ability to monitor the contracts linked to a greatly increased accountability system. The following principles, derived from NIE, have been of central importance:

- separation of ownership and purchase responsibilities;
- separation of policy from operations;
- separation of funding, purchasing and provision of services;
- competition between service providers;
- reallocation of functions for focus, synergy and information. (Scott, 1997: 158)

All of these neoliberal theories assume that individuals are rational utility maximisers and, because of this, the interests of principals and agents will inevitably diverge. In any management context, the problems that the principal will have amount to a range of uncertainties and difficulties in obtaining information. In many senses, both principals and agents have access to information that the other party does not. In addition, agents will have an incentive to exploit their situation to their own advantage. They may, for instance, withhold information that would be to their disadvantage.

What were not noted by the political reformers, however, were the negative consequences of such disaggretative theories. In Britain Hede (1991: 38), Greer

(1992: 223) and Trosa (1994) note negative effects (increased tensions, rivalry, unnecessary duplication of services and resources, etc.) of disaggretative models. They maintain that when policy advice is separated from operations, the emergence of destructive sub-cultures can result, which can in turn lead to the duplication of advice as well as increased distrust and disruption instead of the theorised would-be benefits of greater contestability.

Neoliberal Governmentality and Higher Education

On this model, education is represented as an input-output system which can be reduced to an economic production function. The core dimensions of new public management are: flexibility (in relation to organisations through the use of contracts); clearly defined objectives (both organisational and personal), and a results orientation (measurement of and managerial responsibility for achievement). In addition, new public management in applying quasi market or private sector micro-techniques to the management of public sector organisations has replaced the 'public service ethic' whereby organisations were governed according to norms and values derived from assumptions about the 'common good' or 'public interest' with a new set of contractualist norms and rules. Hence notions of 'professional,' 'trustee' or 'fiduciary' are conceived as 'principal/agent relationships.' When organisations are ruled by new goverance arrangements and models, under relations of managerialised accountability, what happens to the presumption of trust that public servants will act in the public good?

There is also a complex and subtle shift in relation to political philosophy. Under *liberal governmentality*, the 'professions' constituted a mode of institutional organisation characterised by a principle of *autonomy* which characterised a form of power based on 'delegation' (i.e delegated authority) and underpinned by relations of trust. Under *neoliberal governmentality*, principal-agent line management chains replace delegated power with hierachical forms of authoratively structured relation, which erode, and seek to prohibit, an autonomous space from emerging. This shift in regulative modality constitutes a structural shift which is likely to transform the academic's role.

Neoliberalism cuts across the spaces of classical liberalism in other ways as well. The institutionalisation of models of principal-agent chains of line management inserts a hierarchical mode of authority by which the market and state pressures are instituted. For academic staff this carries with it the effect of *de-professionalisation*, involving:

- a shift from collegial or democratic governance in flat structures, to hier-

archical models based on dictated management *specifications* of job performance in principal-agent chains of command;

- the implementation of restructuring initiatives in response to market and
  state demands involves increasing *specifications* by management over work-
  loads and course content by management. Such hierarchically imposed
  specifications erode traditional conceptions of *professional autonomy* over
  work in relation to both teaching and research. Neoliberalism systematically deconstructs the space in terms of which professional autonomy is
  exercised;

- traditional conceptions of *professionalism* involved an ascription of rights
  and powers over work in line with classical liberal notions of freedom of
  the individual. Market pressures increasingly encroach and redesign their
  traditional understandings of rights, as TEIs must adapt to market trends
  (for example, just as individual departments and academics are being told
  of the necessity for acquiring external research grants, so they are also being
  told they must teach summer schools).

The essence of contractual models involves a *specification*, which is fundamentally at odds with the notion of *professionalism*. *Professionalism* conveys the idea of a
subject-directed power based upon the liberal conceptions of rights, freedom and
autonomy. It conveys the idea of a power given to the subject, and of the subject's
ability to make decisions in the workplace. No professional, whether doctor, lawyer
or teacher, has traditionally wanted to have the terms of their practice and conduct
dictated by anyone else but their peers, or determined by groups or structural levers
that are outside of their control. As a particular patterning of power, then, professionalism is systematically at odds with neoliberalism, for neoliberals see the professions as self-interested groups who indulge in rent-seeking behaviour. In
neoliberalism the patterning of power is established on contract, which in turn is
premised upon a need for compliance, monitoring, and accountability organised
in a management line and established through a purchase contract based upon measurable outputs.

Some recent writers have maintained that the impact of neoliberalism on the
nature of professionalism is problematic. For instance, Nixon, et al. (2001) and Du
Gay (1996) argue that professionals have constructed a new form of identity more
suited to managerialism. They have claimed that managerial reforms have restructured the identity of professionals. Also Susan Halford and Peter Leonard (1999:
120) argue "we cannot assume that this is in any way an automatic or linear
process, or that individuals respond in ways in which are consistent or coherent."
Or, as Simkins (2000: 330) suggests:

It is dangerous...to draw sweeping conclusions about the replacement of the traditional bureau-professional organisational order in education by a managerial one. Rather, it is better to view the process as a dynamic one in which growing tensions between 'old' and 'new' are worked out within particular policy and management areas as different value systems and interests of influence.

While we are open to the contention that new 'emergent' possibilities exist, in our view neoliberalism constitutes a 'structural selectivity,' in Offe's (1984) sense, that alters the nature of the professional role. Targets and performance criteria are increasingly applied from *outside* the academic role that diminish the sense in which the academic—their teaching and research—are *autonomous*. The rising importance on 'managed research,' and the pressures to obtain 'funded research' constitute further evidence that academic freedom, at least in terms of the academics' determination over research are concerned, are increasingly 'compromised,' or at least 'under pressure.' The extent to which the ideal expressed by Kant and Newman, of the university as an institutionally autonomous and politically insulated realm, where there are traditional commitments to a liberal conception of professional autonomy, in keeping with a public service ethic, has any relevance in a global economic order, is increasingly seen as an irrelevant concern.

Competitive Neutrality as the Reason of Neoliberalism

One of the major objectives of the reforms in higher education has been to install relations of competition as a way of increasing productivity, accountability and control. Increased competition represents improved quality within neoliberalism. As Marginson (1997: 5) points out:

> Increased competition is meant to increase responsiveness, flexibility and rates of innovation...increase diversity of what is produced and can be chosen...enhance productive and allocative efficiency...improve the quality and volume of production...as well as strengthen accountability to students, employers, and government. More indirect advantages are "internationalisation...fiscal reduction...and university-business links." There is, he says "an imagined line of causation from competition to consumer sovereignty to better efficiency and quality that is the virtuous ideal glowing at the core of micro-economic reform in higher education" (Marginson, 1997: 5).

What such a competitive ordering results in is a new type of approach to academia which, with the addition of a particular funding model, conflicts with and interferes with traditional notions of professional academic autonomy and freedom.

In this process the values of disinterested inquiry and respect for the integrity of the subject matter compete with a new set of pressures to 'dumb' courses down, as well as to demonstrate their relevance to labour market conditions and prospects.

In that competitive neutrality is a state-engineered 'market-driven' programme, it must be considered as a series of supply-side levers introduced to increase responsiveness of the universities to the market order and to market interests of their customers. Yet, it must also be considered as an imperfect programme, for as Marginson (1997: 8) points out, the elite tertiary institutions can rely on their reputations "obtained…in a long slow accumulation of social investment," and in this sense, the top segment of the tertiary education market is not contestable:

> As competitiveness is ratcheted upwards, the seller's market is enhanced. The leading schools and university faculties have long waiting lists. These institutions choose the student-consumer, more than the student choosing them. They do not need to become cheaper, more efficient, or more responsive to gain support, and to expand would be to reduce their positional value. (Marginson, 1997: 7–8)

Marginson (1999) has observed that various organisational changes have accompanied these changes in universities under the period of neoliberal restructuring. In a major study of 'management practices in higher education' in Australia, prepared for publication as *The Enterprise University: Governance, Strategy, Reinvention* (Marginson and Considine, 2000), management practices were examined in some 17 Australian universities. Summarising some of the findings from this study, Marginson (1999: 7–8) notes the following elements as they affect the organisational form of universities:

- the emergence of a new kind of leadership in universities. In this model, the vice-chancellor is a "strategic director and change agent." Universities are now run as corporations according to "formulae, incentives, targets and plans";
- the appointment of vice-chancellors who are 'outsiders' , and who are not organically linked to the institution. This practice is in turn supported by a growing apparatus of DVCs and PVCs, AVCs, executive deans, etc., with loyalty to the centre rather than to disciplines or faculties;
- the partial transformation of governing councils into corporate boards and the sidelining of academic boards;
- the rise of flexible executive-directed systems for internal university consultation and communication, from internal market research to vice-chancellors' advisory groups;
- the rise of new property structures concerning international education, intellectual property, relations with industry, and work-based training;

- the removal from collegial view of key decisions regarding governance;
- the partial breakdown of traditional disciplinary structures in the creation of schools (rather than departments) for teaching purposes;
- the creation of limited life areas of research or research centres, sponsored from above for research funding purposes;
- research management is subject to homogenising systems for assessing performance;
- a diminishment of the role of peer input into decisions about research;
- an increasing irrelevance of the disciplinary organisation of research;
- a prioritisation of research in terms of *quantity of research income* rather than in terms of *numbers of publications* produced or in terms of *quality of scholarship*.

A further consequence of marketisation has been the increased emphasis on performance and accountability assessment, with the accompanying use of performance indicators and personal appraisal systems. This has generated a concern with corporate loyalty and the use of discipline against employees who criticise their universities. Universities in this model have become concerned with their market reputation and become increasingly intolerant of adverse criticism of the institution by the staff. Such policies are the logical outcome of privatisation: in the private sector employees are not permitted to criticise their employer in public. Under neoliberal corporatisation many universities are employing advertising and public relations agencies to ensure that only positive statements appear about the university and its products.

From the neoliberal perspective, however, professionalism is distrusted in that it generates the conditions for opportunism, sets self-serving standards, and is prone to provider-capture. Neoliberalism has thus advocated a shift in the forms of accountability to an emphasis on market processes and quantifiable output measures. We can distinguish two main types of accountability:

> *bureaucratic*—professional accountability, is ex-ante, where rules and regulations are specified in advance and accountability is measured in terms of process; formulated in terms of standards, based on expertise of those who work in a particular area;

> *consumer*—managerial accountability, associated with market systems, based on price; which works in terms of contracts in which the performance is rewarded or punished according to the achievement of pre-set targets and externally imposed objectives.

Under the neoliberal period there has been a shift from 'bureaucratic-professional' forms of accountability to 'consumer-managerial' accountability models. Under consumer-managerial forms of accountability, academics must demonstrate their utility to society by placing themselves in an open market and accordingly competing for students who provide the bulk of core funding through tuition fees. If academic research has value, it can stand up to the rigors of competition for limited funds.

An ideal-type model of the internal governance of universities which indicates the conflict between neoliberal managerial and liberal professional cultures, as we are distinguishing those terms here, is presented in Table 1.

Also occuring in conjunction with the neoliberal policies described above have been developments to make university courses and programmes more relevant to the world of work, as well as changes in the nature of knowledge. The rise of the professional doctorate (see Brunner, Bowden and Laing, 2000) and criticisms of traditional academic programmes and courses are significant here (Clarke, 1998; Harris, 1996; DfEE, 1999; Becher, Henkel and Kogan, 1994; Pearson and Pike, 1989; Pearson et al., 1991). As universities are adapted to the market order there has been growing concern about the limited impact of research on professional practice and a shifting emphasis towards evidence-based practice (Sackett, et al., 1996).

In some disciplinary areas, such as Education, neoliberalism has seen a move towards a concentration on professional work-based (as opposed to academic) practice, such as has occurred in relation to teacher education. This has encouraged not only the growth of professional doctorates but a new theoretical literature, linked to the professional goals now pursued. Schon's *The Reflective Practitioner* (1983) offers an understanding of the process by which practitioners enhance their professional capabilities. In addition, concepts such as 'situated learning' (Lave and Wenger, 1991) and 'communities of practice' (Wenger and Snyder, 2000) link with the concept of the the 'reflective practitioner,' and also with those of 'experiential learning,' 'critical thinking' and 'critical reflection' to constitute a *transformed* theoretical infrastructure to the new understanding of academic theory as preparation for the world of professional work.

As well as trends towards an increased emphasis upon practitioner research and a growing emphasis on work-based learning, there have been a growth in alternative sources of knowledge outside the universities, a shift from an elite system of higher education to a mass system of higher education, an increasing emphasis on transferable skills, and a general shift towards vocationalism and professionalism in higher education generally.

In addition, there has been an increasing legitimacy within the university of new forms of knowledge. Gibbons et al. (1994) distinction between Mode 1 and Mode 2 knowledge is relevant here. Mode 1 knowledge is that which has been traditionally produced in the academy separately from its use. Mode 2 knowledge, by contrast, is knowledge which is produced in-use, linked directly to the functional imperatives of the world of work[4]. According to Bourner, Bowden and Laing (2000: 22) :

Mode 2 knowledge is likely to be produced by practitioners through reflection on practice or as a result of learning their way out of problems encountered in situ at work. It is less likely than mode 1 knowledge to respect traditional academic disciplines, and is work-based knowledge rather than campus-based knowledge

The authors then cite Brennan and Little (1996: 33) who state:

. . . mode 2 knowledge production takes place largely in the market or social arena. Unlike mode 1 knowledge, mode 2 does not require a 'privileged' and 'protected' arena for its development. It (knowledge) is no longer only an 'input' into social and economic processes, it is also an important 'output' of such processes.

Table 1: Ideal-Type Model of Internal Governance of Universities

	Neo-Liberal	Liberal
Mode of operation	private	public
Mode of control	'hard' managerialism; contractual specification between principal-agent; autocratic control	'soft' managerialism; collegial-democratic voting; professional consensus; diffuse control
Management function	managers; line-management; cost centres	leaders; community of scholars; professions; faculty
Goals	maximise outputs; financial profit; efficiency; massification; privatisation	knowledge; research; inquiry; truth; reason; elitist; not-for-profit
Work relations	competitive; hierarchical; workload indexed to market; corporate loyalty; no adverse criticism of university	trust; virtue ethics; professional norms; freedom of expression and criticism; role of public intellectual
Accountability	audit; monitoring; consumer-managerial; performance indicators; output based (ex post)	'soft' managerialism; professional-bureaucratic; peer review and facilitation; rule based (ex ante)
Marketing	centres of excellence; competition; corporate image; branding; public relations	The Kantian ideal of reason; specialisation; communication; truth; democracy
Pedagogy/teaching	semesterisation; slenderisation of courses; modularisation; distance learning; summer schools; vocational; mode 2 knowledge	full year courses; traditional academic methods and course assessment methods; knowledge for its own sake; mode 1 knowledge
Research	externally funded; contestable; separated from teaching; controlled by government or external agency	integrally linked to teaching; controlled from within the university; initiated and undertaken by individual academics

Source: Olssen, 2002, p. 45.

Knowledge As the New Form of Capital Under Neoliberalism

The most significant material change that underpins neoliberalism in the 21st century is the rise in the importance of knowledge as capital. This change, more than any, propels "*the neoliberal project of globalization*"—an outcome of the Washington consensus and modelled by world policy agencies such as the IMF and World Bank—has predominated in world policy forums at the expense of alternative accounts of globalization.[5] It is an account that universalises policies and obscures country and regional differences. It also denies the capacity of local traditions, institutions and cultural values to mediate, negotiate, reinterpret and transmute the dominant model of globalization and the emergent form of knowledge capitalism on which it is based. Yet the voices of criticism, even from mainstream economists, have been raised against this monolithic and homogenizing model of globalization.

For example, Joseph Stiglitz, as former Chief Economist of the World Bank, has recently criticized the policy decisions of the International Monetary Fund (IMF) as "a curious blend of ideology and bad economics." In particular, he argues that the IMF's structural adjustment policies, imposed on developing countries, have led to hunger and riots in many countries and precipitated crises that have led to greater poverty and international inequalities. Elsewhere, Stiglitz identifies the new global "knowledge economy" as one that differs from the traditional industrial economy in terms of the scarcity-defying characteristics of ideas. He suggests "movement to the knowledge economy necessitates a rethinking of economic fundamentals" because, he maintains, knowledge is different from other goods in that it shares many of the properties of a *global* public good which implies a key role for governments in protecting intellectual property rights in a global economy marked by greater potential monopolies than those of the industrial age (Stiglitz, 1999; see also Peters, 2001, 2002b, 2000e, 2000d).

Yet at the heart of Joseph Stiglitz's (2002) analysis of globalization and its discontents is an approach based on the economics of information—in particular, *asymmetries of information*—and its role in challenging standard economic models of the market that assumed perfect information. Information economics provides better foundations for theories of labor and financial markets. His work on the role of information in economics evolved into an analysis of the role of information in political institutions, where he emphasized

> the necessity for increased transparency, improving the information that citizens have about what these institutions do, allowing those who are affected by the policies to have a greater say in their formulation (Stiglitz, 2002: xii).

The transformation of knowledge production and its legitimation, as Stiglitz indicates, are central to an understanding of neoliberal globalization and its effects on education policy. If transformations in knowledge production entail a rethinking of economic fundamentals, the shift to a knowledge economy also requires a profound rethinking of education as emerging forms of knowledge capitalism, involving knowledge creation, acquisition, transmission and organisation.

The term 'knowledge capitalism' emerged only recently to describe the transition to the so-called 'knowledge economy,' which we characterise in terms of the economics of abundance, the annihilation of distance, the de-territorialisation of the state, and, investment in human capital (see Figure 1). As the business development and policy advocate Burton-Jones (1999: vi) puts it "knowledge is fast becoming the most important form of global capital—hence 'knowledge capitalism.'" He views it as a new *generic* form of capitalism as opposed simply to another regional model or variation. For Burton-Jones and analysts of world policy agencies such as the World Bank and OECD, the shift to a knowledge economy involves a fundamental rethinking of the traditional relationships between education, learning and work, focusing on the need for a new coalition between education and industry. 'Knowledge capitalism' and 'knowledge economy' are twin terms that can be traced at the level of public policy to a series of reports that emerged in the late 1990s by the OECD (1996) and the World Bank (1998, 1999), before they were taken up as a policy template by world governments in the late 1990s (see, e.g., Peters, 2001).

In terms of these reports, education is reconfigured as a massively undervalued form of knowledge capital that will determine the future of work, the organisation of knowledge institutions and the shape of society in the years to come. With respect to the economics of knowledge and information today we can tentatively identify at least six important strands, all beginning in the post War period and all but one (i.e., new growth theory) associated with the rise to prominence of the neoclassical second (1960s–70s) and third (1970s–Today) Chicago schools.[6]

1. The economics of information pioneered by Jacob Marschak (and coworkers Miyasawa, and Radner), and George Stigler, who won the Nobel Memorial Prize for his seminal work in the economic theory of information;

2. Fritz Machlup (1962) who laid the groundwork and developed the economics of the production and distribution of knowledge (see Mattessich, 1993);

3. The application of free-market ideas to education by Milton and Rose

Friedman (1962), although Friedman's form of monetarism has become relatively less important;

4. The economics of human capital developed first by Theodore Schultz (1963), and later by Gary Becker (e.g., 1964) in New Social Economics;

5. Public Choice theory developed under James Buchanan and Gordon Tullock (1962);

6. New growth theory, which has highlighted the role of education in the creation of human capital and in the production of new knowledge and explored the possibilities of education-related externalities, not specified by neoclassical theory.

The knowledge economy differs from the traditional economy in several key respects:

1. The economics is not of scarcity, but rather of abundance. Unlike most resources that deplete when used, information and knowledge can be shared, and actually grow through application.

2. The effect of location is diminished. Using appropriate technology and methods, virtual marketplaces and virtual organizations can be created that offer benefits of speed and agility, of round the clock operation and of global reach.

3. Laws, barriers and taxes are difficult to apply on solely a national basis. Knowledge and information 'leak' to where demand is highest and the barriers are lowest.

4. Knowledge enhanced products or services can command price premiums over comparable products with low embedded knowledge or knowledge intensity.

5. Pricing and value depends heavily on context. Thus the same information or knowledge can have vastly different value to different people at different times.

6. Knowledge when locked into systems or processes has higher inherent value than when it can 'walk out of the door' in people's heads.

7. Human capital - competencies - are a key component of value in a knowledge-based company, yet few companies report competency levels in annual reports. In contrast, downsizing is often seen as a positive 'cost cutting' measure.

Source: David Skyrme Associates Home Page
Web page ref http://www.skyrme.com/insights/21gke.htm

Figure 1. Characteristics of the Knowledge Economy

The public policy focus on science and technology, in part, reflects a growing consensus in macroeconomics of 'new growth' or 'endogenous growth theory,' based on the work of Solow (1956, 1994), Lucas (1988) and Romer (1986, 1990, 1994), that the driving force behind economic growth is technological change (i.e., improvements in knowledge about how we transform inputs into outputs in the production process). On this model technological change is *endogenous*, "being determined by the deliberate activities of economic agents acting largely in response to financial incentive" (Snowdon & Vane, 1999: 79). The neoclassical growth model developed by Solow assumed technology to be exogenous and therefore available without limitation across the globe. Romer's endogenous growth model, by contrast, demonstrates that technology is not a pure public good for while ideas are *non-rivalrous* they are also partially *excludable* through the legal system and patents. The policy implication is twofold: knowledge about technology and levels of information flow are critical for economic development and can account for differential growth patterns. Knowledge gaps and information deficiencies can retard growth prospects of poor countries, while technology transfer policies can greatly enhance long-term growth rates and living standards.[7] Let us now turn to three accounts of knowledge capitalism that represent a new orthodoxy.

The Knowledge Economy: Reports of World Policy Agencies

The OECD and New Growth Theory

The OECD report *The Knowledge-based Economy* (1996a) begins with the following statement:

> OECD analysis is increasingly directed to understanding the dynamics of the knowledge-based economy and its relationship to traditional economics, as reflected in *"new growth theory."* The growing codification of knowledge and its transmission through communications and computer networks has led to the emerging *"information society."* The need for workers to acquire a range of skills and to continuously adapt these skills underlies the *"learning economy."* The importance of knowledge and technology diffusion requires better understanding of knowledge networks and *"national innovation systems."*

The report is divided into three sections focusing on trends and implications of the knowledge-based economy, the role of the science system in the knowledge-based economy and indicators, essentially a section dealing with the question of measurement (see also OECD, 1996b, 1996c, 1997; Foray & Lundvall, 1996). In the

Summary, the OECD report discusses *knowledge distribution* (as well as knowledge investments) through formal and informal networks as being essential to economic performance and hypothesises the increasingly codification of knowledge in the emerging *"information society."* In the knowledge-based economy "innovation is driven by the interaction of producers and users in the exchange of both codified and tacit knowledge." The report points to an interactive model of innovation (replacing the old linear model), which consists of knowledge flows and relationships among industry, government and academia in the development of science and technology. With increasing demand for more highly skilled knowledge workers the OECD indicates:

> Governments will need more stress on upgrading human capital through promoting access to a range of skills, and especially the capacity to learn; enhancing the *knowledge distribution power* of the economy through collaborative networks and the diffusion of technology; and providing the enabling conditions for organisational change at the firm level to maximise the benefits of technology for productivity (p. 7).

The science system—public research laboratories and institutions of higher education—is seen as one of the key components of the knowledge economy, and the report identifies the major challenge as one of reconciling traditional functions of knowledge production and training of scientists with its newer role of collaborating with industry in the transfer of knowledge and technology.

In their analysis of the knowledge-based economy in one of the earliest reports to use the concept, the OECD observe that economies are more strongly dependent on knowledge production, distribution and use than ever before and that knowledge-intensive service sectors (especially education, communications and information) are the faster growing parts of western economies, which, in turn, are attracting high levels of public and private investment (spending on research reached an average of 2.3 and education accounts for 12 per cent of GDP, in the early 1990s). The report indicates how knowledge and technology have always been considered external influences on production and that now new approaches are being developed so that knowledge can be include more directly. (The report mentions Friedrich List on knowledge infrastructure and institutions; Schumpeter, Galbraith, Goodwin and Hirschman on innovation; and Romer and Grossman on new growth theory). New growth theory, in particular, demonstrates that investment in knowledge is characterised by increasing rather than decreasing returns, a finding which modifies the neo-classical production function that argues returns diminish as more capital is added to the economy. Knowledge also has spill-over functions from one industry or firm to another, yet types of knowledge vary: some kinds can be easily reproduced and distributed at low cost, while others cannot be easily transferred from one organisation to another or between individuals. Thus, knowledge (as a much broader concept than information) can be considered in terms of "*know-what*" and "*know-why*," broadly what philosophers call propositional knowledge ("knowledge that") embracing both factual knowledge and scientific knowledge, both of which come closest to being market commodities or economic resources that can be fitted into production functions. Other types of knowledge, what the OECD identify as "*know-how*" and "*know-who*" are forms of tacit knowledge (after Polanyi, 1967, see also Polanyi, 1958) which are more difficult to codify and measure. The OECD report indicates that "**Tacit knowledge** in the form of skills needed to handle codified knowledge is more important than ever in labour markets" (p. 13, bold in original) and reason "Education will be the centre of the knowledge-based economy, and learning the tool of individual and organisational advancement" (p. 14), where "*learning-by-doing*" is paramount.[8]

Joseph Stiglitz and the World Bank: 'Knowledge for Development'

The World Development Report *Knowledge for Development* (The World Bank, 1998/99) as its President, James D. Wolfensohn, summarises "examines the role of knowledge in advancing economic and social well being." He indicates, "It [the report] begins with the realization that economics are built not merely through the accumulation of physical and human skill, but on the foundation of information, learning, and adaptation." The World Development Report is significant in that it proposes that we look at the problems of development in a new way—from the perspective of knowledge. Indeed, Joseph Stiglitz, ex-Chief Economist of the World Bank, who resigned over ideological issues, ascribed a new role for the World Bank. He draws an interesting connection between knowledge and development with the strong implication that universities as traditional knowledge institutions have become the leading future service industries and need to be more fully integrated into the prevailing mode of production—a fact not missed by countries like China who are busy restructuring their university systems for the knowledge economy. He asserts that the World Bank has shifted from being a bank for infrastructure finance to being what he calls a "Knowledge Bank." He writes: "We now see economic development as less like the construction business and more like education in the broad and comprehensive sense that covers knowledge, institutions, and culture" (Stiglitz, 1999: 2). Stiglitz argues that the "movement to the knowledge economy necessitates a rethinking of economic fundamentals" because, he maintains, knowledge is different from other goods in that it shares many of the properties of a *global* public good. This means, among other things, a key role for governments in protecting intellectual property rights, although appropriate definitions of such rights are not clear or straightforward. It signals also dangers of monopolization, which, Stiglitz suggests, may be even greater for knowledge economies than for industrial economies.

The World Development Report *Knowledge for Development* focuses on two types of knowledge and two problems that are taken as critical for developing countries—*knowledge about technology*, that is technical knowledge or simply "know-how" such as nutrition, birth control or software engineering, and *knowledge about attributes* such as the quality of a product or the diligence of a worker. Developing countries typically have less "know-how" than advanced countries which the World Bank report calls *knowledge gaps*. Often also developing countries suffer from incomplete knowledge of attributes which the report calls *information problems*. Development, thus, is radically altered in this conceptualisation where it becomes a matter of narrowing knowledge gaps through national policies and strategies for *acquiring*, *absorbing* and *communicating* knowledge, and addressing information problems through national policies designed to process the economy's financial information, increase knowledge of the environment and address information problems that hurt the poor. The actual details are less important than the way in which Hayekian views have inserted themselves in the World Bank's changed picture of development economics, an economics now centrally motivated by questions of knowledge and information.

Let us briefly note the importance of education to this development recipe. Acquiring knowledge not only involves using and adapting knowledge available elsewhere in the world—best acquired, so the report argues, through an open trading regime, foreign investment, and licensing agreements, but also local knowledge creation through research and development and building upon indigenous knowledge. Absorbing knowledge is the set of national policies that centrally concerns education, including universal basic education (with special emphasis on extending girls' education and other disadvantaged groups), creating opportunities for life-long learning, and supporting tertiary education, especially science and engineering. Communicating knowledge involves taking advantage of new information and communications technology, as the report would have it, through increased competition, private sector provision and appropriate regulation. Arguably, without delving further into this substantial report, the World Bank maintains its neoliberal orientation with an emphasis on open trade and privatisation, although it is recast in terms of the perspective of knowledge.

Stiglitz, perhaps, deviates more from the Washington consensus. In a series of related papers delivered in his role as Chief Economist for the World Bank he

(Stiglitz, 1999a) argues that knowledge is a public good because it is non-rivalrous, that is, knowledge once discovered and made public, operates expansively to defy the normal "law" of scarcity that governs most commodity markets.[9] Knowledge in its immaterial or conceptual forms—ideas, information, concepts, functions and abstract objects of thought—are purely non-rivalrous, that is, there is essentially zero marginal costs to adding more users. Yet once materially embodied or encoded, such as in learning or in applications or processes, knowledge becomes costly in time and resources. The pure non-rivalrousness of knowledge can be differentiated from the low cost of its dissemination, resulting from improvements in electronic media and technology, although there may be congestion effects and waiting time (to reserve a book, or download from the Internet). Stiglitz (1999a) delivered his influential paper "Public Policy for a Knowledge Economy" to the United Kingdom's Department for Trade and Industry and Center for Economic Policy Research on the eve of the release of the UK White Paper *Our Competitive Future: Building the Knowledge Driven Economy* (http://www.dti.gov.uk/comp/competitive/main.htm) which subsequently became a template for education policy in England and Scotland (see Peters, 2001). The paper also provides a useful guide for understanding some of the analytics of the knowledge economy (see Figure 2).

While non-rivalrous, knowledge can be *excluded* (the other property of a pure public good) from certain users. The private provision of knowledge normally requires some form of legal protection otherwise firms would have no incentive to produce it. Yet knowledge is not an ordinary property right. Typically, basic ideas, such as mathematical theorems, on which other research depends, are not patentable and, hence, a strong intellectual property right regime might actually inhibit the pace of innovation. Even though knowledge is not a pure public good, there are extensive externalities (spillovers) associated with innovations. As he notes, the full benefits of the transistor, microchip or laser did not accrue to those who contributed to those innovations.

While competition is necessary for a successful knowledge economy, Stiglitz maintains, knowledge gives rise to a form of increasing returns to scale, which may undermine competition for with large network externalities, forms of monopoly knowledge capitalism (e.g., Microsoft) become a possible danger at the international level. New technologies provide greater scope for the suppression of competition and, if creativity is essential for the knowledge economy, then small enterprises may provide a better base for innovation than large bureaucracies. Significantly, Stiglitz provides some grounds for government funding of universities as competitive knowledge corporations within the knowledge economy and for government regulation of knowledge or information monopolies, especially those multinational companies that provide the so-called information infrastructure.

It is argued that the knowledge economy is different from the traditional industrial economy because knowledge is fundamentally different from other commodities, and that these differences, consequently, have fundamental implications both for public policy and for the mode of organization of a knowledge economy.

The Scarcity-defying characteristics of ideas
(i) *Non-Rivalry*
(ii) *Conceptual vs Material Knowledge*

Intellectual property rights
(i) *Excludability*
(ii) *Externalities*
(iii) *Competition*

Organizational dimensions of knowledge
(i) *Knowledge markets*
(ii) *Knowledge transactions within firms*
(iii) *Openness and knowledge transfer*
(iv) *Experimentation*

The marketplace of ideas
(i) *Pluralism in project selection*
(ii) *Robustness*
(ii) *The failure of central planning*
(iii) *Decentralization and participation within firms*
(iv) *Openness in the political process*

Source: Adapted from Joseph Stiglitz (1999) "Public Policy for a Knowledge Economy". Remarks at the Department for Trade and Industry and Center for Economic Policy research, London, UK, January 27. Available at: ⟨http://www.worldbank.org/html/extdr/extme/jssp012799a.htm⟩.

Figure 2. Analytics of the Knowledge Economy

On the basis of this analysis Stiglitz provides a number of pertinent observations on the organisational dimensions of knowledge. He maintains that just as knowledge differs from other commodities so too knowledge markets differ from other markets. If each piece of information differs from every other piece, then information cannot satisfy the essential market property of *homogeneity*. Knowledge market transactions for non-patented knowledge requires that I disclose something and thus risk losing property. Thus, in practice, markets for knowledge and information depend critically on reputation, on repeated interactions, and, also significantly, on trust.

On the supply side, knowledge transactions within firms and organisations require trust and reciprocity if knowledge workers are to share knowledge and codify their tacit knowledge. Hoarding creates a vicious circle of knowledge restriction, whereas trust and reciprocity can create a culture based on a virtuous circle of knowledge sharing. On the demand side, *learning cultures* (my construction) will artificially limit demand for knowledge if they denigrate any requests for knowledge as an admission of ignorance.

He argues that these knowledge principles carry over to knowledge institutions and countries as a whole. If basic intellectual property rights are routinely violated, the supply of knowledge will be diminished. Where trust relationships have been flagrantly violated learning opportunities will vanish. Experimentation is another type of openness, which cannot take place in closed societies or institutions hostile to change. Finally, he argues that changes in economic institutions have counterparts in the political sphere, demanding institutions of the open society such as a free press, transparent government, pluralism, checks and balances, toleration, freedom of thought, and open public debate. This political openness is essential for the success of the transformation towards a knowledge economy.

Alan Burton-Jones and Knowledge Capitalism

Perhaps the most developed 'model' of knowledge capitalism, together with the most worked out implications for education, comes from a book of that title, i.e., *Knowledge Capitalism: Business, Work, and Learning in the New Economy* by Alan Burton-Jones (1999).[10] Burton-Jones states his thesis in the following way:

> The fundamental proposition of the book is that among the various factors currently causing change in the economy, none is more important than the changing role of *knowledge*…As the title of the book suggests, knowledge is fast becoming the most important form of global capital—hence 'knowledge capitalism.' Paradoxically, knowledge is probably the least understood and most undervalued of all economic resources. The central theme of this book is, therefore, the nature and value of knowledge and how it is fundamentally altering the basis of economic activity, thus business, employment, and all of our futures. The central message is that we need to reappraise many of our industrial era notions of business organisation, business ownership, work arrangements, business strategy, and the links between education, learning and work.

He argues that the distinctions between managers and workers, learning and working, are becoming blurred so that we all become owners of our own intellectual capital, all knowledge capitalists—at least in the western advanced economies. And he goes on to chart the shift to the knowledge economy, new models of knowledge-centred organisation, the imperatives of knowledge supply (as opposed to labour supply), the decline in traditional forms of employment and the knowledge characteristics of work. He argues that "economic demand for an increasingly skilled workforce will necessitate a move to lifelong learning" (p. vii) based upon the learning imperative, including the use of learning technologies, that will lead to the development of a global learning industry and to profound "changes to the relationships involving learners, educators and firms" (ibid.). Burton-Jones addresses himself to the question of how governments might assist in the transition to the knowledge economy by focusing on knowledge acquisition (education, learning, skills formation) and knowledge development (research, innovation) policies, suggesting that while most of the changes have occurred as a spontaneous response to the demands of the market rather than through state intervention, the state has an important role to play. He is less enthusiastic than Stiglitz or Thurow about the proposition that the increasing importance of knowledge in the economy might lead to a reversal of current trends leading to an increasing role for the state.

Our speculative hypothesis, not investigated in any length in this chapter, is that knowledge capitalism will exhibit different patterns of production, ownership and innovation according to five basic regional models of capitalism. These five regional models, in part, based on different cultural understandings of knowledge and learning, not only represent cultural differences over the meaning and value of knowledge but also will provide a major index for regional differences in education policy.

We can talk of Anglo-American capitalism, European social market capitalism, French state capitalism and the Japanese model. Clearly, one might also talk of an emergent fifth model based on China's market socialism. A recent World Bank study, for instance, has suggested that the Chinese government must take on the new role of architect of appropriate institutions and provider of incentives to promote and regulate a new socialist market economy based on knowledge (see Dahlman & Aubert, 2001).[11]

Yet the notion of the knowledge economy also represents something of an anomaly. With the massive sweep of neoliberal reforms restructuring and privatising the state sector, national education systems remain overwhelmingly part of the public sector, both state-owned and state-controlled. This is despite the recent wave of reforms in education emphasising choice and diversity through forms of privatisation or joint public-private funding partnerships, such as the Private Finance Initiative (PFI) in the UK. Moreover, the state provision of an increasingly 'massified' system of formal education is still the dominant form of the organisation of knowledge. Advocates of knowledge capitalism argue that state systems are struggling to release themselves from older predominantly industrial organisational forms to take advantage of more flexible and customised forms of delivery, underwritten by developments in ICT and based on notions of 'choice' and 'diversity' (e.g., Burton-Jones). Paradoxically, at a point historically when the interventionist state has been rolled back and when world governments have successfully eased themselves out of the market, often substituting market mechanisms for the allocation of scarce public goods and services, governments find themselves as the major owners and controllers of the means of knowledge production in the new knowledge economy. While some economists and policy analysts have argued that there are new grounds for reappraising the role for the state in the knowledge economy (Stiglitz, 1999; Thurow, 1996), most governments have pursued policies that have followed a process of incremental and parallel privatisation designed to blur the boundaries between the public and the private, learning and work.

In the age of knowledge capitalism, we can expect governments in the West to further ease themselves out of the public provision of education as they begin in earnest to privatise the means of knowledge production and experiment with new ways of designing and promoting a permeable interface between knowledge businesses and public education at all levels. In the last decade educationalists have witnessed the effects of the Hayekian revolution in the economics of knowledge and information, we have experienced the attack on 'big government' and reductions of state provision, funding and regulation. In the age of knowledge capitalism the next great struggle after the 'culture wars' of the 1990s will be the 'education wars,' a struggle not only over the meaning and value of knowledge both internationally and locally, but also over the public means of knowledge production. As Michel Foucault (1991b: 165) argued in the early 1980s in conversation with the Italian communist Duccio Trombadori:

> We live in a social universe in which the formation, circulation, and utilization of knowledge presents a fundamental problem. If the accumulation of capital has been an essential feature of our society, the accumulation of knowledge has not been any less so. Now, the exercise, production, and accumulation of this knowledge cannot be dissociated from the mechanisms of power; complex relations exist which must be analysed.

This chapter has traced the development of a neoliberal model of knowledge capitalism in higher education as a dimension of globalisation during the last thirty years. It charted the influence of Public Choice Theory and neoliberal theories of institutional redesign and concluded with a Foucaultian account of the concept of knowledge capitalism where ower and knowledge are two sides of the same coin.

Notes

1. Hayek's earliest statement is in *The Counter-Revolution of Science: Studies in the Abuse of Reason* (1952) where he defends a qualitative discontinuity between methods of natural and social sciences. There were also Kantian influences on Hayek's subjectivism in that, following Kant, he rejected the idea that knowledge could be constructed from a basis of raw sensory data, seeing order that we find in the world as a product of the creative activity of the human mind but suspecting that there are inherent limitations to the possibility of full explicit knowledge, and, in particular, an impossibility of ever fully explaining a mind as complex as our own (see *New Studies in Philosophy, Politics, Economics and the Study of Ideas*, London: Routledge, 1978, p.45, note 14). In addition, relatedly, Hayek denies the ontological independence of mind a la Descartes, denies the possibility of complete intellectual self-understand-

ing, and denies any foundationalism, seeing all criticism of social life as immanent criticism, and social order itself as spontaneous creation rather than as a rational construction.

2. There is an extensive literature on Agency Theory including Althaus (1997); Bendor (1988); Bergman and Lane (1990); Braun (1993); Boston (1991, 1996a, 1996b); Chan and Rosenbloom (1994); Deane (1989); Eisenhardt (1989); Heymann (1988); Jennings and Cameron (1987); Jensen and Meckling (1976); Kay (1992); Levinthal (1988); Moe (1984, 1990, 1991); Palmer (1993); Perrow (1986a, 1986b); Petersen (1993); Pratt and Zeckhauser (1985); Rees (1985a, 1985b); Scott and Gorringe (1989); Simon (1991); Thompson and Wright (1988); Treblicock (1995); Weingast (1984); Wistrich (1992).

3. For an introduction to Transaction Cost Economics see, Boston (1994), Boston et al. (1996b), Bryson and Smith-Ring (1990), Dow (1987), Perrow (1986a, 1986b), Vining and Weimer (1990), Williamson (1975, 1983, 1985, 1991, 1992).

4. Bourner, Bowden and Laing (2000) describe Mode 1 knowledge in terms of: knowing through contemplation; knowing that; knower as spectator; propositional knowledge; theoretical knowledge; knowledge for its own sake; knowledge about the world; knowledge that is produced and tested in the academy by researchers. Mode 2 knowledge is: knowing through action; knowing how; knower as agent; knowledge as reflection on practice; practical knowledge; working knowledge; knowledge in the world; knowledge that is created and tested in action in the world by practitioners.

5. There is a huge literature criticising globalization and suggesting alternatives. See, for example, Appadurai (2001), Bello (2001), Mandle (2002)

6. See the New School site on the Chicago School: (http://cepa.newschool.edu /het/schools/chicago.htm).

7. This is not to deny that other social sciences have contributed to the discourse on the knowledge economy and its earlier sibling concept of the knowledge society. In sociology, for instance, the notion of postindustrial society was first coined by Daniel Bell (1974) and Alain Touraine (1973) more than twenty years earlier, and developed as the information society and the network society by Manuel Castels (2000). In management theory, knowledge capitalism has been picked up in terms of the burgeoning field of 'knowledge management.'

8. The emphasis on tacit knowledge is developed out of the work of Polanyi (1958, 1967), which is also strongly developed in terms of the concept of practice in both Heidegger and Wittgenstein. The emphasis on *practice*, perhaps, is a major distinguishing characteristic of much twentieth-century philosophy, sociology and cultural analysis (see e.g. Turner, 1994) with a focus on the practical over the theoretical and 'background practices' against which theoretical knowledge is articulated and/or codified. The concept of practice, mostly unexamined figures largely in education and pedagogy and in the relatively new concept of 'communities of practice' that has been developed in the context of business and organisational learning.

9. This section on Stiglitz draws on the section "Analytics of the Knowledge Economy" from my recent paper "University, Globalisation and the Knowledge Economy" (Peters, 2002).

10. For a recent article by Burton-Jones see the inaugural issue of the web-based new start-up journal *Policy Futures in Education* co-edited by myself and Walter Humes, available at Triangle Publications from 2003 (www.triangle.co.uk). The inaugural issue is devoted to "Education and the Knowledge Economy" with contributions from Paul A David & Dominique Forey, Gerarde Delanty, Steve Fuller, and many others.

11. Dahlman & Aubert (2001) argue that improving education is perhaps the most critical reform for the medium and long runs.

4

Neoliberal Governmentality

Foucault on the Birth of Biopolitics

The political, ethical, social, philosophical problem of our days is not to liberate the individual from the State and its institutions, but to liberate ourselves from the State and the type of individualisation linked to it.

Foucault, 1982: 216

Power is exercised only over free subjects, and only insofar as they are free.

Foucault, 1982: 221

IN HIS GOVERNMENTALITY STUDIES IN THE LATE 1970S Foucault held a course at the Collège de France covering the major forms of neoliberalism, examining the three theoretical schools of German ordoliberalism, the Austrian school characterised by Hayek, and American neoliberalism in the form of the Chicago school. Among Foucault's great insights in his work on governmentality was the critical link he observed in liberalism between the governance of the self and government of the state—understood as the exercise of political sovereignty over a territory and its population. He focuses on government as a set of practices legitimated by specific rationalities and saw that these three schools of contemporary economic liberalism focused on the question of too much government—a permanent critique of the state that Foucault considers as a set of techniques for governing the self through the market. Liberal modes of governing, Foucault tells us, are distinguished in general by the ways in which they utilise the capacities of free acting subjects and, consequently, modes of government differ according to the value and definition accorded the concept of freedom. These different mentalities of rule, thus, turn on whether freedom is seen as a natural attribute as with the philosophers of the Scottish Enlightenment, a product of rational choice making, or, as with Hayek, a civilizational artefact theorised as both negative and anti-naturalist. This chapter first briefly discusses Foucault's approach to governmentality, before detailing and analysing Foucault's account of German *ordoliberalism,* a configuration based on the theoretical configuration of economics and law developed at the University of Freiberg by W. Eucken and F. Böhm that views the market contingently as developing historically within a judicial-legal framework. The economy is thus based on a concept of the Rule of Law, anchored in a notion of individual rights, property rights and contractual freedom that constitutes, in effect, an economic constitution. German neoliberal economists (Müller-Armack, Röpke, Rüstow) invented the term "social market economy" which shared certain features with the Freiburg model of law and economics but also differed from it in terms of the 'ethics' of the market (as did Hayek in *The Constitution of Liberty*). This formulation of the "social market economy" proved significant not only in terms of the post-war reconstruction of the (West) German economy but through Erhard, as Minister and Chancellor, became important as the basis of the EEC's and, later, EU's "social model."

Foucault's overriding interest was not in "knowledge as ideology," as Marxists would have it, where bourgeois knowledge, say, modern liberal economics was seen as false knowledge or bad science. Nor was he interested in "knowledge as theory" as classical liberalism has constructed disinterested knowledge, based on inherited distinctions from the Greeks, including Platonic epistemology and endorsed by the Kantian separation of schema/content that distinguishes the analytic enterprise. Rather Foucault examined *practices* of knowledge produced through the relations of power.[1] He examined how these practices, then, were used to augment and refine the efficacy and instrumentality of power in its exercise over both individuals and populations, and also in large measure helped to shape the constitution of subjectivity. Fundamental to his governmentality studies was the understanding that Western society professed to be based on principles of liberty and the Rule of Law and said to derive the legitimation of the State from political philosophies that elucidated these very principles. Yet as a matter of historical fact, Western society employed technologies of power that operated on forms of disciplinary order or were based on biopolitical techniques that bypassed the law and its freedoms altogether. As Colin Gordon (2001: xxvi) puts it so starkly: Foucault embraced Nietzsche as the thinker "who transforms Western philosophy by rejecting its founding disjunction of power and knowledge as myth." By this he means that the rationalities of Western politics, from the time of the Greeks, had incorporated techniques of power specific to Western practices of government, first, in the expert knowledges of the Greek tyrant and, second, in the concept of pastoral power that characterized ecclesiastical government.

It is in this vein that Foucault examines government as a practice and problematic that first emerges in the sixteenth century and is characterized by the insertion of economy into political practice. Foucault (2001: 201) explores the problem of government as it "explodes in the sixteenth century" after the collapse of feudalism and the establishment of new territorial States. Government emerges at this time as a general problem dispersed across quite different questions: Foucault mentions specifically the Stoic revival that focussed on the government of oneself; the government of souls elaborated in Catholic and Protestant pastoral doctrine; the government of children and the problematic of pedagogy; and, last but not least, the government of the State by the prince. Through the reception of Machiavelli's *The Prince* in the sixteenth century and its rediscovery in the nineteenth century, there emerges a literature that sought to replace the power of the prince with the art of government understood in terms of the government of the family, based on the central concept of "economy." The introduction of economy into political practice is for Foucault the essential issue in the establishment of the art of government. As he points out, the problem is still posed for Rousseau, in the mid-18th century, in the same terms—the government of the State is modelled on the management by the head of the family over his family, household and its assets.[2]

It is in the late sixteenth century, then, that the art of government receives its first formulation as "reason of state" that emphasizes a specific rationality intrinsic to the nature of the state, based on principles no longer philosophical and transcendent, or theological and divine, but rather centred on the *problem of population*. This became a science of government conceived of outside the juridical framework of sovereignty characteristic of the feudal territory and firmly focused on the problem of population based on the modern concept which enabled "the creation of new orders of knowledge, new objects of intervention, new forms of subjectivity and....new state forms" (Curtis, 2002: 2). It is this political-statistical concept of population that provided the means by which the government of the state came to involve individualization and totalization, and, thus, married Christian pastoral care with sovereign political authority. The new rationality of "reason of state" focussed on the coupled *population-wealth* as an object of rule, providing conditions for the emergence of political economy as a form of analysis. Foucault investigated the techniques of police science and a new bio-politics,

> which tends to treat the 'population' as a mass of living and co-existing beings, which evidence biological traits and particular kinds of pathologies and which, in consequence, give rise to specific knowledges and techniques (Foucault 1989: 106, cited in Curtis, 2002).

As Foucault (2001) comments in "The Political Technology of Individuals," the "rise and development of our modern political rationality" as "reason of state," that is, as a specific rationality intrinsic to the state, is formulated through "a new relation between politics as a practice and as knowledge" (p. 407), involving specific political knowledge or "political arithmetic" (statistics); "new relationships between politics and history," such that political knowledge helped to strengthen the state and at the same time ushered in an era of politics based on "an irreducible multiplicity of states struggling and competing in a limited history" (p. 409); and, finally, a new relationship between the individual and the state, where "the individual becomes pertinent for the state insofar as he can do something for the strength of the state" (p. 409). In analysing the works of von Justi, Foucault infers that the true object of the police becomes, at the end of the eighteenth century, the population; or, in other words, the state has essentially to take care of men as a population. It wields its power over living beings, and its politics, therefore has to be a biopolitics (p. 416).

Foucault's lectures on governmentality were first delivered in a course he gave at the Collège de France, entitled *Sécurité, Territoire, Population*, during the 1977–78 academic year. While the essays "Governmentality" and "Questions of Method" were published in 1978 and 1980, respectively, and translated into English in the collection *The Foucault Effect: Studies in Governmentality* (Burchell et al., 1991), it is only in the last few years that the course itself has been transcribed from original tapes and published for the first time (Foucault, 2004a), along with the sequel *Naissance de la biopolitique: Cours au Collège de France, 1978–1979* (Foucault, 2004b), although both books remain to be translated.[3] The governmentality literature in English, roughly speaking, dates from the 1991 collection and has now grown quite substantially (see, for example, Miller and Rose, 1990; Barry et al., 1996; Dean, 1999; Rose, 1999).[4] As a number of scholars have pointed out Foucault relied on a group of researchers to help him in his endeavours: François Ewald, Pasquale Pasquino, Daniel Defert, Giovanna Procacci, Jacques Donzelot, on governmentality; François Ewald, Catherine Mevel, Éliane Allo, Nathanie Coppinger and Pasquale Pasquino, François Delaporte and Anne-Marie Moulin, on the birth of biopolitics. These researchers working with Foucault in the late 1970s constitute the first generation of governmentality studies scholars and many have gone on to publish significant works too numerous to list here. In the field of education as yet not a great deal has focussed specifically on governmentality.[5]

Gordon (2001: xxiii) indicates three shifts that took place in Foucault's thinking: a shift from a focus on "specialized practices and knowledges of the individual person" "to the exercise of political sovereignty exercised by the state over an entire population"; the study of government as a *practice* informed and enabled by a specific rationality or succession of different rationalities; and, the understanding that liberalism, by contrast with socialism, possessed a distinctive concept and rationale for the activity of governing. Liberalism and neoliberalism, then, for Foucault represented distinctive innovations in the history of governmental rationality. In his governmentality studies Foucault focussed on the introduction of economy into the practice of politics and in a turn to the contemporary scene studied two examples: German liberalism during the period 1948–62, with an emphasis on the Ordoliberalism of the Freiburg School, and American neoliberalism of the Chicago School. In this chapter I focus of Foucault's reading of German neoliberalism, the emergence of the "social market" which has significance not only for understanding the historical development of an economic constitution and formulation of "social policy" (and the role of education policy within it), but also the development of the European social model, more generally, and the continued relevance for Third Way politics of the "social market economy."

German Neoliberalism and the Birth of Biopolitics

Naissance de la biopolitique (Foucault, 2004b) consists of thirteen lectures delivered by Foucault at the Collège de France (10 January-4th April, 1979). It is helpful to see this course in the series of thirteen courses he gave from 1970 to 1984. The first five courses reflected his early work on knowledge in the human sciences, concerning punishment, penal and psychiatric institutions: "La Volonté de savoir" (1970–71), "Théories et Institutions pénales" (1971–72), "La Société punitive" (1972–73), "Le Pouvoir psychiatrique" (1973–74), "Les Anormaux" (1974–75). The remaining eight courses focussed squarely on governmentality studies, with a clear emphasis also on the problematic (and hermeneutics) of the subject and the relation between subjectivity and truth: "Il faut défendre la société" (1975–76), "Securité, Territoire, Population" (1977–78), "Naissance de la biopolitique" (1978–79), "Du gouvernement des vivants" (1979–80), "Subjectivité et Vérité" (1980–81), "L'Herméneutique du subjet" (1981–82), "Le Gouvernement de soi et des autres" (1982–83), "Le Gouvernement de soi et des autres: le courage de la verite" (1983–84). Even from this list of courses it become readily apparent that the question of government concerns Foucault for the last decade of his life and that for his governmentality studies, politics were inseparable in its modern forms both from biology—biopower and the government of the living—and truth and subjectivity. It is important to note that these same concerns in one form or another enter into Foucault's formulations in *Naissance de la biopolitique.*[6]

In the first lecture, having dealt with the question of method and reviewed the preceding year, Foucault signals his intention to pursue the question of how the introduction of political economy served as an internal (and defining) principle limiting the practice of liberal government. In the second lecture, he considers French radical jurisprudence and English utilitarianism as emerging solutions to the problem of the limitation of the exercise of public power. He begins to specify the novel features of the art of liberal government as consisting in three related aspects: the constitution of the market as a form of truth and not simply a domain of justice; the problem of the limitation of the exercise of public power; and the problem of equilibrium in the internal competition of European states. With Adam Smith and the Physiocrats he charts the birth of a new European model based on the principle of the "freedom of the market" that surface with discussion of international trade, rights of the sea, and perpetual peace in the 18th century. I focus more heavily on lectures 4–8 in the course because they concern German neoliberalism and may be, therefore, more of interest to my German colleagues. They also contain the bulk of the references to Hayek. Lectures 9 and 10 focus of American neoliberalism, and lectures 11 and 12 investigate the model and history of *homo economicus* and the notion of civil society.[7]

Foucault begins the fourth lecture with a discussion of "fear of the State" or State phobia which had surfaced in the 1920s with the calculation debate of Mises and anti-Socialist sentiments of the Austrian School and which came to a head in Germany after the World War II with the experience of National Socialism, postwar reconstruction and the development of the Keynesian interventionist welfare state in Britain and Roosevelt's New Deal in the US. (Foucault also mentions the opposition between Keynes at Cambridge and Hayek at LSE. Hayek was recruited by the Director, Lionel Robbins in the early 1930s). In the context of post-war reconstruction Foucault details the Marshall Plan, adopted in 1948, and the Scientific Council set up in 1947 in Germany with the function, in the Anglo-American zone, of undertaking the reconstruction and administration of the economy. The Council comprised representatives of the Freiburg School (W. Eucken, F. Böhm, A. Müller-Armack, L. Miksch, A. Lampe, O. Veit and others) as well as members of the Christian Socialists. Much of his analysis of post-war Germany in these early years focuses on the role of Ludwig Erhard (1897–1977).

Erhard drafted the memorandum of war financing and debt consolidation and later as a member of the Bavarian Cabinet became Minister of Economics responsible for currency reform. As deputy of the Christian Democrats he was instrumental in introducing the politico-economic concept of the "social market economy" and becomes Minister of Economics in the first Adenauer government in 1949. He later became a council member of the Coal and Steel Community, Governor of the World Bank, appointed Müller-Armack as Secretary of State at the Economics Ministry in Bonn from 1958–63, played a strong role in the EEC, and eventually was elected as the Federal Chancellor of the CDU in 1963 and remained so until 1967.[8] Foucault's emphasis is on the concept of the "social market economy" which Erhard established in 1948, fundamentally changing the West German economy, and with it the whole of post-war society. The social market economy was coined by the national economist Müller-Armack to define an economic system based on the free market principles, aimed at guaranteeing economic efficiency and social justice with a high degree of individual freedom. The crucial aspect for Foucault's governmentality studies is that the social market economy was devised as an economic system combining market freedom with social equilibrium, where the government played a strong regulatory role by creating a juridical-legal framework for market processes that both secured competition and ensured social equity.

In the fifth lecture Foucault begins to outline the German programme of neoliberalism by reference to the theoreticians, Eucken, Böhm, Müller-Armark and Hayek. Eucken was co-founder of the *ordoliberalen* Freiburg School with the jurists, Böhm and Hans Großmann-Doerth, who were united in their concern for constitutional foundations of a free economy and society, an approach that combined law and economics.[9] They were concerned to provide an institutional framework for the competitive order based on transparent rules for the efficient functioning of a private market economy embodied in the concept of "complete competition," which involved State monitoring of monopolies and anti-trust laws. Other aspects of the *ordoliberalen* framework included monetary stability, open markets, private property and ownership of the means of production, and freedom of contract between autonomous economic agents, including liability for one's commitments and actions.

The ordoliberal Freiburg School, as Vanberg (2004: 2) usefully notes, while certainly part of the foundations on which the social market economy was created and generally subsumed under the rubric of *German neoliberalism*, also exhibited differences with neoliberal economists such as Müller-Armack, Röpke and Rüstow.

> For the Freiburg School the market order, as a non-discriminating, privilige-free [sic] order of competition, is in and by itself an ethical order. As far as the need

for "social insurance" is concerned, the Freiburg ordo-liberals recognized that the competitive market order can be, and should be, combined with a system of minimal income guarantees for those who are, temporarily or permanently, unable to earn a living by providing saleable services in the market. They insisted, though, that such social insurance provisions must be of a nondiscriminating, privilege-free nature, and must not be provided in ways—e.g. in the form of subsidies or other privileges granted to particular industries—that corrupt the fundamental ethical principle of the market order, namely its privilege-free nature. Müller-Armack, by contrast, regards the market order as an economically most efficient order, but not as one that has inherent ethical qualities. It is a "technical instrument" that can be used by society to produce wealth, but it does not make itself for a "good" society. It has to be made "ethical" by supplementary policies, in particular "social" policies. The important point is that in Müller-Armack's case, these supplementary "social provisions" that are supposed to make the market economy—beyond its economic efficiency—ethically appealing are not constrained, as they are in for the Freiburg ordoliberals, by the proviso that they must not be in conflict with the privilege-free nature of the rules of the game of the market.[10]

Foucault proceeds to discuss obstacles to political liberalism that had beset Germany since the 19th century, including economic protectionism, the socialism of the Bismarckian State, the role of WWI and economic reconstruction, a type of Keynesian rigidity, and the political economy of National Socialism. The neoliberal critique of National Socialism and State phobia is the starting point for an extension of this critique to both the New Deal in the US and Beveridge's Welfare State in the UK, that is, to the growth and development of the power of the State, and to standardization and massification as infringements of individual liberty defined through competition. Foucault claims that German neoliberalism enjoyed a novel relationship with classical liberalism through its constitutional theory of pure competition.

Lectures 4, 5 and 6 are devoted exclusively to "le néolibéralisme allemande" and Foucault in the last of these three lectures is concerned to discover what distinguishes neoliberalism from classical liberalism. He responds by arguing that the problem of neoliberalism is knowledge (savoir) of how to exercise global political power based on the principles of a market economy and he suggests that a major transformation occurred with the association between the principle of the market economy and the political principle of laissez-faire that presented itself through a theory of pure competition. Pure competition emerged as the formal structure of property that neoliberals saw as means for regulating the economy through the price mechanism.

He traces problems of government in this period in relation to monopolies and political society. He also examines the emergence in post-war Germany of what he calls "politique de société" or *Gesellschaftspolitik,* which I translate as "social policy," and the ordoliberal critique of the welfare state (l'économie de bien-être), where society is modelled on the enterprise society, and enterprise society and the good society come to be seen as one and the same.

The second aspect of social policy according to these German neoliberal thinkers is the problem of right in a society modelled on economic competition of the market which Foucault explores in lecture 8 by reference to a text by Louis Rougier and the idea of a legal-economic order, the question of legal intervention in the economy, and the development of the demand for a judiciary. The concept of order (*Ordnung*) is *the* central concept in the Freiburg school as it is at the basis of an understanding of *economic constitution*, or the *rules of the game*, upon which economies or economic systems are based. Eucken insisted that all economic activity necessarily takes place within a historically evolved framework of rules and institutions (Vanberg, 2004: 6) and that one improves the economy by improving the economic constitution or the institutional framework within which economic activity takes place. This was, in effect, the attempt to create conditions "under which the 'invisible hand' that Adam Smith had described can be expected to do its work" (Vanberg, 2004: 8). The major historical step for German neoliberals was the shift from feudalism to a civil law society where people enjoyed the same rights and status under the law and thus, had the *freedom to contract* with one another. This, in essence, represented their conception of free market economy, which was based on the natural order of free competition where all players met as equals and voluntary exchange and contract enabled coordination of economic activity.

German Neoliberalism and the Birth of the European Social Model

Foucault's prescient analysis in 1979 of German neoliberalism focused on the Freiburg school of ordoliberalism as an innovation in the rationality of government by devising a conception of the market order based squarely on the Rule of Law. This conception, and its related versions in both German neoliberalism (after Müller-Armack and others) and Austrian economics going back to Mises and Hayek, was responsible for a form of constitutional economics that invented the "social market economic" and shaped *Gesellschaftspolitik* or "social policy," as an ethical exception to the rules of the market game. The challenge for scholars, especially in the German context or those with the language skills that permit them to analyse formations of German "social policy" is to provide the genealogical investigation of the change of values and shifting meanings underlying the development of educational policy as part of "the social," and later its shift to being at the centre of economic policy, especially in the decade of 1980s and 1990s when Third Way and EU policies constitute education policy as an aspect of the "knowledge economy."

Foucault's analysis, formulated in the years 1978–79, and then developed in a series of subsequent themes as "the government of the living," "subjectivity and truth," and "the government of self and others," took up an account of the practices neoliberal governmentality as a set of novel practices introduced as a form of economic liberalism, that operated on the premise of a critique of "too much government," what Foucault describes as a permanent critique of State reason. Foucault would not have been unaware of the rise of a particular form of politics referred to as the New Right, which under both Thatcher and Reagan, combined elements of neoliberalism and neoconservativism in a contradictory formulation wielded together through 'great' statesmanship.

In this new neoliberal climate established at a popular level in an Anglo-American model that attained global ambitions under various guises through the old Bretton Woods institutions, the IMF and World Bank, and other formations like the "Washington consensus," the notion of the "social market economy," originally developed through German neoliberalism, offered some new hope as the basis of Third Way economic policies and, more generally, as the basis for the European social model (see, e.g., Joerges, Rödl, 2004).

In the United Kingdom, the Chancellor, Gordon Brown's foray into the discussion of the role and limits of the market in the context of globalisation has helped launch a new debate. In the new BBC4 series The Commanding Heights: The Battle for the World Economy (2003) based on the book by Daniel Yergin and Joseph Stanislaw, Gordon Brown, who heads the key policy-making IMF committee, told Yergin:

> The problem for the Left in the past was that they equated the public interest with public ownership and public regulation, and therefore they assumed that markets were not in the public interest…[Markets] provide opportunities for prosperity, but equally they're not automatically equated with the public interest.

He went on to say:

> The idea that markets must work in the public interest, the idea that governments have a responsibility for the level of employment and prosperity in the economy,

the idea that governments must intervene on occasions–these are increasingly the ideas of our time.

In an age of consumerism, a fundamental question is to what extent, if at all, the "citizen-consumer"—a market-democracy hybrid of the subject—can shape privately funded public services in ways other than through their acts of consumption and whether acts of consumption can genuinely enhance the *social* dimensions of the market (see Peters, 2005c).

Foucault provides us with a means of analysing the centrality of the rule of law to liberalism and the notion of individual property rights, the constitution of freedom in its different historical forms, and, crucially, the link between the government of the state and the government of the self that has become so important to understanding both neoliberalism and Third Way politics, especially insofar as it has institutionalised enterprise culture, the twin notions of performance and accountability, and the generalization of all forms of capitalization of the self, including most prominently the entrepreneurial self. In addition, in his most recently published lectures from the Collège de France Foucault provides us with a complex genealogy of the three main forms of contemporary economic liberalism in outline that confounds standard accounts of liberalism and neoliberalism.

Notes

1. In his Résumé du cours for 1979 (in Foucault, 2004b: 323) Foucault indicates that the method he will adopt is based on Paul Veyne's nominalist history and in this respect he writes:

   Et reprenant un certain nombre de choix de méthode déjà faits, j'ai essayé d'analyser le "libéralisme", non pas une théorie ni comme une idéologie, encore moins, bein entendu, comme une mannière pour la "société" de "se\ représenter"; mais comme une pratique, c'est-à-dire comme une "manière de faire" orientée vers objectifs et se régulant par une réflexion continue. Le libéralisme est à analyser alors comme principe et méthode de rationalisation de l'exercice de gouvernement— rationalisation qui obéit, et c'est là sa spécificité, à la règle interne de l'économie maximale.

   Foucault (in 2001) explains in "Questions of method" his emphasis on practice with an accent on "eventalization" and "the problem of rationalities." He says, "Eventalizing singular ensembles of practices, so as to make them graspable as different regimes of 'jurisdiction' and 'verification'" (p. 230) and he ascribes the method to Veyne with the following remark "it's a matter of the effect on historical knowledge of a nominalist critique itself arrived at by way of historical analysis" (p. 238).

The concept of practice here is crucial to understanding Foucault. Stern (2000: fn 33, p. 358) indicates in a footnote a reference to Dreyfus' course at the NEH Summer Institute on Practices on July 24 1997, under the title "Conclusion: How background practices and skills work to ground norms and intelligibility: the ethico-political implications" and summarises Dreyfus' account of five 'theories' (Wittgenstein and Bourdieu; Hegel and Merleau-Ponty; Heidegger; Derrida; and Foucault). He summarises Foucault's notion as follows: "Problematization. (Foucault) Practices develop in such a way that contradictory actions are felt to be appropriate. Attempts to fix these problems lead to further resistance. This leads to a hyperactive pessimism: showing the contingency of what appears to be necessary and engaging in resistance to established order." See also Schatzki et al. (2001).

2. Rousseau began his famous 1755 text "Discourse on Political Economy" with the following remark: "The word Economy, or OEconomy, is derived from *oikos, a house*, and *vomos, law*, and meant originally only the wise and legitimate government of the house for the common good of the whole family. The meaning of the term was then extended to the government of that great family, the State." Rousseau, as you know, goes on to distinguish between the government of the family and the State, and to deny there is anything in common except the obligations that the head or sovereign owe to their subjects. They are, he argues, based on different rules and that "the first rule of public *economy* is that the administration of justice should be conformable to the laws" and to the general will. For the full text see: http://www.constitution.org/jjr/polecon.htm.

3. The Foucault archives have been recently relocated from the IMEC (Institut Mémoires de l'Édition Contemporaine) Paris address (9, rue Bleue, F-75009 Paris) to Abbaye d'Ardenne (14280 Saint Germaine la Blanche-Herbe), email: bibliotheque@imec-archives.com. "Il faut défendre la société", a course Foucault delivered in 1975–1976, was translated into English by David Macey as *Society Must Be Defended* was published in 2003 by Penguin (Foucault, 2003). While courses for 1977–78, 1978–79, as previously mentioned, and 1981–82 ("L'Herméneutique de sujet") have been recently published (in the Gallimand/Seuill series), courses for the years 1979–80, 1980–81, 1982–83, 1983–84 are still only available from the IMEC Foucault archive as recorded tapes.

4. The governmentality literature has grown up around the journal *Economy and Society*, and includes the work of Cruickshank, Hindess, Hunter, Larner, Minson, O'Malley, Owen, and others, as well as those referred to above, most of who have published in *Economy and Society* (for aims and scope, and table of contents, see http://www.tandf.co.uk/journals/titles/03085147.asp).

5. See my essay "Why Foucault?" (Peters, 2003c) where I discuss Foucault studies in the English-speaking world by reference to the work of Marshall, Olssen, Ball, Popkewitz & Brennan, Besley, Baker, Middleton and myself. My work on Foucault's governmentality dates from Peters (1994), with additional work in 1996 (with

Marshall), Peters (1996), Peters (1997), and Peters (2001a, b, c). For additional work on Foucault see Peters (2003a & b), Peters (2005a & b). A special issue of *Educational Philosophy and Theory* will publish a special issue in 2006 entitled "The Learning Society and Governmentality" edited by Masschelein, Bröckling, Simons and Pongratz.

6. As he writes in his Résumé du cours (in Foucault, 2004b: 323):

> Le thème retenu était doc la "biopolitique": j'entendais par là la manière don't on a essayé, depuis le XVIII siècle, de rationaliser les problèmes posés à la pratique gouvenrement par les phénomènes propres à une ensemble de vivants constitutes en population: santé, hygiene, natalitié, longévité, races . . .

7. Foucault investigates the notion of civil society—a twin notion to *homo economicus* and indissociable elements of the technology of liberal government—by reference to Adam Ferguson (1996), a philosopher of the Scottish Enlightenment, whose An Essay on the History of Civil Society, first published in 1767, as an inquiry into the "natural history of man," seeks to elucidate the general characteristics of human nature (including principles of self-preservation, union, war, etc.), provide a "history of rude nations," policy and arts, and comments on the advancement of civil and commercial arts, as well as "the decline of nations" and "corruption and political slavery."

8. Foucault refers to the work of F. Bilger (1964) *La Pensée économique libérale de l'Allemagne contemporaine.* For a brief chronological biography of Erhard see http://www.dhm.de/lemo/html/biografien/ErhardLudwig/.

9. Foucault (2004b) notes that Eucken knew and met with Husserl. Foucault refers to the phenomenological roots of German ordoliberalism.

10. Vanberg (2004) argues that the constitutional approach of the ordoliberals distanced itself from laissez-faire economics and is closely modelled by James Buchanan's constitutional economics. Vanberg also notes differences that occurred in discussions at the Mont Pelerin Society between Eucken and Mises. While Eucken knew Hayek since the early 1920s, Vanberg argues that ordoliberalism was a German invention that was not influenced by Anglo-Saxon influences or the Austrian School. See also Broyer (1996) and Witt (2002). For the continued relevance of ordoliberalism and the social market model see Joerges, Rödl (2004).

5

Postmodernity, Neoliberalism and the Restructuring of Education

THE CONDITION OF POSTMODERNITY—the postmodern condition—at least on Jean-François Lyotard's (1984) account, represents both a break with the foundational philosophies of the Enlightenment and a crisis of its major secular ideologies—classical liberalism and Marxism. Since the dramatic events of 1989 and 1990 the focus of interest in the West has turned outwards to the collapse of communism in Eastern Europe. These events have temporarily obscured and over-shadowed political and economic developments within liberal-capitalist states.

Lyotard (1984:xxiii) uses the notion of metanarrative to designate the way a particular set of practices and institutions are legitimated. He writes in a now famous passage:

> I will use the term *modern* to designate any science that legitimates itself with reference to a metadiscourse of this kind making explicit appeal to some grand narrative, such as the dialectics of the Spirit, the hermeneutics of meaning, the emancipation of the rational or working subject, or the creation of wealth.

He then defines *postmodern* as an 'incredulity towards metanarratives,' a scepticism and distrust of stories which for ideological purposes purports to justify beliefs, practices and institutions founded upon them by grounding them upon a set of ahistorical and universal principles. The standard interpretation of Lyotard's (1984) work represents modernity encapsulated quintessentially in the idea of reason as the legitimating grand narrative, a narrative which in the postmodern condition we have been freed from in a kind of awakening. In the words of one commentator 'Postmodernity reveals, at last, that reason has only been one narrative among others in history; a grand narrative, certainly, but one of many, which can now be followed by other narratives' (Raulet, 1983:205). Such narratives have varied in their historical form, appealing to various universalist foundations. Classical liberalism has been the dominant metanarrative, which in one form at least, has appealed to reason in the form of an individualism which privileges the rational, knowing subject as the fount of all knowledge, signification, moral authority and action. The particular variant of this metanarrative which informs the economic rationalism of the New Right is construed in classical terms of the assumption of *Homo Economicus*, the assumption that in all of our behaviour we act as self-interested individuals.

The central tenet of the theories underlying public sector restructuring, including changes to both the core and the residual public sectors and the welfare state, is a philosophy of individualism which represents a renewal of the main article of faith underlying classical economic liberalism. It asserts that all human behaviour is dominated by self-interest. Its major innovation in contemporary terms is to extend this principle to the status of a paradigm for understanding politics itself, and, in fact, to understanding all behaviour. It has become the basis for the politics of 'successful reform.'

This chapter has two sections. The first examines the neoliberal philosophy of individualism as providing the universalist foundations for an extreme form of economic rationalism that dominate the policy agenda. It argues that such a philosophy is ultimately destructive of any fully-fledged notion of community, imagined or otherwise. The second section explores and critiques the New Right's project of postmodernity as it has been constructed in official discourse. Here the attention will be on notions of postindustrialism and the information society especially as these terms figure explicitly or implicitly in statements and initiatives focusing on science, technology and education in New Zealand. The purpose of the paper is to describe how New Zealand was currently being restructured by the New Right in the 1980s and 1990s and to create the space to begin the process of reimagining the future of New Zealand.

The Communitarian Critique of Neoliberalism

The communitarian critique of neoliberalism is a useful theoretical antidote to the excesses of an over-confident individualism. On a more technical level, as Friedland and Robertson (1990: 24) demonstrate, neoclassical economic theory is a social construction of 'economic man.' It assumes that individual preferences are exogenous, ordered and stable but because it does not have a theory of the formation of preferences, neoclassical economics, which assumes that individuals make independent choices to maximise their utility, cannot 'take us much beyond the realm of material goods calibrated by relative prices.' They continue:

> That realm is in fact very much restricted: as Sen has pointed out, *rationality* in the model rests on the assumption that preferences are consistently ordered, *maximization* on the assumption that choices 'reveal' preferences, and *individuality* on the assumption that all acts are evaluated in terms of their anticipated consequences for the self . . .

Friedland and Robertson (1990) challenge all three assumptions on the basis of a variety of empirical evidence. Perhaps, an even more damning criticism of the assumption that people should be treated as rational utility maximisers in all of their behaviour is that it is reductionistic in the extreme: *homo economicus* simply summarises the reduction of cultural, gender and family attributes into one individual who is described in masculine terms. This reduction reflects the lack of any social or collective dimension in explaining behaviour. By accepting a priori assumptions on universalist grounds about human behaviour explained solely in terms of an individualistic and self-interested economic rationality, different cultural (eg. Maori) and gender values are covertly screened out. This line of criticism has been employed effectively by feminist writers. Friedman (1989:280), for instance, argues that males are theorised to seek autonomy, individuation, separateness and moral ideals that are thought to depend on a highly individuated conception of persons. From her feminist perspective such a concept of persons is viewed as a problem because socialisation in terms of this model breeds people 'incapable of of human attachments based on mutuality and trust' and ultimately creates social institutions 'which tolerate, even legitimise violence and aggression.'

The second position outlined above is, in my view, more interesting and more productive for it exposes more clearly the individualism of the New Right as an ideology. This position which is characteristic of poststructuralism argues that the discourse of the self or, more precisely, the philosophy of the subject, is exhausted. Both the humanistic and reductionist neoliberal versions of this 'construction' of the individual subject are based on (European) logocentric and homocentric illusions which have served to subjugate and mask the histories and 'voices' of Others who have been consigned to the forgotten margins—women, ethnic minorities, indigenous peoples, and so on.

The analyses of the poststructuralists like Foucault and Derrida critique and repeal the humanism of Descartes' cogito and the tradition of European philosophy that grants privilege to the epistemological and political subject. Derrida (1982:119) has indicated how the critique of humanism and anthropologism has been a dominant and guiding motif of contemporary French thought. His philosophical project has been directed towards the goal of showing us that the unity of the subject as self-presence is more a fiction of linguistic practice than a genuine entity. In one sense Derrida and Foucault stand in a tradition of French twentieth-century thought which has sought to specify the subject in terms of its finitude, its historical and temporal boundaries, its physical embodiment. This tradition, drawing on psychoanalytic theory, has emphasised the so-called 'splitting' (Lacan), 'displacement' (Derrida) and 'death' (Foucault, Deleuze) of the Hegelian subject (Butler, 1987).

Foucault is often presented as someone who eclipses the subject in his neostructuralist phase. In *The Order of Things* (1973) he suggests that 'man' is a very recent invention and one who is perhaps approaching its end. I think we can read this against Heidegger's 'Letter on Humanism' and the insight that 'man,' 'subject,' 'citizen' and 'individual' are all ideological constructs, effects of discourse, that express certain political values in relation to an age.

In 'The Political Technology of Individuals' Foucault (1988a) moves into the realm of European humanism and the tradition of philosophical anthropology initiated by Kant's question 'What are we today?" consider as a form of historical reflection on ourselves and what we have become as it characterizes a tradition of thought continued by the Frankfurt school.

In terms of this tradition he suggests that his own work is an attempt to 'to show how we have indirectly constituted ourselves through the exclusion of some others' (p. 141) In the seminar called *Technologies of the Self* (Foucault, 1988b) he tries to understand 'how we we directly constitute our identity through some ethical techniques of the self which developed through antiquity down to now' (ibid), that is how we produce ourselves through ethical self-understanding. The history of the subject especially in the macrological structures of power of the state initiated through a combination of juridical and state power in political economy, education and the law produces a certain kind of historical subject. Governmentality is Foucault's ultimate attempt to situate this liberal subject historically in relation to a concept of freedom; indeed, a subject that requires consent in order to be governed and one that is define through the introduction of political economy as a set of governmental practices.

In 'The Political Technology of Individuals' Foucault (1988a) suggests that the reason of state is intimately bound up with the development of 'political arithmetic,' the evolving science of statistics (state-istics) and new relations between politics and history that defines the position of the individual against the state in terms of 'rights' and 'obligations.' The techniques and practices of the state define individuals by which they could be integrated into society. In German and French the word 'police' characterizes both the productive and negative aspects of life, not only working lives but also death and dying, and those who required help like the poor, orphans and the aged. 'Police' here then refers to an administrative state that produces a governable order based on the lives of individuals and their ability to contribute to the society. Administrative practices covered all aspects of life and regulated society by controlling the relations between individuals and by defining the relation of the individual to the state. The true pursuit of politics is happiness which becomes a major focus in political philosophy. This changes to individuals as social beings, which becomes the focus of administrative practices and 'police' work becomes a science or a discipline that is concerned with a biopolitics that is the lives of human beings as a population of the territory. Foucault (1988a: 161) writes:

> it is possible to analyze political rationality, as it is possible to analyze any scientific rationality. Of course, this political rationality is linked with other forms of rationality. Its development in large part is dependent upon economical, social, cultural, and technical processes. It is always embodied in institutions and strategies and has its own specificity.

He goes on to argue:

> I think that the main characteristic of our political rationality is the fact that this integration of the individuals in a community or in a totality results from a constant correlation between an increasing individualization and the reinforcement of this totality. From this point of view we can understand why the modern political rationality is permitted by the antinomy between law and order (Foucault, 1988a; 161–2).

And he ends by maintaining that the rise of social science cannot be separated from the rise of this political rationality, this new political technology. A Foucauldian radical political economy of education must also follow the rise of this political technology and the ways in which its transmutes itself in the liberal sciences especially of psychology and the new psy-science, child development, to produce individuals as part of the schools and universities of advanced liberal societies.

Neoliberalism and Postmodernity

'Postmodernity' bears some relation to 'modernity' but its exact relation is a matter of some dispute. Sometimes the term is used to indicate that we are witnessing a change as great as the shift from an agrarian way of life to industrial society. Sometimes it is used to indicate a radicalisation of modernity—its last phase. In conjunction with this view but from a critical standpoint, postmodernity is seen as a myth which simply disguises the way the term is used to mask the restoration or resurgence of past ideologies. In the sociological literature it is often taken as a periodising concept. In this way the notion of postmodernity is substantively associated with theories of postindustrialism and of the information society. I will argue that this discourse represents the neoliberal attempt to develop a new metanarrative, a unifying and totalising story, as a basis to reimagine the future. While this grand narrative is couched in terms of a periodising concept which draws explicitly on notions of the postindustrialism and of the information society, it also functions as a myth to mask the ideological purposes that it serves. Postmodernity as a neoliberal project is anchored in the individualism described above: it represents an extreme form of economic rationalism which restructures science, technology and education as the future leading economic sectors and basis for national competitive advantage in the global economy.

Western representations of modernisation are at the heart of a set of theories about the postindustrial and information society. In neoliberal terms, it is seen to be based on an economic instrumental rationality which has universalist value, especially since the failures of communist and nationalist modernisations. Yet it is constituted as an outcome of natural laws of progress and the rationality of the global economic system rather than in terms of any reference to social actors or social movements or what they imply for a workable notion of democracy. The neoliberal discourse that I have christened the 'project of postmodernity' depicts the future in largely technocratic and celebratory terms. It is this version rather than the critical, 'technophobic' version, which serves as a critique of postindustrialism, that figures in international and national policy documents (see Peters, 1991).

The OECD, as an international policy agency, has, for instance, made a great deal of the importance of the new technologies in the 1990s as a basis for a socioeconomic strategy. One OECD document (1988:11) concluded that information technologies represent a 'key structural break' which offers considerable productivity potential because 'based on a cluster of interrelated innovations in micro-electronics, computers and telecommunications, [IT] is an extraordinary pervasive technology.' In OECD terms the focal point of the strategy is the generation of advanced capacity for continuing innovation which requires advanced R&D capacity and social and institutional innovations to facilitate rapid diffusion. This strategy is said to require, among other things, greater flexibility in enterprise (a shift from the 'Tayloristic' model of production to decentralised organisational structures) and a more responsive education system with greater emphasis on enterprise and entrepreneurship. In a more recent document (1991:13), the OECD spells out the connections between information technology and economic growth: increased productivity (better use of input factors) and flexibility (customised production); better quality of products and services; new means of organising and linking together basic functions of the production, delivery and consumption processes of the economy; new means for collecting, assembling and arranging information to thus drive the process of innovation and create new basic knowledge. The new opportunities afforded by information technology are said to have significant implications for the location and structure of industrial activities as well as for the international division of labour. Interestingly, the OECD indicate that policy intervention in the IT sector can be justified because the market is unlikely to provide the necessary infrastructure.

From the early 1980s the OECD has been insistent that education and science must be restructured to accommodate the needs of postindustrial economic growth and as a basis for greater international competitiveness and survival. One example must suffice here. The OECD publication *Universities Under Scrutiny* (1987:3) indicates that current problems pose a 'fundamental question concerning the very purposes and functions of higher education institutions in postindustrial societies' and recommends means to encourage existing institutions to adapt: more career-oriented courses; greater emphasis on applied research and development; planning for technology transfer and knowledge diffusion; greater accountability and responsiveness of institutions; increased productivity and efficiency. Behind these policy statements is a recognition of the basic tenets of a crude postindustrialism based on the axial principle of the centrality of theoretical knowledge as both a source of continuous innovation and as the new factor of production. Alongside this central belief, which requires the explicit harnessing and restructuring of science, technology and education for economic purposes, are a series of ideas emphasising the importance of the new information technologies as the necessary infrastructure for the postindustrial economy, and the general change which western societies are thought to be experiencing from a goods-producing to a service economy.

The revival of the classical theory of market exchange as the basis for a spontaneously ordered society, has been extended in its application to all forms of human behaviour, to politics and the politics of reform. This economic theory of politics underlies theories underpinning what Christopher Hood (1991:3) has called 'new public management,' the rise of which is associated with a number of trends: the attempt to reverse or slow down government growth in terms of public spending; the shift towards privatisation and quasi-privatisation; the development of automation, particularly in information technology, in the production and distribution of public services; and the growth of a more international agenda focused on issues of public management and policy design.

This has lead to a number of changes in a much scaled-down public sector in many western countries: the separation of trading activities from social service functions; changes in the relationship between the Chief Executive Officer (CEO) and the government, in the name of greater accountability; a greater stress on private sector styles of management practice and greater discretion to CEOs to manage freely without political interference; a shift to favouring greater competition; the introduction of explicit standards and measures of performance; a greater emphasis on output controls; a greater emphasis on discipline and parsimony in resource use.

It is clear that the elements of the new discourse I have called the 'project of postmodernity' focus around a host of interrelated concepts which allegedly signal an epochal break with the previous and dominant socioeconomic system. One of the central tenets of this view is the way a series of developments in science and technology point to a new condition called the information age. In Australia and New Zealand this discourse has been framed up within a neoliberal ideology of individualism, which motivated by an extreme form of economic rationalism, projects a totalising story onto the future. The key operators here are national competitive advantage and economic growth. Yet in all this there is little reflection on fundamental questions: on how knowledge and the status of knowledge changes as societies enter the so-called information age; on how the relations of knowledge and power in this changed context raises new legal and ethical issues concerning the state; on how new language formations within electronic media alter significantly the network of social relations, restructuring those relations and the subjects they constitute.

The work of Jean-François Lyotard (1984) serves as a basis for raising these kind of issues. His analysis, while predicated on the same epochal transition, is neither technocratic nor celebratory. It serves to call into question the naive and crude thesis of postindustrialism underlying the neoliberal project of postmodernity. Lyotard's (1984) point of departure in describing the transition of western societies into the postindustrial age is scientific knowledge. He argues that the 'leading' sciences and technologies—cybernetics, telematics, informatics, and the growth of computer languages—are all significantly *language-based* and have transformed the two principal functions of knowledge: research and education (as the transmission of acquired learning). Knowledge and the status of knowledge is redefined within this context of transformation. Anything in the body of knowledge which is not directly translatable into *quantities* of information, that is, into a computer language, will be abandoned. Knowledge, in other words, loses its 'use-value.' Knowledge is exteriorised with respect to the 'knower' and the status of the learner and the teacher is transformed into a commodity relationship of 'supplier' and 'user': 'Knowledge is and will be produced in order to be sold, it is and will be consumed in order to be valorised in a new production: in both cases, the goal is exchange' (Lyotard, 1984:4). The technical transformations wrought by a continued miniaturisation and commercialisation of knowledge machines will further change the way in which learning is acquired, classified, made available, and exploited.

Already knowledge has become the principal force of production, severely altering the composition of the work force in developed countries. The mercantilisation of knowledge will further widen the gap between developed and developing countries. It will bring about the new distinction between individuals and groups within developed countries based on the availability of and access to information. It will disrupt the traditional view that learning falls within the purview of the state and raise new legal and ethical questions for the relationship between the state and the 'information-rich' multinational corporations.

This scenario, as Lyotard admits, is neither original nor necessarily true, but it does have strategic value in allowing us to see the effects of the transformation of knowledge on public power and civil institutions, and it raises afresh the central problem of the legitimation: who decides what is 'true' or what is to be regarded as 'scientific'? Who has the right to decide what is just? In the postindustrial society where knowledge and power have been revealed as simply two sides of the same question, the idea of legitimation becomes an over-riding imperative: 'In the computer age, the question of knowledge is now more than ever a question of government' (Lyotard, 1984:9). While as Lyotard argues the postmodern condition is to be defined by an 'incredulity towards metanarratives,' a distrust of stories that purport to justify certain practices or institutions by grounding them upon a set of universal principles and while there are in fact many different stories or narratives which are incommensurable and cannot be reduced to one another, present decision-makers and governments proceed on the assumption that there is commensurability, that there is common ground and that the whole is determinable:

> They allocate our lives for the growth of power. In matters of social justice and scientific truth alike, the legitimation of that power is based on its optimising the system's performance—efficiency (Lyotard, 1984:xxiv).

In Lyotard's terms, the scientific 'game' has increasingly fallen under the sway and control of another game, that of technology. The game of technology, as opposed to science whose goal is truth, follows the principle of optimal performance (ie. maximising output, minimising input). Its goal is efficiency rather than truth or justice. Progress in knowledge becomes subordinated to investment in technology, and science and education become forces of production—moments in the circulation of capital—and the old humanist (emancipatory) narratives of legitimation are replaced by the new ideological legitimation of science and education promulgated by the state and multinational corporations in terms of the value of efficiency. The goal of education, under these conditions, becomes its optimal contribution to the best performance of the system. This goal demands the creation of two kinds of skill indispensable to the maintenance of the economic and social system: those necessary to enhance competitiveness in the world market and those necessary for fulfilling the need for its internal cohesion.

Other social commentators have begun to theorise the effects of the 'mode of information' on social relations. Some have emphasised how the introduction of the new information technologies is something more than the simple evolution of technical efficiencies in communications. It represents a series of social arenas for negotiating issues crucial to the conduct of social life, including: who may speak and who may not; who has authority and who has not; who may be believed and who may not.

On a more theoretical level, the basic configurations of language brought about by the mode of information alters the way in which the subject processes signs into meanings. Electronic media, for instance, permit the exchange of symbols in ways less subject to the constraints of space and time. By doing so, as Mark Poster argues, (1989:3, 4), it 'heightens the fragility of social networks.' His examples include the speed at which computer viruses spread and the way in which 'the communications network that ties the world's financial hubs together…also threatens them with instant economic collapse.' He asserts that in the information mode 'the self is decentered, dispersed, and multiplied in continuous instability' (*ibid.*: 6) and echoing Jean Baudrillard, draws attention to the way in which the representational character of language has become especially fragile and problematic:

> These reconfigurations…of language, in turn impose a new relation between science and power, between the state and the individual, between the individual and the community, between *authority* and the law, between family members, between the consumer and the retailer. In sum the solid institutional routines that have characterised modern society for some two hundred years are being shaken by the earthquake of electronically mediated communication and recomposed into new routines whose outlines are as yet by no means clear (*ibid.*:14).

He argues that the mode of information puts into questions 'the very shape of subjectivity' destabilising it because the subject no longer can be located in a point in absolute space/time. Instead the subject is:

> multiplied by databases, dispersed by computer messaging and conferencing, decontextualised and reidentified by TV ads, dissolved and materialised continuously in the electronic transmission of symbols (*ibid.*:15).

What these observations tell us is that the statements which recast questions of postindustrialism and the information age in terms of an economic rationalism based on neoliberal individualism—based on a new metanarrative restoring an old ideology—are not only open to serious scrutiny but that they are wrong-headed.

6

The New Zealand
Education Experiment

HISTORICALLY SPEAKING, THE DEVELOPMENT OF EDUCATION in New Zealand was shaped and maintained by two ideas central to the welfare state: the ideal of social welfare and the ideal of egalitarian democracy. In return, education contributed to the maintenance of the welfare state and social integration. One of the hoped for functions of schooling was at the level of social class and religious and racial integration, providing shared experiences as the basis of community development.

The introduction in 1877 of a "universal, compulsory, and secular" primary education system in New Zealand reflected the egalitarian principles of early policy makers and was based on a number of historically important rights and claims. The "positive" rights associated with social-democratic liberalism entailed that a universal and free education was the necessary prerequisite to the freedom of the individual. Such education was to be compulsory for a variety of reasons: children needed to be protected against the individual self-interest of their parents, especially in a white-settler society; a basic elementary education was deemed to be essential to the development of moral and personal autonomy; education, it was considered, should be accessible to all children irrespective of class, race or creed. Such rights underpinned the goals of a democratic society, to ensure its reproduction through a common set of skills and values. Universal and compulsory education thus served the community by addressing social needs. Schools provided students with a common set of values and knowledge, thus helping create the basis for citizenship and the democratic functioning of society. Schooling also helped lay the foundation for scientific and cultural progress and played an important role in economic and social growth, contributing to creating the conditions for full employment.

The first Labour Government introduced a comprehensive model of the welfare state from 1936. As part of this reform agenda, the state commitment to universal, free, and compulsory education was extended.

Universal education would be provided in a package of benefits and services that would be "non-contributory, universal, comprehensive, and adequate" and which were to be provided by the state "as a citizen's right, not as an act of charity." In addition to a commitment to free, universal and compulsory education, at the basis of all welfare policies was the accepted goal of full employment, which it was claimed made possible the dignified self-help of every member of the community.

This welfare ideology was cemented into place during the 1930s and progressively refined thereafter. It prevailed in the New Zealand education system up until the mid-1980s when David Lange's Fourth Labour Government, against traditional union and Left-wing affiliations, initiated a complex series of policy changes that restructured both economy and society. In retrospect we can describe these "reforms" under the economic ideology of neoliberalism and "structural adjustment," although New Zealand developed its own distinctive spin on these principles and policies, and came to occupy a unique place in the world story of neoliberalism. New Zealand was acknowledged by the World Bank, OECD and IMF as *the* example of successful reform to illustrate the change from a regulated to an open economy.

For instance, David Henderson (1999: 5), previously Head of the Economics and Statistics Department for the OECD, argues that "The extension and exercise of economic freedoms make for closer *economic integration*, both within and across national boundaries" (emphasis in the original). Liberalism, which for Henderson implies restricting the power and functions of governments so as to give full scope for individual and enterprises, after a hundred years of decline has regained ground in the economics profession, especially after the period of the 1930s–1970s. The economic policies enacted by a variety of world governments on the basis of principles of economic liberalisation emphasise a "strong association between political and economic freedoms" (Henderson, 1999: 46). He reviews "economic freedom ratings" over the period 1975–95 to map the geography of reform, purportedly demonstrating that core OECD countries are all "reforming" governments. In the so-called "economic freedom ratings," on Henderson's analysis, New Zealand emerges clearly as the leading reformer, in policy areas privatisation and deregulation, trade liberalisation, taxation, and labour market reform (before the Employment Contracts Act was repealed).[1]

Historically and symbolically, 1984 represents the end of welfare state ideology in New Zealand, a profound shift in the principles of social and political philosophy, and the promotion of the neoliberal political project of globalisation. It signalled that the "economy" had become an abstract and reified object, no longer part of the society as a whole and no longer subject to socially defined ends. It also initiated a programme of educational reform, which, at the levels of early childhood, primary and secondary, has had disastrous social consequences, and at the level of tertiary education has seriously eroded our knowledge cultures. I refer to neoliberal education policy paradigm as "The New Zealand Education Experiment" (after Kelsey, 1997) arguing that it has involved a shift from participatory democracy to self-management within a quasi-market economy and, in higher education, it has involved a shift from universal welfare entitlement to a model of private investment.

The reform of education in light of broader principles of economic and public sector restructuring, took place quite late in the reform process. Changes to compulsory education in 1988 were initiated under *Administering for Excellence: Effective Administration in Education*, known as the Picot Report, after its chairman, Brian Picot, (Department of Education, 1988) and *Tomorrow's Schools: The Reform of Educational Administration in New Zealand* (Department of Education, 1988). Since the introduction of these changes, the system has become increasingly consumer-driven, seriously eroding the notion of education as a welfare right, with the consequence that access and provision of education have become increasingly unequal. The policy regimes in both early childhood education and higher education, followed the so-called Picot model, which contained all elements of contractualism, the ideology of self-management, and decentralization rather than genuine devolution, that became the basis for the neoliberal paradigm of education reform in the succeeding decade.

The Policy Context: Economic Liberalisation and Public Sector Restructuring

The reform of education and training in New Zealand must be understood within the wider context of public sector restructuring, and as a subset of the reforms of the state sector based on the same principles, just as the restructuring of the public sector must be understood as a part of the radical structural economic reform embarked upon by the fourth Labour Government (1984–1990). On the whole, this "experiment" has been both accepted and consolidated by the National and Coalition administrations that succeeded Labour in 1990, only to be partially rolled back by the election of a Labour-led Coalition, under Helen Clarke, in 2000. To be sure, the commitment by Thatcher and Reagan administrations to monetarism and supply-side economics, and the general move towards economic liberalisation[2] by Western governments—especially the so-called "Washington consensus"—provided a global context for structural reform in New Zealand. This international development was reinforced by the rapid dissemination of a particular set of theoretical developments in microeconomic theory (to the control departments of the New Zealand bureaucracy the Treasury and State Services Commission), emphasising notions of public choice, contestability and property rights. Public choice theory, originating with Gordon Tullock and James Buchanan (1962) at Virginia, represents a renewal of the main article of faith underlying classical economic liberalism. It asserts that all behaviour is dominated by self-interest and its major innovation is to extend this principle to the status of a paradigm for understanding politics. On this view individuals are rational utility-maximizers, and while it is accepted that the pursuit of self-interest in the market place will yield socially desirable outcomes, similar behaviour in politics needs to be structured and controlled in various ways.

Criticism of the "Think Big" projects in New Zealand (which emphasised the failure of a huge public investment program in the 1970s) was ultimately directed at the nature of *direct* government intervention in the economy. This criticism was to be ritually reiterated later with the break-up of the centrally planned economies in Soviet Russia and Eastern Europe. It was thought that New Zealand had performed poorly in terms of productivity and growth since the mid-1970s; there was a record of devaluation, inflation and stabilisation attempts, and the *ad hoc* development of a set of "restrictive" regulatory government interventions since the 1970s (Duncan & Bollard, 1992).

Labour, historically, a party of the welfare state and the regulated economy with strong and traditional links to the union movement, on becoming government "discarded this tradition without warning and became a party of the New Right" (Jesson 1992, p.37). Constitutionally, operating on the basis of a "thin" political system (a two party system with a single parliamentary chamber and few checks and balances to the exercise of executive power), the Labour Government pushed through its reforms at an astonishingly rapid rate based on a deliberate "politics of reform" aimed at neutralising opposition (Douglas, 1989). In the six years to 1990 when Labour was in power it almost completely deregulated the New Zealand economy:

it deregulated the financial sector; it terminated subsidies for agricultural products and exports; it abolished import licensing, heavily reduced tariffs, removed controls on international capital, liberalised foreign investment, and floated the exchange rate (Duncan & Bollard, 1992: 6). From being the welfare state laboratory during the 1930s, admired by the rest of the world for the extent of its social provision, New Zealand became in the 1980s the "experiment" in structural adjustment, touted as the most open economy in the world, and referred to in glowing terms by the World Bank, IMF and OECD.

A review of the role of the state and the "restructuring" of the public sector was seen as a necessary part of the wider structural economic reform. In particular, the new micro-economic theories argued that state-owned and controlled trading organisations performed poorly because they were constrained by the institutional environment and lacked the same incentives as the private sector. From the mid-1980s the Government pursued a programme of corporatisation and, later, privatisation, as twin strategies for improving the efficiency and accountability of departmental trading departments. Under these strategies, social functions were separated out from the commercial functions of state trading organisations and "managers" were required to run departments as successful businesses, which involved pricing and marketing within performance objectives set by Ministers. The new state enterprises, modelled on the private sector, each with its own board of directors, were required to operate in a competitively neutral environment. The operating principles were enshrined in the State-Owned Enterprises (SOEs) Act (1986). Nine SOEs were created from former government trading departments on 1 April 1987. Subsequently other SOEs were created.[3] Under this Act trading departments became state corporations regulated by company law, to be run to make a profit and to be as efficient as their private sector counterparts. User charges were introduced for government services purchased from the corporations and the SOEs, in the newly established competitively neutral environment, were required to pay dividends and taxes. Ministers became "shareholders," and chief executive officers who had been purposely given the freedom to manage without political interference, must provide a "statement of corporate intent" and annual reports.

A privatisation programme followed corporatisation, against an explicit election promise. Advocates of state sector reform had seen corporatisation as a preliminary and partial solution (Treasury 1984, 1987; Dean 1989). In general, the arguments for privatisation centred on alleged operational weaknesses in the SOE model, which arose from differences with the private sector, e.g., no threat of takeovers or bankruptcy, non-shareholding directors, state guarantees and monitoring roles. The Treasury (1987) and the Business Roundtable were the strongest voices in favour of privatisation arguing that a transfer of assets to the private sector would address efficiency shortfalls of the SOEs, help reduce the public debt, continue the process of "load-shedding," and aid capital accumulation in the private sector. Opposition to privatisation came from a variety of sources. Maori contested the Government's right to sell off public assets under the Treaty of Waitangi, which in 1840 had guaranteed them rights to land, forest and fisheries. Unions not only feared huge redundancies but also critiqued the "emerging privatised market society" focusing on the way a *political* debate over the role of the state and democracy had been reduced to or subsumed by economic arguments (PSA, 1989).

Labour's state asset sales programme which took place from 1988 to (June) 1990 included fifteen major businesses totalling a massive $9 billion approximately. (The sale of Telecom at $4.25 billion in 1990 was the fourth largest global sale that year). The timing of the sales was problematic. The first sales followed rapidly on the huge stock market crash of 1987 in which a fall in value of over 50 per cent was experienced, and the economy was in a deep recession. Also the valuation and marketisation processes were open to question. Sale by treaty and tender followed by negotiation was criticised as a process open to political interference. No full market floatations occurred. Many of the agreed asset prices, it has been justly asserted, were much too low: the assets sold off had been greatly under-valued. It is not even clear to what extent the level of public debt was reduced through the privatisation programme. Whether the sales programme was in the best long-term interests of New Zealand is another matter.

The reform of the remaining core public sector (i.e. the residual non-SOE public sector) including defence, policing and justice, social services such as health and education, and research and development (among others), was based on two major pieces of legislation: the State Sector Act 1988 and the Public Finance Act 1989. Reforms based on these Acts have been described as "the most far-reaching and ambitious of any of their kind in the world" (State Services Commission 1991). Christopher Hood (1990, p.210), commenting on the Treasury's (1987) treatise, *Government Management*—the basis and inspiration for the reforms—described it as "remarkable," implying that it was vastly more coherent and intellectually sophisticated than its equivalents elsewhere: "Neither Canberra nor Whitehall has produced anything remotely comparable in quality or quantity to the New Zealand Treasury's 'NPM manifesto.'" He cites the cardinal principles of what he terms "New Public Management" set in place by Treasury: goal clarity, transparency, contestability, avoidance of bureaucratic or provider capture, congruent incentive structures, enhancement of accountability, and cost-effective use of information.

The impetus for the reforms was economic efficiency and accordingly the reforms "focused upon generating improvement by clarifying objectives and allowing managers to manage within a framework of accountability and performance"

(State Services Commission, 1991: 5). The State Sector Act had two main aims: to redefine the relationship between ministers and permanent heads from one based on the Westminster system (e.g., permanent tenure, independently set remuneration) to one based on a performance contract; and to apply similar labour-market regulations to both state and private-sector employment (Scott et al., 1990:153). Where the State Sector Act made changes in industrial relations and in the appointment and employment of senior managers, the Public Finance Act 1989 clarified the meaning of "performance" in the Public Service by establishing criteria for monitoring. The reforms of financial management under the Finance Act have followed changes adopted in Britain and Australia with two important differences: the first is the distinction between purchase and ownership; and the second is the distinction between outputs and outcomes. The tension between the government's aims as owner of its agencies and its aims as consumer of their outputs can be resolved through the market, i.e., contestability. Chief executive officers are directly responsible for the outputs (the goods and services) produced by their departments and the ministers are responsible for choosing which outputs should be produced and therefore also the outcomes (the effects of those outputs on the community). The first task of policy advice, according to this model of management, is to identify the connection between the outputs and the outcomes, the trade-offs between different outcomes and the best source for the supply of outputs. The justification for public expenditure is related to the directness and quality of the connection. These two major differences have also influenced methods of appropriation (which are now directly linked to performance), the nature of reporting, and the nature of policy advice (Scott et al., 1990: 156).

Neoliberals and advocates of New Right policies in New Zealand increasingly focused their attention on the rising and apparently irreversible tide of welfare expectations. They argued that the welfare state has evaded both investment and work incentives, directly contributing to economic recession. The combined effects of social policies—including guaranteed minimum wages, superannuation, and the growth of spending in health and education sectors—allegedly had strengthened organised labour against capital, augmenting wages as against capital goods. It had also, they claimed, substantially led to increased State borrowings, leading to a decline of profitability.

Neoliberals[4] argued that the so-called "perverse effects" lead to greater state interventionism in both social and economic terms, but the more the state helps, they argued, the more it will have to help and at diminishing levels of effectiveness. It is alleged that increasing levels of intervention, while leading to the current crisis of an imbalance between state receipts and expenditure, tend in the long term to rob economic liberalism of its vitality. The bottom line is that the perverse effects of economic and social intervention represent to these critics a fundamental threat to individual political and democratic freedom.

While the restructuring of the state under Labour was not restricted to the core public sector—education, health and local government underwent major reorganisation—it was with the National Government, which came to power in 1990, that the "residual" public sector was re-defined in terms of a more limited or minimal state. The National Government embarked on the most significant changes to the welfare state since its establishment in the 1930s. The major initiatives have included substantial cuts in benefits and other forms of income support, together with much stricter eligibility criteria, greater targeting of social assistance and changes to the method of targeting, and "a radical redesign of the means by which the state provides assistance," particularly in the areas of housing, health care and tertiary education (Boston, 1992: 1). While the changes have been justified in terms of the need for fiscal stringency, given the country's high external debt and the failure of the previous policy regime, it is clear that, as Boston (1992: 1) notes, the changes "also originate from a marked shift in political philosophy" which focuses on the question of the nature and scope of the state.

The National Government, in addition, committed itself to a privatisation programme and to the corporatisation of the remaining public sector organisations, including Electricity Companies, Crown Research Institutes and Crown Health Enterprises. Perhaps, most importantly the National Government introduced the Employment Contracts Act (1991) which complements social welfare changes in the sense that it was "decidedly anti-collectivist in philosophy and intent," shifting as it does "the focus of labour law from the collective to the individual" (Walsh, 1992: 59 & 64). The Act, designed to liberalise the labour market through deregulation, focuses on six components: "freedom of association"; enterprise bargaining; personal grievance; enforceability of contracts; strike and lock-out rights; the redesign of the Employment Court; a code of minimum wages and conditions. In general, then, it can be argued, that the National Government accepted, continued with and attempted to complete the transformation initiated under the neoliberal ideology of the Labour Government.

The New Zealand Treasury and the Restructuring of Education

During the 1980s the Treasury came to exert increasing influence on government policy. Their adoption of market-liberal principles influenced the move to a market model of welfare in New Zealand, although their implementation in various reforms and legislation has taken some time and occurred across successive governments. In 1984, the incoming Labour Government received from the Treasury briefing papers that were later published under the title *Economic Management* (Treasury, 1984). This documented Treasury thinking at the time which was based on neoliberal strategies for improving the New Zealand economy. The implication of such policies for education was to become clearer in 1987. In that year, the Treasury produced for the re-elected Labour Government its brief entitled *Government Management* (Treasury, 1987). This was published in two volumes, with the second devoted to education issues setting forth the Treasury's arguments specifically in relation to education (see Treasury, 1987). Here it was maintained that:

1. Education shares the main characteristics of other commodities traded in the marketplace, and it cannot be analysed successfully as a "public good" (p. 33);

2. New Zealanders are too optimistic about the ability of education to contribute to economic growth and equality of opportunity (p. 8);

3. increased expenditure in education does not necessarily improve educational standards or equality of opportunity, or lead to improved economic performance (pp. 8, 18, 39, 130, 132, 141 and 142);

4. not only has the education system not adjusted to changed circumstances but it has performed badly despite increased expenditure on it (pp. 6, 16, 18 and 140);

5. the reason it has performed badly is because teachers and the educational establishments have pursued their own self-interest rather than those of pupils and parents; i.e., they are not responsive enough to consumer interests and desires (pp. 37–38);

6. specifically, the educational system lacks a rigorous system of accountability. There is a lack of national monitoring procedures or of any satisfactory ways of comparing the effectiveness of schools in order to account for the public resources employed (p. 108);

7. government intervention and control has interrupted the "natural" free-market contract between producer and consumer causing bureaucratic inflexibility, credential inflation and hence, educational inequality (pp. 37–39, 41, 132 and 137).

In short, Treasury argued that state-provided and controlled education meant that education had performed badly and would continue to do so unless changes of a radical sort were implemented. The Treasury sought to buttress its arguments for the necessity of change by reference to "falling standards" and "rising mediocrity," and by discrediting the notion of education as a "public good." The central issues under review were those of *efficiency* and *equity* in education. In relation to these issues, the key subject-themes on which recommendations were made included:

- school governance, with implications for the administration, management, and funding of schools (e.g., bulk funding and Boards of Trustees);
- the role of the State in the provision, management and funding of education;
- the merits of market or quasi-market models relating to issues such as consumer choice in relation to participation and access in education;
- the nature of education as a public or private good and the respective merits of public versus private provision in education; i.e., whether the benefits accrue to the community or to individuals;
- parental choice, including the issues of zoning and targeted individual entitlements.

In its critique of education, the Treasury drew on the work of research that criticised the inability of the welfare state to adequately distribute resources, especially Le Grand's research (1982 and 1987) which sought to document the distributional failures of the old welfare state, claiming on the basis of empirical data that the welfare state was not redistributive across class lines but that most redistribution is intra-class and over the course of the individual's life time. The Treasury adopted the concept of "middle class and professional capture" both to criticise the welfare state for its deficiencies of existing welfare policies in terms of egalitarian objectives and to advocate a shift to neoliberal solutions based on the minimal state and individual choice (see Bertram, 1988).

School Reform: From Participatory Democracy to Self-Management

The *Picot Report* (*Administering For Excellence*, 1988), a report issued by the taskforce set up to restructure the administration of primary and secondary education, echoed the Treasury's analysis and recommendations with regard to education. Its terms of reference were individualist in orientation, emphasising the concept of consumer choice in education, along with individual competence, cultural sensitivity and good management practices. The Report focused heavily on standard neoliberal criticisms of the welfare state: the Department of Education, as part of the state welfare bureaucratic apparatus, was considered to be over-centralised; decision-making processes were too complex; there was a huge lack of information and virtually no choice in the system; and finally, as a consequence of these factors, the Committee maintained, parents felt disempowered.

The policy solutions recommended by the Picot Committee in large measure reflected the wider political economy of reform, emphasising, in particular, the principles devised by the Treasury to reform the core public sector: an emphasis on greater accountability; a clearer specification of responsibilities and goals; devolution of management control and first indication of "self-management"; the separation of policy advice from policy implementation; the disaggregation of large bureaucracies into autonomous agencies; a greater emphasis of management rather than policy; the development of a performance management system. In general, it was held: that policies which encouraged individuals to make choices for their own good is the best means for achieving welfare objectives; that the way to improve schools is to ensure that they are consumer-driven; that the user should pay; and, that private schools are better than state schools and should be encouraged. These principles and beliefs reflected substantially the theoretical underpinnings to public sector reform in terms of the new institutional economics, public choice theory, principal-agency analysis, transaction cost analysis, and contract theory (Scott and Gorringe, 1989; Boston, 1991).

The main elements of the reform proposals that were to follow as a consequence of the *Tomorrow's Schools* reforms can be summarised in terms of the following principles:

- transfer of responsibility for the control and co-ordination of education away from the state to elected boards, associations and councils;
- transfer of responsibility for employment of staff away from the state to elected local boards;
- transfer of responsibility for the management of assets, property and money spent in education away from the state to institution based boards;
- increased emphasis on the market discipline of 'choice' in the early childhood, primary and secondary sectors, and the introduction of user-pays in tertiary education;
- greater state control over essential educational services in the form of charters, national curriculum guidelines, and assessment procedures.

From 1988, a large number of other reports and policies were produced by government and their various advisory bodies of direct or indirect relevance to the restructuring of education. With the plethora of reports came dramatic changes in the operation and functioning of education at the early childhood, primary, secondary and tertiary levels. The very notion of education also changed. For the first time in New Zealand's history, the conception of education as a private good partially subject to market conditions (i.e., a quasi-market) became a reality. The central issue of equality of opportunity which dominated the educational debate up until the end of the 1970s gave way to talk about "efficiency," "choice," "competition" and "accountability." Schooling would be reoriented in terms of the themes of devolution and efficiency and schools would be modelled on structures similar to that of private business enterprises.

In 1990, the old "over-centralised" Department of Education was disaggregated or broken up into a number of autonomous agencies, including a new streamlined Ministry devoted only to policy advice, the prototype of the New Zealand Qualifications Authority, and the Education Review Office. As part of a deliberate policy of devolution, a great deal of administration of education was allocated to individual schools. "Boards of Trustees"—which replaced the old Boards of Governors and School Committees—became the link, through the Ministry, between the school and central government.

This new structure increased the responsibilities of individual schools at the local community level, although whether it increased actual effective control over key issues in education is more questionable and has been strongly challenged. At a superficial level, the Boards of Trustees were given a whole series of new responsibilities including staff employment, management of the institution's property, and the design and implementation of a "Charter" (based on a contract). The Education Review Office (ERO) and the New Zealand Qualifications Authority (NZQA) were also established. These changes were instituted through the Education Act 1989, the Education Amendment Act 1990 and the Education Amendment Act 1991. These Acts laid the framework for bulk funding for both teachers' salaries and school operations, revoked compulsory registration for teachers, and abolished zoning for schools. In 1991, a "user pays" system of student fees in tertiary education was introduced which laid the basis for the later modifications and changes introduced by the National government resulting in the introduction of student loans.

The reforms appeared to be based on a notion of devolution, with community representation on Boards of Trustees working in partnership with the principal and teachers. This appearance of devolution was bolstered by appeals to the notion of community in the original Picot Report and *Tomorrow's Schools*. For instance, at the district level there was reference to community education forums which were designed: to represent the interests of the wider community; to identify and gather together the different views; to discuss and settle conflicts of interests; to discuss policy initiatives; and even to initiate policy ideas. At one point the *Picot Report* states (s. 5.8.4, p. 55):

> We cannot emphasise too strongly the importance of community education forums. In many submissions to us, we read that one particular sector of education or another did not have the opportunity of finding out the views of others locally and so could not present a community viewpoint to us. Similarly, we were told of syllabus committees and such groups that have had trouble in finding people to represent a broad-based community view. We believe the establishment of community education forums would help overcome that kind of difficulty.

There is a clear attempt to ensure genuine community representation, the essence of participatory democracy. Besides the community education forums, an Education Policy Council (a national organisation of eight members to provide independent policy advice), and the Parent Advocacy Council (an independent body, funded by the state and reporting directly to Parliament) was envisaged. Together with an emphasis on the Treaty of Waitangi and wider provisions for equity in school charters, these appeals to community and public representation seemed to promise genuine devolution and participatory democracy. *Tomorrow's Schools* (1988), for example, graced its opening pages with the following quotation from Thomas Jefferson in both Maori and English:

> I know of no safe depository of the ultimate power of the society but the people themselves and if we think them not enlightened enough to exercise their control with a wholesome direction, the remedy is not to take it from them, but to inform their discretion.

Tomorrow's Schools went out under David Lange's name, then both Minister of Education and Prime Minister. His opening statement as Minister of Education reinforced the appeal to principles of participatory democracy and the importance of investment in education. The community education forums and the Parent Advocacy Council were abolished and many of the original Treaty of Waitangi and equity requirements of the charters have been abandoned.

The originally intended form of *devolution* was never a genuine option, given the political economy of reform established by the Treasury. Its promise of community and participatory democracy was replaced by a form of *delegation*, developed according to principal-agency theory, and the doctrine of self-managing schools. Agency theory was seen as a means of minimising costs of economic transactions related to the monitoring and enforcement of a set of contracts with agents whose interests may diverge from those of the principal. As delegation, "devolution" becomes a contract relationship between individuals which is controlled through monitored performance and applying incentives and sanctions to encourage managers to act to meet agreed objectives rather than to follow their own goals.

Against the original policy intent, the Treasury's model of accountability—reflecting principles of New Public Management—prevailed, with the crucial accountability mechanisms consisting in a set of contractual relationships between the government and chief executives of educational agencies and educational providers (i.e. councils and boards). Charters set out intended outcomes and performance objectives measures, and audits of performance are measured against charter objectives.

From the perspective of supporters of the welfare state, or those who subscribe to a notion of democracy like John Dewey (1916), choice proposals have several undesirable effects: they protect privilege; they deny all students equal access to education; they deny all students exposure to alternative social experiences; they limit the community's progress as a democratic community, and they undermine the basis of its integration socially and politically (see also Ball et al., 2000; Gillborn and Youdell, 2000).

In New Zealand, research also attests to the negative effects of quasi-market choice policies on issues of welfare within the community. Wylie (1994) has documented the broad effects of increasing competition under schemes of choice, citing changes in ethnic and socio-economic composition of schools as well as deterioration in the relations between schools. The Smithfield Project (Lauder, 1994) also documents the negative social effects of choice proposals. For instance, the abolition of zoning in 1991 had markedly increased competition and had significantly affected the rolls and composition of the schools. The overall effects of "choice" have been to magnify existing trends. Hence a school at the "bottom of the heap" had almost halved its first-year intake since 1990, while a successful school which served able middle class students was increasing its roll rapidly. One of the key findings to emerge from the Smithfield study was that structural social and economic conditions affect individual consumer choices in crucial ways, frequently rendering them completely inconsequential. Where schools experience excess demand for attendance, for instance, it is they, and not the parents or students, who are the *effective* choosers. In a more general sense the Smithfield study also reinforces the point that consumer choices (whether "voice" or "exit") must be seen as effectively diminished or enhanced according to financial and socio-economic circumstances.

Such conclusions are also supported by Gordon's (1994) research in relation to the effect of social class on school choice. Her studies concluded that the status of a neighbourhood was a powerful factor influencing school choice. While poorer parents frequently do not have the option to shift their children from one school to another, more affluent parents do. An implication of this trend, says Gordon "is that within schools, there will be increasingly homogenous class groupings, while between schools differences will be enhanced" (p. 15). Similar patterns of segregation operate in respect to ethnicity. The class exclusivity of a school's population is enforced through the adoption of "enrolment schemes" which place limits on numbers, and effectively enable schools to determine which type of pupils they will accept. Hence "because patterns of residence are themselves linked closely to ethnicity, Maori and Pacific Island students tend to be maintained in schools at the lower end of the market hierarchy" (idem.). The net consequence of this process is that "schools at the bottom of the local market tend to lose pupils to neighbouring schools," which, in turn, promotes a "spiral of decline" (Gordon, 1994: 15–16). The issue of access to a school is a very important matter. Under systems of consumer choice, it is clear that it is the school rather than the consumer which effectively chooses its intake. In fact, the freedom presupposed in relation to theories of consumer choice depends ultimately on economic criteria, and in this sense the freedom is "illusory" as the promises it makes cannot be provided for *all*— for within the zero-sum context in which the competitive market choice is structured, the "freedom" of few is premised on the "non-freedom" of many.

Higher Education in Crisis: From Welfare Entitlement to Private Investment[5]

The transformation of higher education in New Zealand from a universal welfare entitlement first into a private investment in "human capital" and finally to a fully consumer-driven system, has followed a now familiar pattern: a transparent alignment of the university system to reflect the needs of an emerging "postindustrial" economy, with increasing demands for highly-trained, multi-skilled, tertiary-educated workers; the introduction of new forms of corporate managerialism and the emulation of private sector management styles; the corporatisation of the university system; the introduction of corporate and "ownership monitoring" to reduce the financial risk of the State; an attack on faculty and student representation in university governance and the general attempt to discredit democratic forms of governance on "efficiency" grounds; the introduction of user-charges, student loans, and the creeping privatisation of the system as a whole.

In its brief to government, the Treasury (1987) argued that the education system had performed badly in spite of increased expenditure because teachers pursued their own self-interest rather than being responsive to the consumer needs of parents and pupils, and government intervention had created bureaucratic inflexibility disrupting the natural market contract between producer and consumer. The Treasury concluded that New Zealanders had been too optimistic about the ability of education to contribute to economic growth and equality of opportunity. *Tomorrow's Schools* involved the transfer of responsibility for property management, employment of staff, and control of education away from the State to the institutions themselves or elected boards, with a greater emphasis on the market discipline of choice.[6]

The reform of tertiary education in New Zealand followed a similar pattern, based on the same Treasury principles of public sector restructuring, with the publication of the *Hawke Report* and *Learning for Life* I and II in the late 1980s, and the appearance of the white paper, *Tertiary Education in New Zealand: Policy Directions for the 21st Century*, a decade later (see Peters & Roberts, 1999). The policy directions offered did not differ greatly from those neoliberal initiatives first mentioned in the *Hawke Report*: a consolidation of the formula funding model and stronger support to private training establishments; greater emphasis on quality assurance mechanisms; separation of the funding for teaching and research; greater monitoring and accountability, and perhaps most troubling, changes to the governance arrangements of tertiary institutions. While New Zealand experienced massive growth of participation rates during the early nineties, this largely self-financed growth of student numbers attending tertiary institutions slowed down in the late 1990s as the weight of the accumulated student debt, standing at 3 billion dollars at the end of the century, began to accumulate. New Zealand universities are now, perhaps, the most efficient in the world. They provide roughly a similar education for a fraction of the cost of their British and American counterparts and there is little fat left in the system. The trouble is the process has been very punishing to tertiary institutions, especially when the priority (at least under the National Government) had been to prioritise early childhood education. There have been large staff cutbacks and morale is low; overseas recruitment of staff is increasingly difficult because of the comparatively low salaries; many academics have sought jobs elsewhere; class sizes have not been significantly reduced across the disciplines. With a commitment to the so-called "knowledge economy" this seems like a recipe for disaster, especially when the most influential human capital and new growth theories strongly emphasise investment in higher education and research.

The "massification" of higher education has been based on new formula funding mechanisms involving an ever-increasing proportion of income from student fees and contestable research funding through the Public Good Science Fund. Even with the diversification of funding sources, universities have struggled to cope financially. The decade of the 1990s was destined to become an era of closure for some departments, especially as the spectacular growth in participation experienced during the early 1990s levelled out and institutions were forced not only to compete with each other in the market for student places but also absorb the cost of providing extra, unfunded, student places, at declining levels of State funding.

The *Report of the Working Group on Post Compulsory Education and Training* (1988) (called the *Hawke Report*, after its chairman) and *Learning for Life* I & II (1989) identified inefficiency and a lack of accountability as shortcomings in tertiary education. The neoliberal answer was clear: increased competition, the introduction of user charges, corporate planning, the adoption of a managerialist ideology and a private sector industrial relations framework. In other words, the ultimate policy goal was the establishment of a pure market model of tertiary education and a fully consumer-driven system.

Learning for Life, the policy translation of the *Hawke Report*, strongly advocated a model of devolution and accountability which is based closely on that developed under Brian Picot as Chairman of the Taskforce to Review Education Administration in New Zealand (the *Picot Report*). The introduction to the *Report on Post Compulsory Education and Training in New Zealand* (the *Hawke Report*) stated:

> The Picot Report advocates essentially devolution and accountability, opportunities for local initiatives within national guidelines. It argues that the essential features of a new structure are:
>
> - a simple administrative structure;
> - decisions made as close as possible to where they are executed;
> - national objectives, clear responsibilities and goals;
> - co-ordination in a structure in which decision makers have control over available resources and are accountable for outcomes;
> - the system should be open to scrutiny;
> - the system should promote responsiveness to client demands.

These are equally appropriate for PCET. All the debate is about how to achieve the right mixture of devolution and accountability, and the right balance of local initiative and national uniformity (pp. 4–5).

Later, in the body of the text (section 3.9) the crucial accountability mechanisms are identified as consisting of a set of contractual relationships between the government, on the one hand, and the chief executives of the Ministry of Education and other educational agencies (such as the Educational Review Office, National Education Qualifications Authority) on the other; and between tertiary educational providers (councils and boards) and their chief executives. Charters were the principal contractual mechanism setting out intended outcomes and performance measures, which emphasised regular audits of performance. Universities, polytechnics and colleges of education were expected to develop forms of asset value accounting in order to promote greater public financial accountability.

The charter forms the basis of agreement between the council of an institution and the Government. It outlines education, financial and social goals, in consultation with the community it serves, which becomes a basis for negotiation with the Ministry "within funding parameters and provide the basis for performance review" (p. 4). Accountability requires a statement of goals (a charter): "a statement which translates these goals to measurable objectives" (a corporate plan); "the capacity to manage efficiently (which requires ownership and/or control of assets)"; and a variety of reporting mechanisms. The main accountability mechanisms are deemed to be: clarity of objectives; freedom to manage; incentives and sanctions; adequate information flows; effective assessment with a basis for judgements and comparisons. Institutions are required to provide an annual report, including audited accounts and information about educational, financial and equity performance allowing comparisons with previous years.

In addition, external monitoring was conducted by the Ministry Educational Review Office (ERO) and (the re-titled) New Zealand Qualifications Authority (NZQA) and lastly, self, peer and internal reviews were instituted. Traditional forms of professional accountability received minimal recognition and were overshadowed by external forms of monitoring. The major stakeholder identified was the Government who has an interest in accountability to reflect its role both as "provider of assets" and as "principal founder for outputs on behalf of students." Students and communities were recognised as having an interest in accountability for the quality and quantity of outputs. Additionally "some communities have a particular interest in the equity provisions provided" (p. 6). It is abundantly clear that the model of accountability developed here is managerialist in orientation, heavily emphasising an economic perspective which centres around questions concerning the control of assets/resources and a potentially technocratic measurement of relative performance, both individually and institutionally.

It is evident that accountability in the Picot model conforms to the economic perspective advocated by Treasury analysts Bushnell and Scott (1988:20) which views devolution as a form of delegation. They define devolution within the context of principal/agency theory:

> In our view accountability is inseparable from devolution or delegation. A principal (Government, Board or Council) would be willing to delegate duties or devolve processes if confident that the agent would act in line with the intentions of the principal. Of particular importance is the ability to hold the agent to account for the performance of the duties. Devolution, therefore, should be favoured to the extent that this furthers the objectives of the principal.

The overriding consideration here is one to do with "the efficiency of relationships between agents and their principals." In this approach to accountability, once objectives and goals are agreed upon, performance is measured, and any tendency to opportunism by the agent is countered through the use of incentives and sanctions. The State Sector Act, 1988, performs the function of formalising and structuring the contractual relationship between agent and principal, allowing a "more explicit accountability of performance" (p. 28).

Martin Carnoy (1995: 653) comments that "structural adjustment is normally associated with the correction of imbalances in foreign accounts and domestic consumption...and with the deregulation and privatization of the economy." He suggests that, therefore, such policies are identified with a fiscal austerity programme designed to shrink the public sector, and in some countries, with growing poverty and the unequal distribution of income. Yet, as Carnoy observes, the practice of structural adjustment followed by the high-income OECD countries and the newly industrialising countries (NICs) of Asia does not usually conform to this picture. In these countries the focus has been on increased exports, reduced domestic demand, constraints on government spending, together with some privatisation. Educational systems in most OECD countries have not suffered.

Drawing upon this difference in practice, Carnoy surmises that there are several categories of structural adjustment and that in the case of the richer OECD nations the term stands for *a set of policies* which originated in the United States during the 1970s as the dominant view of how economies in crisis, typically those of developing countries characterised by high indebtedness, should reorganise to achieve growth. Such policies called for cuts in public expenditure on services, including education, precisely at the point when a shift to a global information economy required massive public investment in an information infrastructure necessary to take advantage of changes in the nature of the world economy.

The so-called "New Zealand experiment" is something of an anomaly in terms of Carnoy's analysis. While it started the process of structural adjustment relatively late in comparison to the United States and the United Kingdom (i.e., in the mid 1980s rather than the late 1970s), it did so under conditions of crisis management, which enabled the Labour Government, to gain a kind of legitimacy and momentum for neoliberal policies that ran against the historical mission of a left wing party traditionally affiliated to the labour movement.[7] It is also the case that New Zealand, during the period 1984–96, sustained a programme of reform across different and successive governments which, contrary to the main thrust of Carnoy's analysis, has clearly resulted in both increased poverty and social inequalities.

The potential of the combined effects of the new institutional economics and a managerialist ideology has been to seriously erode the *democratic* nature of universities in a twin action of "restructuring" universities. First, internally, the strategy has been to grant managers, rather than academics, greater operational freedom to act commercially. Second, the strategy has also been to replace traditional faculty and student representation on governing councils with ministerial appointees who have managerial or business experience, or simply to substitute the model of a trust for that of a council, again with ministerial appointees from the private sector. In terms of this double strategy the traditional democratic governance arrangements of the university undergo profound change: "freedom" in this context no longer registers the traditional liberal concern for institutional autonomy and academic freedom but rather accentuates a neoliberal variant of negative freedom— the freedom to manage and make commercial decisions without interference from the State or academics.

In effect, the university, like other public institutions, once transformed by the government bureaucrats impressed with the new institutional economics—through clarification of objectives, separation of commercial and social functions etc.— becomes yet another "privatised" public institution, that is, a business which must be managed and run commercially to make a profit. Paradoxically, the policy arguments for the reduction of universities and all public institutions to same "performance" logic and model is phrased in terms of "accountability," construed not in terms of democratic theory (in which the term has its home) but in terms of a narrow construction of financial accountancy.

The Government's vision for tertiary education has been spelt out in terms that are very familiar to us from the UK and elsewhere—"lifelong learning for a knowledge society"—which has been adopted as the slogan by the Tertiary Education Advisory Commission (TEAC), itself the centrepiece of Government policy. The terms that distinguish the Government's direction from the previous regime are "co-operation," "collaboration," and "partnership." The emphasis on the "knowledge society" is no different from the previous National-led administration. "The nature of the knowledge society" is also the starting point for TEAC's shared vision, yet the concept is never analysed, defined or clearly distinguished from the knowledge economy. TEAC simply asserts that all fields of knowledge are of value. And while I agree with TEAC's conclusion that there has been excessive reliance on demand-driven funding, I am not convinced that the Tertiary Education Commission is not simply a return to central bureaucracy and planning. One would expect TEAC, as a Labour-appointed body, to want to jettison the market approach. Its finding that the central-steering mechanism is weak should, therefore, come as no surprise. The strengthening of charters and the introduction of profiles and "functional classifications," may provide the basis for a more integrated and strategic approach, but the important questions concerning the impact of forces of globalisation and opportunities of the knowledge economy seem to have been submerged, or at least have not received the analysis they deserve.

Conclusion

To summarise: the development of neoliberalism in New Zealand represents a clear example of the neoliberal shift in political philosophy and policy development that occurred during the 1980s. From being the so-called "social laboratory" of the Western world in the 1930s in terms of social welfare provision, New Zealand became the "neoliberal experiment" in the 1980s and the 1990s. With this historical reversal of social principles and philosophy, as I have previously mentioned, New Zealand has been described as a "successful" experiment of structural adjustment by a number of powerful world policy institutions, such as the World Bank, IMF, and the OECD. The neoliberal era in New Zealand can be conceived historically as the period stretching from the election of the fourth Labour government in 1984, through the election of successive administrations of the National government, lasting until the election of a reconstituted left-wing Labour government in 1999. The 1984 Labour Government jettisoned its traditional affiliation with the labour movement to base its policies upon contemporary forms of American neoliberalism (Chicago school economics, public choice theory, transaction cost analysis, and new institutional economics), reforming the labour market by introducing the Employment Contracts Act, privatizing state assets and restructuring the social realm. Led by Jim Bolger and Jenny Shipley, national governments which came to power following the decline of the fourth Labour government and its loss of the Treasury benches in 1990 consolidated and extended neoliberal policies, especially in the field of social and education policy.

New Zealand with a "thin" democracy (that is, one house and a strong executive) and a small population geographically confined, makes New Zealand an ideal country for social experiment. A distinctive brand of neoliberalism emerged in New

Zealand as the dominant paradigm of public policy: citizens have been redefined as individual consumers of newly competitive public services, and citizen rights have been re-defined as consumer rights; the public sector itself has undergone considerable downsizing as successive government have pursued the privatization agenda; management has been delegated or devolved while executive power has been concentrated even more at the centre. Nowhere is this shift more evident than in social welfare and education. There has been a clear shift away from universality to a "modest safety net." The old welfare goals of participation and belonging have been abolished. User-charges for social services and education have been introduced across the board. Since 1991, there have been substantial cuts in benefits and other forms of income support. Eligibility criteria have been tightened up. Targeting of social assistance has become the new social philosophy and there is a greater policing of welfare recipients aimed at reducing benefit fraud. The stated goal of neoliberals has been to free New Zealanders from the dependence on state welfare. The old welfare policies, allegedly, discouraged effort and self-reliance and, in the eyes of neoliberals, can be held responsible for *producing* young illiterates, juvenile delinquents, alcoholics, substance abusers, school truants, "dysfunctional families" and drug addicts.

International assessments of the recent reform experience of New Zealand have not been as compelling or as praiseworthy those of the World Bank or OECD. For instance, John Gray (1999), Professor of European Thought at the London School of Economics, writes:

> The neoliberal experiment in New Zealand is the most ambitious attempt at constructing the free market as a social institution to be implemented anywhere this century. It is a clearer example of the costs and limits of reinventing the free market in a late-twentieth-century context than the Thatcherite experiment in Britain. Among the many novel effects of neoliberal policy in New Zealand has been the creation of an underclass in a country that did not have one before....One of the world's most comprehensive social democracies became a neoliberal state (p. 39).[8]

He continues:

> In New Zealand, the theories of the American New Right achieved a rare and curious feat—self-refutation by their practical application. Contrary to the Right's confident claims, the abolition of nearly all universal social services and the stratification of income groups for the purpose of targeting welfare benefits selectively created a neoliberal poverty trap (p. 42).

He concludes that many of the changes instituted during the neoliberal period are irreversible. In strictly economic terms, neoliberalism achieved many of its objectives—a restructuring of the economy that would have been necessary in any case—yet it could have carried out its policies without the huge social costs. He suggests that while neoliberal reforms will not be overturned they have had the effect of narrowing the scope of future governments to reinstitute social democratic policies, despite the fact that criticism of the excesses of neoliberalism will become part of the new political consensus.

Ramesh Mishra (1999), Professor of Social Policy at York University (Canada) concurs. He remarks:

> New Zealand provides a good example of the role the OECD and IMF in promoting deregulation and privatization in individual countries. The drastic reforms in New Zealand which began in 1984 and continued into the early 1990s changed its economy from being one of the most closed to one of the most open among OECD countries…The OECD evaluated these reforms and the subsequent economic performances of the country in glowing terms and remonstrated with governments for not carrying projected changes far enough…Admitting that these changes involved short-term pain, the report asserts that they are sure to bring long terms gain (p. 10).

He suggests that the OECD plays up the neoliberal reforms, praising their consequences, while the success of the social market economies is glossed over. His assessment is that globalisation is as much a political and ideological project as it is market-driven and he argues that globalisation has "weakened very considerably the influence of domestic national policies on social policy" (p. 3, see Figure 2). In other words, "globalization virtually sounds the death-knell of the classical social democratic strategy of full employment, high levels of public expenditure and progressive taxation" (p. 6).

The argument of this chapter has been that since the introduction of changes to compulsory education in New Zealand in 1988 initiated under the *Picot Report* and *Tomorrow's Schools*, the system has become increasingly consumer-driven, seriously eroding the notion of education as a welfare right. In higher education with the introduction of "user-pays," there has been a shift from education as a universal welfare entitlement to a model of private investment whereby students have to pay a substantial portion of the costs of their education. The end point of a pure neoliberal approach to education policy is a fully consumer-driven model, where social or state welfare functions disappear completely. In contrast to a neoliberal model of education policy it can be argued that today there is even more reason to regard education as a form of welfare; indeed, in a postindustrial society or in the emerging global knowledge economy, education becomes the single most important means for easing the transition from dependency on state welfare to economic and social self-responsibility. There are, of course, different accounts to be offered of this process with different sets of moral meanings attached to the notion of "work," from a more or less draconian, forced transition from state welfare to state workfare, to an enabling cultural and education-based transition based upon a reconceptualisation of education as a twentieth-first century welfare right.

Appendix:
Major Education Reports and Policy Documents

Early Childhood Education

Report of the Early Childhood Care and Education Working Group (Meade Report), 1988, Department of Education, Wellington.
Before Five: Early Childhood Care and Education in New Zealand, 1988, Department of Education, Wellington.

Primary and Secondary Education

Administering for Excellence: Effective Administration in Education (Picot Report), 1988, Department of Education, Wellington.
Tomorrow's Schools: The Reform of Educational Administration in New Zealand, 1988, Department of Education, Wellington.
Today's Schools: A Review of the Educational Implementation Process (Lough Report), 1990, Ministry of Education, Wellington.
The National Curriculum of New Zealand, 1991, Ministry of Education, Wellington.
The New Zealand Curriculum Framework, 1993, Ministry of Education, Wellington.

Tertiary Education

New Zealand's Universities: Partners in National Development (Watts Report), 1987, New Zealand Vice-Chancellors' Committee.
Report of the Working Groups on Post-Compulsory Education and Training (Hawke Report), 1988, Department of Education, Wellington.
Reforming Tertiary Education in New Zealand, 1988, New Zealand Business Roundtable.
Learning for Life, Vols. I & II, 1988, Department of Education, Wellington.
The Report of the Ministerial Consultative Group (Todd Report), 1994, Ministry of Education.
The Tertiary Reviews, 1994, Treasury, Wellington.

General Significance: Education and the Economy

Economic Management, 1984, Treasury, Wellington.

Government Management, Vol. II: Education Issues, 1987, Treasury, Wellington.

Bulk Funding: Wage Bargaining in the Education Sector, 1991, Treasury, Wellington.

Designing the Framework: A Discussion About Restructuring National Qualifications, 1991, New Zealand Qualifications Authority, Wellington.

Upgrading New Zealand's Competitive Advantage (Porter Project), Crocombe et al. (1991).

Learning to Learn: An Introduction to the New National Qualifications Framework, 1992, New Zealand Qualifications Authority, Wellington.

Education for the 21st Century, 1993, Ministry of Education, Wellington.

Economic Surveys, 1992–1993, OECD, Paris.

Towards an Enterprise Culture, 1993, New Zealand Business Roundtable, Wellington.

Notes

1. Yet as he notes in the annex devoted to measuring economic freedoms and assessing its benefits:

   > Since the reform process was set under way in New Zealand in mid-1984, liberalisation has been taken further there than in Ireland, and on most reckonings the New Zealand economy would now show up as the freer of the two: both these conclusions emerge from the respective figures [given]…But if we compare 1984 with 1997 GDP per head in New Zealand appears as having increased by only some 10 per cent, as compared with over 90 per cent for Ireland. It seems obvious that this remarkable divergence between the two countries cannot be chiefly explained with reference to the comparative extent of economic freedom or differences in the recent progress of liberalisation (Henderson, 1999: 99–100).

2. In New Zealand the term "economic rationalism" (after Pusey, 1991), favoured in Australia, was not commonly used. Commentators tended to use terms such as the neutral "economic liberalisation," or the more ideological "New Right," or the term that I prefer "neoliberalism," which I take to refer to the revival of the assumptions of neoclassical economics (especially in the form of *homo economicus*) particularly in the third Chicago school (1970s to today). American neoliberalism—e.g., monetarism of Friedman, public choice economics of Tullock and Buchanan, human capital theory of Becker, principal-agency analysis, and so on—proved very influential with the NZ Treasury. This is not to deny the importance of other influences from the UK (the Institute of Economic Affairs) and also the quasi-world policy agencies such as the World Bank, IMF, OECD and WTO. Unlike Mok & Welch, I do not run the term "postmodernism" together with "neoliberalism" or "economic rationalism," even although postmodernism has been referred to as "the cultural logic of late capitalism" (Fredric Jameson) or the first international cultural style. I think these

claims have to be treated very carefully and that we should distinguish between "post-modernism" and "poststructuralism" (see e.g., Peters, 1995; 1996; 2001b).

3. The nine SOEs were: Electricity and Coal Corporations (from the Ministry of Energy); NZ Post, Post Office Bank and Telecom (from the former Post Office); Land and Forestry Corporations (from NZ Forest Service and the Lands and Survey Department; Airways Corporation; and Government Property services. Subsequently, the Works Corporation was set up from the old Ministry of Works and Development (1988); the Government Supply Brokerage Company was formed from the old government Stores Board; public sector superannuation funds were separated from Treasury; the Government Computing services was split from the State Services Commission. Under the National Government the health system has been 'restructured,' as has the science policy regime: the larger hospitals have become Crown Health Enterprises and the old Department of Science and Industrial Research (DSIR), along with other science departments, have been broken up into ten Crown Research Institutes.

4. As examples of neoliberals in New Zealand we can cite the National government's, Minister of Health, Simon Upton, and Minister of Social Welfare, Jenny Shipley, (later to be Prime Minister)—both in Jim Bolger's administration. We might also regard the one-time Secretary of Treasury, Graham Scott, Rod Dean (government official and one–time chairman of Telecom), Don Brash (chairman of the Reserve Bank), as well as the disaffected Labour Ministers, Roger Douglas and Richard Prebble, neoliberals of one form or other. The New Zealand political spectrum was dominated by a two-party system until the introduction of proportional representation in the late 1990s—the Labour party, with traditional affiliations to the labour movement, and the National Party, a center-right party, that traditionally favoured farmers and the rural heartland of NZ. After the election of the 1984 'neoliberal' Labour government, especially with Douglas as Finance Minister and Prebble as Minister of State Owned Enterprises, the political scene became confused, with Labour reneging on its traditional values and support base. Douglas and Prebble split off from the Labour party to form a right-wing party called ACT to take advantage of the new proportional representation.

5. This section draws on material from my "Introduction: The University in Crisis" (Peters, 1997).

6. The negative effects of quasi-market choice policies on issues of welfare within the community has been documented by Wylie (1994) who has investigated the broad effects of increasing competition under schemes of choice, citing changes in ethnic and socio-economic composition of schools as well as deterioration in the relations between schools. The Smithfield Project (Lauder, 1994) also documents the negative social effects of choice proposals. Gordon's (1994) research concluded that the status of a neighbourhood was a powerful factor influencing school choice. While poorer parents frequently do not have the option to shift their children from one

school to another, more affluent parents do. An implication of this trend, says Gordon "is that within schools, there will be increasingly homogenous class group-ings, while between schools differences will be enhanced" (p. 15). Similar patterns of segregation operate in respect to ethnicity.

7. New Zealand's late start to its experiment (vis-a-vis the UK), and the paradox of a Labour government fostering neoliberal policies, parallels the Australian experience. See Welch, 1997 and Welch (2001, this volume).

8. It is debatable whether it can be fairly maintained that New Zealand never had an underclass. It could be argued that Maori constituted an underclass, although their visibility as such was hidden through rural dispersion up until the rapid urban migration that occurred during the 1960s and 70s. I owe this point to Anthony Welch.

7

Rethinking Education as a Welfare Right

...none of the so-called rights of man goes beyond egoistic man,....An individual withdrawn behind his private interests and whims and separated from the community.

Karl Marx "On the Jewish Question," in *Karl Marx: Selected Writings*, ed. David McLellan, Oxford, 1977: 54

The concept of human rights is a historical product which evolves in Europe, out of foundations in Christianity, Stoicism and Roman law with its *jus gentium*, but which gains force and direction only with the contractual and pluralist nature of European feudalism, church struggles, the rise of Protestantism and of cities. It sees society as an association of individuals, as founded—logically or historically—on a contract between them, and it elevates the individual human person and his freedom and happiness to be the goal and end of all human association. In the vast majority of human societies, in time and space, until very recently such a view of human society would have been hotly contested; indeed, most cultures and languages would not have had the words in which to express it plausibly.

Eugene Kamenka (1978) "The Anatomy of an Idea" in Kamenka, Eugene and Alice Erh-Soon Tay, (eds.) *Human Rights*, New York, St. Martin's Press.

MY ARGUMENT WILL BE THAT SINCE THE INTRODUCTION of changes to compulsory education in New Zealand in 1988 initiated under the *Picot Report* and *Tomorrow's Schools*, the system has become increasingly consumer-driven, seriously eroding the notion of education as a welfare right. The end point of a pure neoliberal approach to education policy is a fully consumer-driven model, where social or state welfare functions disappear completely. In contrast to a neoliberal model of education policy it can be argued that today there is even more reason to regard education as a form of welfare; indeed, in a postindustrial society or in the emerging global knowledge/information economy, education becomes the single most important means for easing the transition from dependency on state welfare to economic and social self-responsibility. There are, of course, different accounts to be offered of this process with different set of moral meanings attached to the notion of 'work,' from a more or less draconian, forced transition from state welfare to state workfare, to an enabling cultural and education-based transition based upon a reconceptualisation of education as a twentieth-first century welfare right, together with the responsibilisation and empowerment of the self, *whanau* (Maori: family), and community.

This chapter comprises three main sections. First, an historical narrative concerning the development of a political culture under the first Labour government in New Zealand which established education as a universal social right and, paradoxically, the reversal of this right (at least at the tertiary level) under a neoliberal Fourth Labour government fifty years later. Second, a philosophical discussion of the nature of rights aimed at providing a sketch of a non-foundationalist account of rights, that is, an account which argues that a theory of human rights does not require or depend upon a theory of human nature or an essentialist or foundational account of what it is to be human. Third, an argument for considering education as a (non-foundationalist) welfare right within the changed circumstances of the so-called 'knowledge economy.'

The middle section—the philosophical discussion—underlies the other two sections for I want to argue that we should give up all sorts of foundationalism, not only the epistemological kind but also and especially the moral and political kind. I am sceptical both of the very idea of foundational reasoning about political morality and of the attempt to provide a foundation to human rights by anchoring it in facts about human nature or universal rationality. Accordingly, I argue we should learn to give up on a foundational notion of morality that is seen to rest upon or spring from a perceived essence of human nature. Indeed, like many postmodern and neopragmatist philosophers, I would argue that there is no political philosophy that can underpin and justify the public culture of the liberal state; there is only the political culture itself, which has to be struggled for. 'Reforms' or changes to protect the less fortunate members of society must be forced on the statue books.

Education and Welfare: Building a Political Culture[1]

The development of education in New Zealand was shaped and maintained by the ideal of social welfare and the ideal of egalitarianism. Education was seen to contribute to the maintenance of the welfare state and social integration as Garrett and Bates (1977: 61) argue:

> The contribution of education to social welfare has been seen, first, as providing the means of promoting an increasingly better society in which individuals are able to realise and exercise their abilities…The schools were also seen as providing a means of civilising those whose abilities were limited or perverse. In other words educators' tasks have been to promote social welfare, equality of opportunity and social control.

One of the hoped for functions of schooling was at the level of social class and religious and racial integration providing shared experiences as the basis of community development. Sutch (1971: 123) says, for instance:

> New Zealanders do not perhaps realise what an integrating effect our free and universal education system has had in the country. State education has avoided becoming a low quality system and, most importantly, it is socially approved, that is, there is no stigma, no sense of inferiority, no loss of family or of individual self-respect in attending primary or secondary school.

Since the introduction of changes to compulsory education in 1988 initiated under the *Picot Report* and *Tomorrow's Schools*, the system has become increasingly consumer-driven, seriously eroding the notion of education as a welfare right, with the consequence that access and provision of education have become increasingly unequal. At the tertiary level, since the late 1980s governments—both Labour and National—have aimed at creating a fully consumer-driven system with the consequence that the system as a whole has incrementally edged towards privatisation (see Peters and Roberts, 1999).

The introduction in 1877 of a 'universal, compulsory, and secular' primary education system in New Zealand reflected the egalitarian principles of early policy makers and was based on a number of historically important rights and claims. The 'positive' rights associated with social-democratic liberalism entailed that a universal and free education was the necessary prerequisite to the freedom of the individual. Such education was to be compulsory for a variety of reasons. First, children needed to be protected against the individual self-interest of their parents. This was because settler parents often ranked the labour a child could contribute to the family economy ahead of schooling. Second, because a basic elementary education was deemed to be essential to the development of moral and personal autonomy, it was considered that it should be accessible to all children irrespective of class, race or creed. Such rights underpinned the goals of a democratic society to ensure its reproduction through a common set of skills and values. Universal and compulsory education thus served the community by addressing social needs. Schools provided students with a common set of values and knowledge, thus helping create the basis for citizenship and the democratic functioning of society. Schooling also helped lay the foundation for scientific and cultural progress and played an important role in economic and social growth, contributing to creating the conditions for full employment.

The public benefits of education were additional to the sum of individual private benefits. Early New Zealand educators claimed that in order that public benefits might be derived from schooling all children should receive an education with common features, no matter whether they lived in town or in rural districts. This safeguarding of a universal schooling experience was not possible in a private system. Where education was privately funded some parents could not afford to obtain schooling for their children at all; others might seek schooling that reinforced sectarian political, ethnic or cultural ends. As a consequence, important issues to do with the regulation and control over such things as the 'quality of teacher training' or 'the nature of the curriculum' would not be possible. Universal and compulsory education established common uniform features in order to guarantee skills such as universal literacy and numeracy as the common basis necessary for active citizenship and democratic participation.

By 1914, the principle of universality, already firmly established in the political culture, was extended to secondary schooling, as long as the pupil had passed the Proficiency Examination at the end of primary school. In this way, while private schools and denominational schools continued to cater for the secondary pupils whose parents could afford to pay the required fees, future generations of New Zealanders were guaranteed access to a secondary education (Olssen & Morris Matthews, 1997: 8). The first Labour Government introduced a comprehensive model of the welfare state from 1936. As part of this reform agenda, the state commitment to universal, free, and compulsory education was extended. As expressed by Fraser's famous statement in 1939 (*AJHR*, 1939, Vol. E, pp. 2–3):

> The Government's objective, broadly expressed, is that every person, whatever the level of his academic ability, whether he be rich or poor, whether he live in town or country, has a right as a citizen to a free education of a kind for which he is best fitted and to the fullest extent of his powers.

Universal education would be provided in a package of benefits and services that would be 'non-contributory, universal, comprehensive, and adequate' and which were to be provided by the state 'as a citizen's right, not as an act of charity' (Hanson, 1975: 49). By the end of the war the Minister of Social Security could say 'we have the best social security system in the world: everything is done' (reported in Sutch, 1966: 341). The period 1945 to 1960 was a period of consolidation without significant new action. In addition to a commitment to free, universal and compulsory education, at the basis of all welfare policies was the accepted goal of full employment, which it was claimed made possible the dignified self-help of every member of the community (Rosenberg, 1977: 53).

Fraser and Education: Biography of a Minister

The building of the political culture in New Zealand during the years of the first Labour government, and the central importance of education considered as a social right, can be gained from a study of the influence and biography of Peter Fraser. Fraser was a Highland Scot, born in 1884, whose interest in politics grew out of anti-landlordism, the poetry of Robbie Burns, prohibitionism (the Independent Order of the Templars) and New Testament Presbyterianism "as a source of democratic procedure and tradition" (King, 1998: 23). He became Prime Minister in 1940, after the death of Michael Savage, and he remained in that post until 1949. Fraser had a passion for education. He became Minister of Education in 1935 and remained in that position for four and a half years. Having arrived in Auckland in 1911 he rapidly became a founding member of the New Zealand Labour Party and Workers' Educational Association. During the 1920s the main educational influences upon his thinking were Percy Nunn (on individual development), John Dewey, Maria Montessori, Caldwell Cook (play-way). James Shelly, an Englishman who was appointed to the first chair in education at Canterbury College in 1920 (education had only become a university discipline three years earlier), was also a strong local influence on Fraser's educational thinking, and along with Labour party activists such as "Walter Nash, Harry Holland, T. H. McCombs, W. B. Sutch, Tommy Hunter, P. Martin Smith, C. E. Beeby, F. L. McCombs and A. E. Campbell…had helped develop Labour's education policy in preparation for office" (Carter, 1993: 198).

Shelly's student and protégé, C. E. Beeby, who was responsible for establishing the New Zealand Council of Educational Research in 1934 (and of giving the institutions a psychological measurement and testing orientation), later became Assistant Director General, then Director General of Education in New Zealand under Fraser as Minister, a post he was to hold until 1960. The popular or received view of the educational community in New Zealand is that Beeby was responsible for or authored the famous statement on equality of educational opportunity, a fact Beeby emphasised to me when I interviewed him in 1992, shortly before his death in 1998. As Noeline Alcorn (1999: 98) comments:

> Although he was friendly with individual members of the left-wing educational groups which advised Fraser before and after the Labour Party came to power, Beeby had never been personally involved. He saw himself as a researcher and psychologist studying education rather than an educationalist.

William Renwick (1998: 68), himself at one time Director General of Education, suggests that Fraser's contributions to education after 1940 have been overlooked precisely because of Beeby's "dominant place" which he held "in the collective memory of the teaching profession during the years 1940–60 when he was Director of Education." As he goes on to argue:

> Beeby's own memoir, furthermore, has recently, provided an account of the period that many readers will find sufficient for their purposes. But without a similar account of Fraser's role in those reforms the historical record remains unbalanced, and one unintended effect of Beeby's memoir has been to distance Fraser from the educational reforms he himself authored. For, without detracting from Beeby's singular achievement, public servants do not determine the policies they administer, even though they may claim a hand in their authorship" (Renwick, 1998: 68).

Fraser's first substantive speech in the House in 1919 was on education and "He was appointed to the Education Committee in 1921 and served on it continuously until his death" (Renwick, 1998: 71). He believed in state-funded education: for kindergartens and primary schools (up to the age of twelve) with no drafting of children into academic and technical streams. He insisted that all children "should receive what he called a 'cultural' education until the age of fifteen" (Renwick, 1998: 72). He supported special schools, accreditation rather than examination and held that school boards should be elected and teachers should have a say in governance. Nevertheless, formal education was considered only one instrument of social reconstruction along with the means to promote children's health and well-being.

Renwick's (1998: 77) assessment:

> Fraser's abiding legacy was the reorientation of public education in the name of
> equality of educational opportunity...By the time that objective became the pol-
> icy of Western governments in the generation after World War II, the reconstruc-
> tion of education in New Zealand was already well advanced.

The powerful nature of the 1939 statement of equality of educational opportunity which dominated education policy in New Zealand in a formal sense from 1935,
when Fraser became Minister of Education, through to 1960—the end Beeby's
director-generalship of education—really laid the basis for a political culture that
accepted as a new commonsense the notion that education was a fundamental citizen right. Writing in National Education in 1938 Fraser expressed the notion in
the following words:

> Every child, whatever his social and economic position and whatever his level of
> academic ability has a right as a citizen to a free education of the kind and length
> to which his powers best (fit) him (cited in Alcorn, 1999: 99).

It was this notion of education as a citizen right and the policy ideology and political culture upon which it was built that was attacked and abolished by neoliberal thinkers and policy actors in the late 1980s.

The Neoliberal Reversal of the Right to Education

Although there are different accounts as to the relative importance of the Treasury
vis-à-vis other state agencies (Dale and Jesson, 1992), the position that is adopted
here, and the most widely maintained view, is that the Treasury is the dominant
state department influencing the reforms (see e.g., Easton, 1990; Boston and
Cooper, 1989: 123; Oliver, 1989: 11–12; Kelsey 1993: 64–65). The power and
influence of the Treasury within the policy process reflect partly the high ranking
of the finance portfolio within the government, partly the priority afforded to maintaining the stability and growth of the country's economy, and partly historical factors related to the development of the state bureaucracy in New Zealand.

During the 1980s the Treasury came to exert increasing influence on government policy. Their adoption of market-liberal principles influenced the move to a
market model of welfare in New Zealand, although their implementation in various reforms and legislation has taken some time and occurred across successive governments. In 1984, the incoming Labour Government received from the Treasury
briefing papers which were later published under the title *Economic Management*

(Treasury, 1984). This documented Treasury thinking at the time which was based on 'New Right' theory and strategies for improving the New Zealand economy. The implication of such policies for education was to become clearer in 1987. In that year, the Treasury produced for the re-elected Labour Government its brief entitled *Government Management* (Treasury, 1987). This was published in two volumes, with the second devoted to *Education Issues* setting forth the Treasury's arguments specifically in relation to education. Here it was maintained that:

- education shares the main characteristics of other commodities traded in the marketplace, and it cannot be analysed successfully as a 'public good' (p. 33);
- New Zealanders are too optimistic about the ability of education to contribute to economic growth and equality of opportunity (p. 8);
- increased expenditure in education does not necessarily improve educational standards or equality of opportunity, or lead to improved economic performance (pp. 8, 18, 39, 130, 132, 141 and 142);
- not only has the education system not adjusted to changed circumstances but it has performed badly despite increased expenditure on it (pp. 6, 16, 18 and 140);
- the reason it has performed badly is because teachers and the educational establishment have pursued their own self-interest rather than those of pupils and parents; i.e., they are not responsive enough to consumer interests and desires (pp. 37–38);
- specifically, the educational system lacks a rigorous system of accountability. There is a lack of national monitoring procedures or of any satisfactory ways of comparing the effectiveness of schools in order to account for the public resources employed (p. 108);
- government intervention and control has interrupted the 'natural' free-market contract between producer and consumer causing bureaucratic inflexibility, credential inflation and hence, educational inequality (pp. 37–39, 41, 132 and 137).

In short, Treasury argued that state-provided and controlled education meant that education had performed badly and would continue to do so unless changes of a radical sort were implemented. The Treasury sought to buttress its arguments for the necessity of change by reference to 'falling standards' and 'rising mediocrity,' and by discrediting the notion of education as a 'public good.' The central issues under review were those of *efficiency* and *equity* in education. In relation to these issues, the key subject-themes on which recommendations were made included:

- school governance, with implications for the administration, management, and funding of schools (e.g., bulk funding and Boards of Trustees);
- the role of the State in the provision, management and funding of education;
- the merits of market or quasi-market models relating to issues such as consumer choice in relation to participation and access in education;
- the nature of education as a public or private good and the respective merits of public versus private provision in education; i.e., whether the benefits accrue to the community or to individuals;
- parental choice, including the issues of zoning and targeted individual entitlements.

In its critique of education, the Treasury drew on the work of research that criticised the inability of the welfare state to adequately distribute resources. Influential here was research in England by Julien Le Grand (1982, 1987) which sought to document the distributional failures of the old welfare state, claiming on the basis of empirical data that the welfare state was not redistributive across class lines but that most redistribution is intra-class and over the course of the individual's life time. Le Grand's studies also argued that middle and upper classes secured a disproportionate amount in terms of per capita share of the total available equity of state-provided resources and services. Indicative of their new found interest in neoliberal theoretical models, the Treasury adopted the theoretical concept of 'capture' to ground their critique of the welfare state (see Bertram, 1988). This concept is used both to account for the deficiencies of existing welfare policies in terms of egalitarian objectives and to advocate a shift to neoliberal solutions based on the minimal state and individual choice.

The full story of the reversal of education as a citizen right has been told elsewhere (see Peters and Olssen, 1999, for a review of this literature). The crucial point here for my purposes is that the New Zealand Treasury, along with neoliberal politicians and other policy actors both within the Ministry of Education and related agencies (including, New Zealand Qualification Authority and The Educational Review Office), moved deliberately to disestablish education as a citizen right by substituting the notion of consumer sovereignty and consumer rights for those of the citizen. In this sense just as Margaret Thatcher's Government in the United Kingdom moved to reverse the welfare rights to education, so too did successive governments in New Zealand over the period 1988–1999. This reversal took place through a variety of strategies: a process of incremental privatisation at the tertiary level with the introduction of user-charges, students loans, and subsidies to private training establishments, and a process of 'dezoning' and deregulation of the schooling sector, with increased public funding of private schools and the move to establish a fully consumer-driven model.

Foundationalism and Human Rights

Generally a right is considered a special advantage—a liberty, a power, entitlement—that someone gains because of his or her particular status as a human being or a citizen (or a member of a definable group—a woman, a minority, an animal, a child). It applies in both legal and morals contexts. I want to advance a negative conception of rights, 'negative' in the sense that it avoids: (1) any suggestion that we can infer rights or rights talk from a theory of human nature; (2) the notion that there is a *telos* to history which guarantees both rights and rights talk (a kind of historical inevitability, as in the Hegelian-inspired work of Italian philosopher of jurisprudence, Norberto Bobbio [1995]), and; (3) the idea that rights are or should be conceived purely as citizen entitlements dependent solely upon the State. While I am sceptical of rights talk and think that we should take a pragmatic stance and judge the usefulness of rights talk in terms of its consequences, nevertheless, I think the discourse can be made to do more work, especially in the context of globalisation and in relation to education. I raise the argument for adopting the notion of education as a global welfare right under the changed conditions of "the knowledge economy," including reference to some recent work completed by Joseph Stiglitz (1998, 1999a, 1999b) who analyses education as a global public good.

The notion of education as a social or welfare right advanced by the early architects of the welfare state in New Zealand and elsewhere in the West was seen to rest implicitly upon a theory of citizenship; rights were conferred upon individuals by virtue of their membership as a citizen of a particular State. A whole host of reasons were advanced for the necessity of conceiving education as a social right based upon an education system that was "secular, compulsory, and free" at the primary and secondary levels and universally accessible on the basis of merit at the tertiary level. Most of these reasons derived from two sources: a vision of the State and/or of the society, with a strong appeal to egalitarianism, and a theory of human nature, that is the positing of an ontology that accorded human beings a certain essential nature (often involving appeals to freedom, equality and fraternity). In parliamentary debates and in political discussion of the theory of the welfare state, there was little, if any, probing of the philosophical assumptions behind political positions, although there was a fair amount of reasoning from social and economic consequences (i.e., the economic and social benefits of equality).

Even today, often education is simply conceived as a "right" without examination of grounds or of theoretical basis for such an ascription. A good example is the UNESCO World Conference on Higher Education held in October 1998 which focused upon higher education as a "fundamental right," equitable access to higher education as a world-wide problem, and the biggest challenge to be how countries will "provide their citizens with broadened access to postsecondary education and thereby afford them the opportunity to prepare for citizenship and work in the knowledge based global economy" (Miller, 1999: 1). By 2025 the world tertiary institutions will be expected to accommodate 200 million students (more than double the 85 million of 1995) and the *World Declaration on Higher Education for the Twenty-First Century*, declaring access to higher education a fundamental right based on the merit of the individual, indicates that such access ought not to be limited by inability to pay.

If we look back a little into the past century we can see that "free primary education, and accessible education at all levels" was included in the UN Covenant on Economic, Social, and Cultural Rights, along with the basic economic, social, and cultural rights of individuals and nations, including the right to: self-determination, wages sufficient to support a minimum standard of living, equal pay for equal work, equal opportunity for advancement, form trade unions, strike, paid or otherwise compensated maternity leave, copyright, patent, and trademark protection for intellectual property. The text of this covenant was finalized in 1966 but has not yet been ratified.

Article 26 of the Universal declaration of Human Right in respect of education specifically states:

1. Everyone has the right to education. Education shall be free, at least in the elementary and fundamental stages. Elementary education shall be compulsory. Technical and professional education shall be made generally available and higher education shall be equally accessible to all on the basis of merit.
2. Education shall be directed to the full development of the human personality and to the strengthening of respect for human rights and fundamental freedoms. It shall promote understanding, tolerance and friendship among all nations, racial or religious groups, and shall further the activities of the United Nations for the maintenance of peace.
3. Parents have a prior right to choose the kind of education that shall be given to their children.

These are the most influential statements of contemporary human rights in rela-tion to education and education as a right was included in the earliest of declara-tions. Indeed, as Charles Leben (1991:75) writes:

> the first French Constitution of 3 September 1791 states in the first Title head-ed 'Fundamental Provisions Guaranteed by the Constitution' that '[a] general sys-tem of public assistance shall be established and organized, to bring up abandoned children, comfort the poor when they are sick, and provide work for the able-bod-ied poor who have been unable to find any.' And the following paragraph states: 'Public education shall be established and organized, common to all citizens, free as regards the elements of education indispensable to all men.'

As Leben goes on to note these 'second-generation' rights are re-asserted with more force in the Montaignard Constitution of 24 June 1793, which includes them in its new Declaration of the Rights of Man and the Citizen. Article 22 states: '[e]ducation is a requirement for all. Society must with all its power promote the progress of public reason, and put education within the reach of all its citizens' (cited in Leben, 1999: 75).

The concept of human rights, itself, has existed in one form or another in European thought for many centuries, dating back to King John of England and the signing of the Magna Carta. Non-Western political and religious traditions have also proclaimed "human rights," at least in the sense of delineating limits of the sov-ereign's power over the lives and property of their citizens. The concept of "natur-al rights" was proposed in the 18th and 19th centuries. This concept suggested that rights belonged to a person by nature and because he was a human being, not by virtue of his citizenship in a particular country or membership in a particular reli-gious or ethnic group but this concept was increasingly rejected by both philoso-phers and jurists as theoretically unjustifiable, even though it underpinned the two declarations based on the revolutions of the 1700s (the US Declaration of Independence and the French Declaration of the Rights of Man). As Thomas Paine, John Stuart Mill, and Henry David Thoreau developed the concept the notion of "universal human rights" took over from the notion of "natural rights." It was this notion that served at the forefront of human rights issues including slav-ery, child labour, women's rights, and the US Civil Rights during the late 19th and 20th centuries.

Michael Freeman (1994: 16) argues that there are no *uncontested* foundations of human rights. They are, he suggests, two approaches to questions concerning such foundations:

The first approach emphasizes contingency, construction, and relativity. Laclau and Mouffe [1985], Rorty [1993], Dworkin[1977], MacIntyre [1981] and Donnelly [1989] all adopt some form of this approach....MacIntyre is hostile to the concept of human rights. Laclau, Rorty, and Dworkin support human rights on the basis of a prerational commitment to liberal culture. Donnelly endorses the particular list of rights in international texts on the grounds that they are required to protect human dignity under modern conditions. All these theorists hold that under different conditions different lists of rights, different conceptions of human rights, or even quite different moral concepts might properly be defended.

The second approach, Freeman describes as that which attempts to locate "objective foundations for human rights in reason and morality." On this approach that he attributes to Gewirth (1982), the "doctrine of human rights is objectively and universally true."

I have already professed my intellectual sympathies for the former approach, although it is clear that within that approach there are numerous positions. One may, like Donnelly (1989) believe that there is, as a matter of contingent fact, a consensus on human rights, but that does not imply a consensus on their theoretical foundations (Freeman, 1994: 3). One might, like Rorty and Laclau, claim that "the 'universality' of our values is a precarious, pragmatic and non-necessary construction" (Freeman, 1994: 5) (i.e., that there are no theoretical foundations) though asserting the contingency of human rights does nothing to justify them. One may argue that the foundational concepts are "essentially contested" and that there is no logical method for resolving conceptual disputes unambiguously. One may argue, like MacIntyre (1981) that human rights doctrine is not simply 'contingent' but false. As Freeman (1994: 6) comments "Anti-foundationalism proceeds, at least in part, on the premise of the death of God. A further project of anti-foundationalism is to disallow God-substitutes, such as Reason, nature, etc." (see Peters, 2000).[2]

There is another position which we might call "relativism" that, in my view, does not proceed from the so-called "death of God" for the arguments are drawn up by people from cultures outside the Western tradition, outside Judaic-Christian culture, and, therefore, not having ever subscribed to "God" in the Judaic-Christian sense, cannot be seen to subscribe to the "death of God." This form of non-foundationalism, which has raised its head recently in the debate over "Asian values," is based on the criticism that the question is not simply whether the doctrine of human rights is "Western" and therefore simply a matter of contingent historical fact, but more problematically, whether the doctrine is irretrievably "Western," that is, based upon individualistic and ontological assumptions that other cultures could not possibly share or could only share by themselves jettisoning some of their own cultural and ontological baggage. Such a radical relativism might then militate against any possible world consensus from emerging. This form of objection has been in evidence from the very moment the United Nations voted to adopt the Universal Declaration. On the eve of the vote the American Anthropological Association (AAA) submitted a statement to the draft committee stating the cultural relativist case against the Declaration arguing that respect for the individual entails a respect for cultural differences since the individual realises his or her personality through his culture and that no technique of qualitatively evaluating cultures has been discovered:

> Standards and values are relative to the culture from which they derive so that any attempt to formulate postulates that have grown out of the beliefs or moral codes of one culture must to that extent detract from the applicability of any Declaration of Human Rights to mankind as a whole (cited in Li, 1998: 1).

Xiaorong Li (1998) poses the theoretical difficulties involved in the challenge to universal human rights in terms of the relativist challenge that has been made forcefully by the Chinese president Jiang Zemin:

> Fifty years later, challenges to universality of human rights have continued and, more specifically, have flared up in China, where government leaders have asserted particularist cultural values. Confucianism and other traditions of thought were long derided in favor of Marxism. Having faced the need to counter international criticisms of its human rights record since 1989, the Chinese authorities now claim that their political repression is justified by traditional "cultural values." Replying to questions about human rights during Clinton's visit, Chinese president Jiang Zemin thus defended the government's authoritarian policies: "[t]he two countries differ in social system, ideology, historical tradition and cultural background, the two countries have different means and ways in realizing human rights and fundamental freedoms." Official statements…have declared that China has its own unique cultural values (such as obedience to authority, collectivism, family, and other dispositions), which are said to be opposed to human rights ideals that cherish individual freedom and tolerance.

The question highlighted here, which must be considered in light of particular historical readings of past episodes of Western imperialism and colonisation, is the problem of values in relation to cultural pluralism and the normative force of the idea that one culture should not impose on other cultures its own values or ethical standards. For China, as Li points out, international human rights are merely disguised Western cultural ideas. One of the central issues is whether relativists' insistence on an incommensurability of cultural values—that each culture and its values are unique and cannot be compared with other cultures—constitutes a denial in principle of *universal* human rights (see also, O'Manique, 1992; Howard, 1993; Zechenter, 1997).

The relativist question is central to education within liberal cultures, not only as regards rights, but also as regards matters concerning the curriculum. It is not self-evident that migrants or members of indigenous cultures should automatically subscribe to the notion of rights as it is promulgated in the dominant liberal culture. One of the strongest challenges to liberal political theory (and, therefore, to liberal political theory of education) comes from the argument from minority, group and cultural rights to the maintenance of one's language, identity, and culture. Whether liberal theory is able to reform its core individualistic assumptions to accommodate such challenges is beyond the scope of the chapter. So the question of the universal is as complex within liberal culture as it is among cultures.

Some scholars, like Donnelly (1989) argue for the consensus view, the notion that there are, as a matter of contingent fact, overlapping values between different cultures in human history and that we are moving towards a convergence. He sketches an "analytic theory of the concept of human rights" which lays out the case for the universality of these rights despite their undeniable origins in historic Western liberalism. He argues that nonliberal regimes may advance one or another conception of human dignity, but that only the "liberal" (i.e., "social democratic") state can champion this goal through the defence of human rights. Yet he also argues that "historic particularity" of the norms and conceptions characteristic of human rights do not require us to accept the cultural relativity of these rights.

Leben (1998: 75) frames up the problem in the following way:

Does the deep-rootedness in history mean that doubt is cast on the universal character of the European/western doctrine of human rights or, conversely, that this doctrine represents the only possible path which all the civilizations of the world must follow?

And he responds to his own question thus: "It seems to me that the answer to both questions must be 'No'" (p. 25), quoting Professor P. H. Imbert (Director of Human Rights at the Council of Europe) "for anybody, humanity is accessible only through his own particular culture. In this there is *a priori* no contradiction with the requirement of the universality of human rights" (cited in Leben, 1998: 76).

Leben goes on to argue that "the path toward the universal may be found in any civilization. The crux, however, is to discover how, in a given culture, it is possible to progress towards this conception of the universal" (Leben, 1998: 77) which, he maintains, takes place through the labour of self-examination. Certainly, there is a good *prima facie* case concerning the historical particularity of mathematics or science, in terms of their cultural beginning, though few of us would want to deny their universality. We might talk here of a *bootstrap theory of rights*, which, while not conferring any special cultural privilege on the West because of it, provide the world with the current notion of human rights, allowed philosophers, jurists, and civil and human rights activists—through a learning process, argumentation, precedent, and the experience of case law—enabled us to develop a universal notion. I would argue for a *naturalised* view of human rights. Naturalising human rights simply means that judgements concerning universality of categories of rights cannot be based upon any theory that ascribes a nature or essence to human beings and it suggests, paradoxically perhaps, that such universality is a contingent feature that develops out of particular cultures. It may be at this moment we are witnessing the historical effects of globalisation of cultures on establishing human rights.

Certainly, within the liberal tradition of rights going back to the early declarations and beyond—back further to the origins the development of the idea of 'equality' in Christianity and, ultimately, to the Greeks for notions of 'justice' and 'democracy,' it is possible *within* liberal states to make strong appeals to tradition as a basis for rights and such 'second-generation' rights as education. It is in terms of these general theoretical parameters that I want to make a case for establishing education as a universal human right in the so-called global knowledge society/economy.

Education as a Welfare Right in the Knowledge Economy

The body of literature on the concept of the "knowledge economy" is both recent and rapidly growing, especially in the related fields of economics and management, yet both less recognised and less established in the field of education. It is a concept that has inspired many national governments and world policy institutions such as the OECD[3] (1996a; 1996b; 1997) and the World Bank (see e.g., Stiglitz, 1999a, 1999b) to talk of the global "knowledge economy" of the future, and to emphasise the fundamental importance of education considered as an investment both in human capital (see Becker, 1964) and in the production of research or new knowledge.

In February 2000 the executive body of the European Union (EU) launched an ambitious new strategy to promote job creation and skills for the new knowledge-based economy, designed to overcome the gap with the United States in access to the Internet and the use of information and communication technology. The strategy sets out a range of specific recommendations in four main areas (learning, work, public services and enterprises) and, specifically, calls for: linking all schools to the Internet by 2002; teacher competency in information society skills; an inclusiveness where all workers have the opportunity to achieve the key new skills of information society; and the establishment of flexible frameworks for tele-working to meet the new needs of business and employment. The EU Commissioner for Employment, Anna Diamantopoulou, suggested that the main goal of the union is to build an inclusive knowledge-oriented economy as she considers it the only route to create jobs and growth in Europe in coming years. Diamantopoulou also pointed out that the next generation of the work force—the "net generation"—is in school today and nations of the EU must properly equip this generation so that the EU can grasp the challenges and opportunities of the knowledge society that are considered vital to the EU's future economic and social development.

The concept of the "knowledge economy" and its associated discourse is anchored in a diverse literature that is now almost fifty years old, beginning, perhaps, with Peter Drucker's (1959) predictions in *Landmarks of Tomorrow*, developed further by Fritz Machlup's (1962) empirical analyses of the growth of the service sector of the American economy in the early 1960's, and taken up by the sociologists of postindustrialism, Daniel Bell (1973) and Alain Touraine (1972), in the 1970s.

The 'knowledge economy' allegedly differs from the traditional economy with an emphasis on what I shall call the 'economics of abundance,' the 'annihilation of distance,' 'de-territoralisation of the state,' the importance of 'local knowledge,' and 'investment in human capital' (and its embedding in processes). Let me briefly expand on each of these characteristics:

1. *Economics of abundance*: The economics is not of scarcity, but rather of abundance for unlike most resources that become depleted when used, information and knowledge can be shared, and actually grow through application.
2. *The annihilation of distance*: The effect of location is diminished through new information and communications technologies; virtual marketplaces and organisations offer round-the-clock operation and global reach.

3. *The de-territoralisation of the state*: Laws, barriers and taxes are difficult to apply on solely a national basis as knowledge and information 'leak' to where demand is highest and the barriers are lowest.

4. *The importance of local knowledge*: Pricing and value depends heavily on context as the same information or knowledge can have vastly different value to different people at different times.

5. *Investment in human capital*: Human capital (i.e., competencies) is the key component of value in a knowledge-based economy and knowledge-based companies seek knowledge locked into systems or processes rather than in workers because it has a higher inherent value.

It is policy understandings based upon these characteristics that recently have helped shape national policy constructions of the 'knowledge economy' in the USA, United Kingdom, Ireland, Australia, Canada and New Zealand. The United Kingdom's White Paper *Our Competitive Future: Building the Knowledge Driven Economy* (Department of Trade and Industry, 1998), for example, begins by acknowledging the fact that the World Bank's 1998 *World Development Report* took knowledge as its theme, citing the report as follows:

> For countries in the vanguard of the world economy, the balance between knowledge and resources has shifted so far towards the former that knowledge has become perhaps the most important factor determining the standard of living...... . Today's most technologically advanced economies are truly knowledge-based (http://www.dti.gov.uk/comp/competitive/main.htm.)

The White Paper also mentions that the OECD has drawn attention to the growing importance of knowledge indicating that the emergence of knowledge based economies has significant policy implications for the organisation of production and its effect on employment and skill requirements. The report suggests that already other countries including, US, Canada, Denmark and Finland have identified the growing importance of knowledge and reflected it in their approach to economic policy.

It defines a knowledge based economy in the following terms:

> A knowledge driven economy is one in which the generation and the exploitation of knowledge has come to play the predominant part in the creation of wealth. It is not simply about pushing back the frontiers of knowledge; it is also about the more effective use and exploitation of all types of knowledge in all manner of activity (http://www.dti.gov.uk/comp/competitive/main.htm.)

The report suggests that "knowledge" is more than just information and it goes on to distinguish between two types of knowledge: "codified" and "tacit." Codifiable knowledge can be written down and transferred easily to others whereas tacit knowledge is "often slow to acquire and much more difficult to transfer."

Much of the report follows Paul Romer's (1986, 1990) work in so-called "new growth theory," charting the ways in which education and technology are now viewed as central to economic growth. One of the limitations of neo-classical economics is that it does not specify how knowledge accumulation occurs. As a result there is no mention of human capital and there is no direct role for education. Further, in the neo-classical model there is no income 'left over' (all output is paid to either capital or labour) to act as a reward or incentive for knowledge accumulation. Accordingly, there are no externalities to knowledge accumulation. By contrast, new growth theory has highlighted the role of education in the creation of human capital and in the production of new knowledge (see, for example, Solow, 1956, 1994). On this basis it has explored the possibilities of education-related externalities. In short, while the evidence is far from conclusive at this stage there is a consensus emerging in economic theory that education is important for successful research activities (e.g., by producing scientists and engineers), which is, in turn, important for productivity growth, and education creates human capital, which directly affects knowledge accumulation and therefore productivity growth.

New Zealand's Ministry of Research Science and Technology (MoRST) completed a comprehensive review of the priorities for public good science and technology, under the umbrella of the so-called Foresight Project. The Foresight Project links government investment with the vision of New Zealand as a "knowledge society."

On this account knowledge is said to include "information in any form, but also includes know-how and know-why, and involves the way we interact as individuals and as a community" (MoRST, 1998). The project defines "knowledge economies" in the following terms:

> Knowledge economies are those which are directly based on the production, distribution and use of knowledge and information. This is reflected in the trend towards growth in high-technology investments, high-technology industries, more highly-skilled labour and associated productivity gains. Knowledge, as embodied in people (as 'human capital') and in technology, has always been central to economic development. But it is only over the last few years that its relative importance has been recognised, just as that importance is growing (http://www.morst.govt.nz/foresight/font.html).

The policy constructions do not recognise, for instance, either knowledge as *a global public good* or the key role governments have in promoting *public* education or protecting and regulating intellectual property rights. I shall briefly elaborate this criticism by reference to the work of Joseph Stiglitz (1999a, 1999b) when he was Senior Vice President and Chief Economist at the World Bank. Simply put, Stiglitz combines two concepts that have been developed over the last twenty-five years: the concept of global public goods and the notion of knowledge as a global public good. A public good has two properties: non-rivalrousness and non-excludability. Knowledge qualifies as a public good on these two criteria: it is non-rivalrous because "there is a zero marginal cost from an additional individual enjoying the benefits of knowledge" (Stiglitz, 1999c) which has the implication that "Even if one could exclude someone from enjoying the benefits of knowledge, it would be undesirable to do so because there are no marginal costs to sharing its benefits" (ibid.) The non-excludability property of knowledge (which means that no one can be excluded) also has a strong implication: "it means that knowledge cannot be provided privately" (ibid.). (It is the case, however, that knowledge can be appropriated through the patent process so there is some degree of non-excludability.)

Stiglitz (1999c) indicates shortly after Samuelson developed his general theory of pure public goods it became recognised that some public goods were limited geographically, yet most knowledge is a global public good, especially if we are talking of scientific knowledge for its 'truth' is considered universal. Stiglitz (1999c) argues that one of the central implications of knowledge as a global public good is that the state must play some role in the provision of such goods, otherwise they will be undersupplied. As he writes:

> National public goods provide one of the central rationales for national collective action and for the role of government. Efficiency requires public provision, and to avoid the free rider problem, the provision must be supported by compulsory taxation.

He argues further that "knowledge is one of the critical keys to development and that knowledge is complementary to private and public capital. Knowledge is a global good requiring public support at the global level" (Stiglitz, 1999c).

If there is an argument for the public provision of knowledge as a local and global good, there is also an argument for considering education as a local and global good and for its public support through taxation. Certainly, it is the case that the knowledge economy depends upon the fostering of higher order cognitive skills, the development of the knowledge infrastructure, and an understanding of the institutional complexities of knowledge cultures, both public and private. I believe that government approaches to the fostering of higher order cognitive skills requires a more complete understanding of the concept of knowledge, its different forms and aspects, and an understanding of the ways in which intellectual cultures operate. This means that governments ought to be looking more closely at the synergistic effects of research collaboration and the collegiality, and peer networking that characterize traditional intellectual cultures like universities and technical institutes as well as research teams, think-tanks and the like.

It is of fundamental importance that economists of information and knowledge consider the wider societal and cultural parameters of knowledge. In this context, it is also important to draw the distinction between "knowledge *economy*" and "knowledge *society*." Both locally (and nationally) and globally, I want to argue, governments and world institutions, have a joint role and responsibility: to provide the public goods of knowledge and education and to support the right to education. In the transformed global context of the "knowledge economy" education must be considered as a *universal welfare right*, perhaps, *the* global welfare right that has the power to determine individual citizenship, employment status, and income. Indeed, we might say that within the global knowledge economy/society a new set of rights are beginning to emerge: the set of rights to knowledge and education that will determine individual, cultural, national and global development well into the third millennium. This set of rights, I would argue, should be central to the future concerns of the Left, which should define and prosecute the struggle for equality in the related realms of knowledge and education, as never before.

Appendix:
The United Nations International Covenant on Economic, Social and Cultural Rights

Article 13

1. The States Parties to the present Covenant recognize the right of everyone to education. They agree that education shall be directed to the full development of the human personality and the sense of its dignity, and shall strengthen the respect for human rights and fundamental freedoms. They further agree that education shall enable all persons to participate effectively in a free society, promote understanding, tolerance and friendship among all nations and all racial, ethnic or religious groups, and further the activities of the United Nations for the maintenance of peace.

2. The States Parties to the present Covenant recognize that, with a view to achieving the full realization of this right:
   a. Primary education shall be compulsory and available free to all;
   b. Secondary education in its different forms, including technical and vocational secondary education, shall be made generally available and accessible to all by ever appropriate means, and in particular by the progressive introduction of free education;
   c. Higher education shall be made equally accessible to all, on the basis of capacity, by every appropriate means, and in particular by the progressive introduction of free education;
   d. Fundamental education shall be encouraged or intensified as far as possible for those persons who have not received or completed the whole period of their primary education;
   e. The development of a system of schools at all levels shall be actively pursued, an adequate fellowship system shall be established, and the material conditions of teaching staff shall be continuously improved.
3. The States Parties to the present Covenant undertake to have respect for the liberty of parents and, when applicable, legal guardians to choose for their children schools, other than those established by the public authorities, which conform to such minimum educational standards as may be laid down or approved by the State and to ensure the religious and moral education of their children in conformity with their own convictions.
4. No part of this article shall be construed so as to interfere with the liberty of individuals and bodies to establish and direct educational institutions, subject always to the observance of the principles set forth in paragraph 1 of this article and to the requirement that the education given in such institutions shall conform to such minimum standards as may be laid down by the State.

Notes

1. The first part of this section is based upon Peters & Olssen (1999).
2. Walzer (1983) argues for a non-foundational account based upon a notion of *complex equality*: that there are no universal laws of justice except in the sense that minimal requirements—prohibitions against murder, deception and cruelty—run across all culture. Justice, by contrast, is the creation of a particular political community at a particular time: it follows that any account of justice must be given from within that community.

In formal terms, complex equality means that no citizen's standing in one sphere or with regard to one social good can be undercut by his standing in some other sphere, with regard to some other good. Thus, citizen X may be chosen over citizen Y for political office, and then the two of them will be unequal in the sphere of politics. But they will not be unequal generally so long as X's office gives him no advantages over Y in any other sphere—superior medical care, access to better schools for his children, entrepreneurial opportunities, and so on (Walzer, 1983: 19).

Walzer (1995) in *Spheres of Justice* indicates that education is a good example of complex equality. As he says (Walzer, 1995: 282) education obviously has no singular meaning and "Education for citizenship and basic social competence and education for the professions require different distributive principles."

3. For OECD on "Information Economy" http://www.oecd.org/dsti/sti/it/infosoc/prod/online.htm

8

Postmodernity and the Philosophy of Educational Reform

Our institutions are no longer fit for anything: everyone is unanimous about that. But the fault lies not with them but in *us*. Having lost all instincts out of which institutions grow, we are losing the institutions themselves, because *we* are no longer fit for them....For institutions to exist there must exist the kind of will, instinct, imperative which is anti-liberal to the point of malice: the will to tradition, to authority, to cen-turies-long responsibility, to *solidarity* between succeeding generations backwards and forwards *ad infinitum*....The entire West has lost those instincts out of which institutions grow, out of which the future grows: perhaps nothing goes so much against the grain of its 'modern' spirit as this. One lives for today, one lives very fast—one lives very irresponsi-bly: it is precisely this which one calls 'freedom.'

Friedrich Nietzsche, 1968: 93–94

The movement toward the neoliberal utopia of a pure and perfect mar-ket is made possible by the politics of financial deregulation. And it is achieved through the transformation and, it must be said, *destructive* action of all the political measures (of which the most recent is the Multilateral Agreement on Investment [MAI] designed to protect foreign corporations and their investments from national states) that aim to *call into question any and all collective structures* that could serve as an obstacle to the logic of the pure market: the nation, whose space to manoeuvre continually decreases; work groups, for example through the individualisation of salaries and of careers as a function of individual competences with the consequent atomisation of workers; collectives for the defence of the rights of workers, unions, associations, cooperatives; even the family, which loses part of its control over consumption through the constitution of market by age groups.

Pierre Bourdieu "Utopia of Endless Exploitation: The Essence of Neoliberalism," *Le Monde diplomatique,* December, 1998, p. 2. Available at: (http://www.mode-diplomatique.fr/en/1998/12/08bourdieu)

FOR THE PURPOSES OF THIS CHAPTER, I want to argue that postmodernity can be pursued as the *question of value* after the event Nietzsche called the "death of God," the re-examination of our traditional sources and orientations of normativity, and the search for new ethical and political directions for our major institutions. In the Western world since 1979 (with the election of the Thatcher Government) postmodernity and the question of value has been dominated by contemporary forms of neoliberalism, which have colonised the future with a view of the market and globalisation as political project of world economic integration.

New Zealand represents a clear example of the neoliberal shift in political philosophy and policy development. From being the so-called "social laboratory" of the Western world in the 1930s in terms of social welfare provision, New Zealand became the "neoliberal experiment" in the 1980s and the 1990s. This historical reversal of social principles and philosophy epitomised in the establishment of the welfare state, singled out New Zealand as a "successful" experiment pointed to by a number of powerful world policy institutions, such as the World Bank, the International Monetary Fund and the OECD New Zealand with a "thin" democracy (that is, one house and a strong executive) and a small population geographically confined, made New Zealand an ideal country for social experiment. In New Zealand during the 1980s a distinctive strand of neoliberalism emerged as the dominant paradigm of public policy: citizens were redefined as individual consumers of newly competitive public services with the consequence that "welfare rights" became consumer rights; the public sector itself underwent considerable "downsizing" as successive governments—both Labour and National—pursued an agenda of commercialisation, corporatisation and privatisation; management was delegated rather than devolved, while executive power became concentrated even more at the centre.

The continuing thread of my argument concerns the *value* of education in postmodernity. Education, to quote from political party manifestos of both conservative and new labour or their equivalents, is more than ever in the global knowledge economy the passport to a relatively secure job and income and, therefore, also to active participation in society as a knowledge worker and as a citizen. Education in the so-called new knowledge economy more than ever before is intimately tied up with welfare and with democracy. In this chapter I shall be offering a number of arguments that shows the importance of relationships among these three concepts. Indeed, I think there is a distinctive view of postmodernity that runs against the standard neoliberal model or construction.

I want to begin by talking in broad philosophical terms about the concept of postmodernity about which there is much confusion and also fiercely held views. I want to provide a clearer understanding of this term, especially in relation to its sibling concept "modernity" and to suggest how both terms apply to Aotearoa/New Zealand.

Nietzsche, Postmodernity and the Question of Value[1]

Accounts of the concept of "postmodernity" and so-called postmodern philosophy that attribute its source and power of inspiration to Nietzsche typically begin with Nietzsche's revelation that "God is dead." Often on the basis of a rudimentary understanding of this remark, commentators falsely attribute a nihilism to Nietzsche (and to postmodern philosophy), as though Nietzsche was advocating nihilism. Nihilism, from the Latin *nihil* meaning "nothing" or "that which does not exist," is the belief that there is no legitimate foundation to values or, more simply, that the world is meaningless. Nihilistic themes have dominated twentieth century art, literature and philosophy. It is evidenced as a kind of existential despair in the work of Albert Camus and Jean-Paul Sartre, who suggested in *Existentialism is a Humanism* that "man is condemned to be free"—meaning that in a world of pure contingency we have no choice but to make choices, however, terrible the options might be. Nihilism surfaces in contemporary themes of the destruction of the earth, identity crisis, cosmological purposelessness, and the desperate search for meaning and identity.

Yet to attribute this intensely sceptical doctrine to Nietzsche is wrongheaded— nothing could be further from Nietzsche's purpose. While it is true for Nietzsche that nihilism proceeds as a consequence from the fact that "God is dead," it is also the starting point for a philosophy of the future that promotes the *revaluation of all values* "to pursue the problem of the total health of a people, time, race or of humanity," aimed at "growth, power, life" (1974: 35). It is also the case that those who follow Nietzsche, particularly Martin Heidegger, but also those contemporary

French philosophers we call "postmodern," sympathetically understand Nietzsche's philosophy as a basis to overcome the desire to substitute any surrogate or replacement for God as the transcendental truth, centre, or eternal guarantee for morality and self-certainty. And this is so, whether that replacement be Reason, Science, or—perhaps the greatest temptation of all—Man or Humankind.

Nietzsche's famous parable and formulation occurs at #125 in *The Gay Science*, where the madman runs into the marketplace with a lantern in the early morning, crying repeatedly, "I seek God!," only to be laughed at and ridiculed by bystanders. The madman asks again "Whither is God?" and continues: "I will tell you. We have killed him—you and I" (1974: 181). After an extended poetic elaboration and questioning of this momentous event, the madman finally throws down his lantern and says: "I have come too early…my time is not yet. This tremendous event is still on its way….This deed is still more distant from them than the most distant stars— and yet they have done it to themselves" (182). The parable must be understood in relation to relevant sections (from #108 to #125) and also in relation to reformulations of the "death of God" that occur in Nietzsche's other works, including *Thus Spake Zarathrustra*, *The Anti-Christ*, and *The Will to Power*.

The relevant passages in *The Gay Science* begin by discussing "our aesthetic anthropomorphisms" that characterize our beliefs that the world is a living being, and the universe a machine, when the character of the world is, in fact, "in all eternity chaos," understood as "a lack of order" (#109, 168). Nietzsche says there are only necessities in nature: "there is nobody who commands, nobody who obeys, nobody who trespasses. Once you know there are no purposes, you also know that there is no accident….There are no eternally enduring substances" (168). And Nietzsche ends his 'scientific' observation with two important questions: "When will we complete our de-deification of nature? When may we begin to 'naturalize' humanity in terms of a pure, newly discovered, newly redeemed nature?" (169) Nietzsche's goal here is clearly the naturalization of humanity, of knowledge and 'morality'—the de-deification of humanity, science, nature and morality. His discussion thereafter of the origin of knowledge, of logic, and of cause and effect, extends to the moral sphere, and is essentially a discussion of the way in which humans have been educated through his "four errors" of anthropomorphism.

There is considerable disagreement in interpretation concerning the status of Nietzsche's "death of God" pronouncement. The fable of the Madman has been taken as an attack on the adherents of secularized versions of the old Christian moral ideal. On this view the bystanders listening to the madman display a curious kind of "bad faith." While convinced by historical criticism of biblical texts about the mythical presuppositions of Christianity, these bystanders, who no longer believe, nevertheless retain the underlying Christian morality. Nietzsche's historical and genealogical criticisms of Christianity, said to reveal a purely reactive morality of resentment, are to be replaced by an active morality of self-expression and self-overcoming, based upon a "revaluation of all values."

In the final volume of his *Nietzsche*, Heidegger traces the philosophical use of the word nihilism to Friedrich Jacobi, later to Turgeniev, Jean Paul, and Dostoievsky. Against these early uses, Heidegger claims:

> Nietzsche uses nihilism as the name for the historical movement that he was the first to recognize and that already governed the previous century while defining the century to come, the movement whose essential interpretation he concentrates in the terse sentence: "God is dead." That is to say, "the Christian God" has lost His power over beings and over the determination of man. "Christian God" also stands for the "transcendent" in general in its various meanings—for "ideals" and "norms," "principles" and "rules," "ends" and "values," which are set "above" the being, in order to give being as a whole a purpose, and order, and—as it is succinctly expressed—"meaning" (1961, IV: 4).

For Heidegger, drawing heavily on the fragments of *The Will To Power*, Nietzsche's sense of nihilism is interpreted in terms of the historical process completing the modern era, culminating in the "end of metaphysics" and a "revaluation [that] thinks Being for the first time as value" (IV:6).

Some would argue that it is the Christian reactive response to the all-too-human origin of our values in declaring existence or life meaningless that is the real source of nihilism. That is, once the transcendental guarantees of (Christian) morality and grand expectations based upon them have collapsed or been exposed for what they really are, an active nihilism ensues. And yet the same genealogical critique, the loss of faith in the categories of reason, can also inspire a revolutionary demand for things to be different. One can tell the story of contemporary Continental philosophy by emphasising the importance of central notions of practice, a critique of the present, the production of crisis (especially in relation to modernity), and anti-scientism (as a modernist metanarrative) in defining a tradition that recognises the essential historicity of philosophy and, therefore, also the radical finitude of the human subject and the contingent character of human experience. We might argue that post-Nietzschean philosophy not only provides a critique of the rational, autonomous (Christian-liberal) subject but also redirects our attention to historical sources of normativity that are embedded in cultures. It provides, in other words, a path for moral reconstruction after the so-called "death of God"—a way forward and a positive response to the question of nihilism that demands the revaluation of values. In doing so it belongs to the counter-enlightenment tradition of thought that asserts the historicity of human reason and experience on the basis of a radical questioning of the transcendental guarantee and moral authority of God, and of all possible substitutes for God (Humanity, Reason, Science, the transcendental signifier).]

Gianni Vattimo (1991), the Italian philosopher, begins his book *The End of Modernity* by emphasising the theoretical links between Nietzsche and Heidegger in relation to the question of postmodernity. He takes Nietzsche's analysis of nihilism and Heidegger's critique of humanism "as 'positive' moments for a philosophical reconstruction, and not merely as symptoms and declarations of decadance" (Vattimo, 1991: 1). Vattimo goes on to suggest that such an interpretation is possible "only of we have the courage...to listen attentively to the various discourses concerning postmodernity and it specific traits that are at present being developed in the arts, literary criticism, and sociology" (Vattimo, 1991: 1–2). For Vattimo the vital link between Nietzsche and Heidegger is that together they call the heritage of European thought into question *without* proposing the means for a critical 'overcoming.' For both Nietzsche and Heidegger, despite their differences, Vattimo argues:

> Modernity is in fact dominated by the idea that the history of thought is a progressive 'enlightenment' which develops through an ever more complete appropriation and reappropriation of its own 'foundations.' These are often also understood to be 'origins,' so that the theoretical and practical revolutions of Western history are presented and legitimated for the most part as 'recoveries,' rebirths, or returns. The idea of 'overcoming,' which is so important in all modern philosophy, understands the course of thought as being a progressive development in which the new is identified with value through the mediation of the recovery and appropriation of the foundation-origin (Vattimo, 1991: 2).

As Vattimo goes on to explain, both Nietzsche and Heidegger take up a critical attitude to European and Enlightenment thought insofar as its represents in one way or another, *forms of foundational thinking*; the difficulty is that they do so but *not* in the name of another, truer, more real, or more enlightened, foundation. It is this feature, Vattimo claims that distinguish Nietzsche and Heidegger as philosophers of postmodernity.

> The 'post-' in the term 'post-modernity' indicates in fact a taking leave of modernity. In its search to free itself from the logic of development inherent in modernity—namely the idea of a critical 'overcoming' directed toward a new foundation—post-modernity seeks exactly what Nietzsche and Heidegger seek in their own peculiar 'critical' relationship with Western thought (Vattimo, 1991: 3).

I find Vattimo's observation here particularly helpful in distinguishing the critical attitude and ethos between neoliberalism, considered as a distinct Anglo-American continuation, mutation or reinvention, of the tradition of European liberal thought, and poststructuralism, precisely as a critique of that same tradition (and, more broadly, the culture of modernity to which it belongs) but not one which criticises in the name of a better, truer, more 'real,' foundation.

Neoliberalism as Metanarrative

"Postmodern" philosophy can be characterised as seeking a positive answer to nihilism—a way forward that suggests while there may be no foundation for values, or for knowledge, this does not mean that knowledge is not possible or that the creation of new value is denied. Jean-François Lyotard (1984), the French philosopher, defines postmodernism as an "incredulity toward metanarratives," that is, a scepticism of those "big stories" that purport to ground our cultural practices and to legitimate our institutions—narratives on which we have relied to make sense of the world and our place in it.

In *The Postmodern Condition* Jean-François Lyotard was concerned with metanarratives which had grown out of the Enlightenment and had come to mark modernity. In *The Postmodern Explained to Children* Lyotard (1992: 29) mentions:

> the progressive emancipation of reason and freedom, the progressive or catastrophic emancipation of labour…, the enrichment of all through the progress of capitalist technoscience, and even…the salvation of creatures through the conversion of souls to the Christian narrative of martyred love.

These metanarratives which have the goal of legitimating our institutions and our practices all have centrally involved education. Indeed, education is not merely one of the institutions which have been shaped or legitimated by the dominant metanarratives, at the lower levels it has been instrumentally involved with their systematic reproduction, elucidation, and preservation and, at the higher levels, it has been concerned with their ideological production, dissemination and refinement (see Peters, 1995; Peters & Marshall, 1996).

Certainly, the first mentioned of these metanarratives which we can also refer to as the complex skein of liberalism considered as both a political tradition and an economic doctrine, has been the dominant metanarrative in education in the West. Since the early 1980s a particularly narrow variant—neoliberalism—has become the dominant metanarrative. (The publication of Lyotard's *The Postmodern Condition* coincided with the election to power of Margaret Thatcher's Conservative

Government in Britain.) This particular variant, which revitalises the master discourse of neoclassical economic liberalism, has been remarkably successful in advancing a *foundationalist* and *universalist* individualised reason as a basis for a radical global reconstruction of all aspects of society and economy. A form of economic reason encapsulated in the notion of *homo economicus*, with its abstract and universalist assumptions of individuality, rationality and self-interest, has captured the policy agendas of OECD countries. Part of its innovation has been the way in which the neoliberal master narrative has successfully imperialistically extended the principle of self-interest into the status of a paradigm for understanding politics itself, and, in fact, not merely market but *all* behaviour and human action. Consequently, in the realm of education policy, especially in OECD countries but also in developing countries, at every opportunity the market has been substituted for the state: students are now "customers" or "clients" and teachers are "providers." The notion of vouchers is suggested as a universal panacea to problems of funding and quality. The teaching/learning relation has been reduced to an implicit contract between buyer and seller. As Lyotard argued prophetically in *The Postmodern Condition* not only has knowledge and research become commodified but so have the relations of the production of knowledge in a new logic of *performativity*.

Postmodernity, then, is a cultural, political and socio-economic phenomenon: it emphasises the break not only with traditionally modern ways of understanding the world but also transformations of the dominant mode of economic organisation, including changes in production and marketing, corporate and financial organisation, as well as the labour market and patterns of work. In the economic domain, 'postmodernity' is sometimes referred to as "late capitalism," "multinational capitalism," "post-Fordism," or "flexible specialisation." Together these descriptions emphasise a new techno-information and communications infrastructure, which supports the global networked knowledge economy. While the internationalisation of the new economy is itself not a novel feature, there is no doubt that the technological infrastructure, which permits complex economic transactions to be completed at an unprecedented speed, certainly is new. As Manuel Castells (2000: 52) argues:

> Productivity and competitiveness are, by and large, a function of knowledge generation and information processing; firms and territories are organised in networks of production, management, and distribution; the core economic activities are global—that is, they have the capacity to work as a unit in real time, or chosen time, on a planetary scale.

This new techno-infrastructure and the info-capitalism based upon it, together with the new technologies, has already transformed both our institutions and our subjectivities. As a first approximation at outlining the concept of postmodernity, I shall present it as a complex or multi-layed concept involving three elements: socio-economic postmodernisation; cultural transformation, and; the emergence of new political forms (see Figure 1, *Postmodernity*). It is these world-historical transformations that represent the challenge for Aotearoa/New Zealand. Education and culture, as you can see, are central elements in the shift from an industrial (or in New Zealand's case agro-industrial) to knowledge economy. They are also central ingredients in my overall argument for the conception of the relationship between education and culture is critical in the transition to the knowledge economy, particularly when we speak of the development of education as knowledge cultures.

More precisely, I shall define postmodernity, in relation to Aotearoa/New Zealand, as beginning in 1984 with the election of the Fourth Labour government. Historically and symbolically, this represents the end of the welfare state, a profound shift in the principles of social and political philosophy, and the promotion of the neoliberal political project of globalisation. It signalled that the "economy" had become an abstract and reified object, no longer part of the society as a whole and no longer subject to socially defined ends. It also initiated a programme of educational reform, which, at the levels of early childhood, primary and secondary, has had disastrous social consequences, and at the level of tertiary education has seriously eroded our knowledge cultures (see Peters & Marshall, 1996). In various publications I have referred to the neoliberal education policy as "The New Zealand Education Experiment" arguing that it has involved a shift from participatory democracy to self-management within a quasi-market economy (see Peters, 1999; 2001).

In its brief to government, the Treasury (1987) argued that the education system had performed badly in spite of increased expenditure because teachers pursued their own self-interest rather than being responsive to the consumer needs of parents and pupils, and government intervention had created bureaucratic inflexibility disrupting the natural market contract between producer and consumer. The Treasury concluded that New Zealanders had been too optimistic about the ability of education to contribute to economic growth and equality of opportunity. Largely as a consequence, *Tomorrow's Schools* involved the transfer of responsibility for property management, employment of staff, and control of education away from the State to the institutions themselves or elected boards, with a greater emphasis on the market discipline of choice.

The policy directions offered did not differ greatly from those neoliberal initiatives first mentioned in the *Hawke Report*: a consolidation of the formula funding model and stronger support to private training establishments; greater emphasis on quality assurance mechanisms; separation of the funding for teaching and research; greater monitoring and accountability, and; perhaps, most troubling, changes to the governance arrangements of tertiary institutions. While New Zealand experienced massive growth of participation rates during the early nineties, this largely self-financed growth of student numbers attending tertiary institutions slowed down in the late 1990s as the weight of the accumulated student debt, standing at 3 billion dollars at the end of the century, started to kick in. The trouble is the process has been very punishing to tertiary institutions, especially when the priority (at least under National) has been to prioritise early childhood education; there have been large staff cutbacks and morale is low; overseas recruitment of staff is increasingly difficult because of the comparatively low salaries; many academics have sought jobs elsewhere; class sizes have not been significantly reduced across the disciplines. With a commitment to the so-called knowledge economy this seems like a recipe for disaster, especially when the most influential human capital and new growth theories, strongly emphasise investment in higher education and research.

Understanding Neoliberalism in Aotearoa/New Zealand

Assessments of the global force of neoliberalism differ. Thus, for instance, David Henderson (1999: 1), previously Head of the Economics and Statistics Department for the OECD, comments upon the way in which economic policies across the world have changed their character with the effect of "making their economies freer, more open and less regulated." In *The Changing Fortunes of Economic Liberalism*, jointly sponsored by the Institute of Public Affairs and the New Zealand Business Roundtable, Henderson suggests that it is a mistake to interpret these developments as a victory for conservatism:

> More justly, the recent evolution of economic policies can be seen as the latest chapter in a continuing story which goes back at any rate to the mid-18th century, the hero of which is economic liberalism. Recent events have involved a shift, not from left to right, but in the balance between liberalism and interventionism in economic systems (Henderson, 1999: 2).

Here he is using the term liberalism in the European sense of "the realisation, enlargement and defence of individual freedom" (p. 4) and he argues that "The extension and exercise of economic freedoms make for closer *economic integration*, both within and across national boundaries" (p. 5). He states "Liberalism is individualist, in that it defines the interests of national states, and the scope and purposes of government, with reference to individuals who are subject to them" (p. 7). Liberalism, which for Henderson implies restricting the power and functions of governments so as to give full scope for individuals and enterprises, after a hundred years of decline has regained ground in the economics profession, especially after the period of the 1930s–1970s. The economic policies enacted by a variety of world governments on the basis of principles of economic liberalization emphasise a "strong association between political and economic freedoms" (p. 46). He reviews "economic freedom ratings" over the period 1975–95 to map the geography of reform, purportedly demonstrating that core OECD countries are all "reforming" governments and while he examines overlapping areas of policy (financial markets, international transactions, privatisation, energy, agricultural, labour and public spending) he is unable to draw any conclusions concerning so-called "reforming" policies (i.e., greater economic liberalization) and increased levels of national prosperity.

In the "economic freedom ratings" New Zealand emerges clearly as the leading reformer, in policy areas of privatisation and deregulation, trade liberalisation, taxation, and labour market reform (before the Employment Contracts Act was repealed). Yet as he notes in the annex devoted to measuring economic freedoms and assessing its benefits:

> Since the reform process was set under way in New Zealand in mid-1984, liberalisation has been taken further there than in Ireland, and on most reckonings the New Zealand economy would now show up as the freer of the two: both these conclusions emerge from the respective figures [given]…But if we compare 1984 with 1997 GDP per head in New Zealand appears as having increased by only some 10 per cent, as compared with over 90 per cent for Ireland. It seems obvious that this remarkable divergence between the two countries cannot be chiefly explained with reference to the comparative extent of economic freedom or differences in the recent progress of liberalisation (Henderson, 1999: 99–100).

Henderson (1999), following Milton and Rose Friedman, who also provide the foreword, indicates that while *the battle of ideas has been won* insofar as both economists and governments hold to the revival of economic liberalism (i.e., neoliberalism), its victory has so far been disappointing and its chronic weakness lies in the fact that it has "*no solid basis of general support*" (p. 58). It is in this context that he comments on what he calls anti-liberal ideas and their increasing support which he lists in relation to three related developments: opposition to greater freedom of international trade and capital flows; the "excessive drive to equality" (the phrase is taken from the Friedmans), and; the spread of "cultural studies" in the universities. He is worth quoting on the last of these developments:

> Economists have given little attention to this trend, probably because their own subject has so far escaped the ravages of "deconstruction," "post-modernism" and related tendencies, while these movements in turn have not developed a systematic economic orientation or philosophy of their own which has claims to be taken seriously…(p. 65).

He continues:

> Both post-modernism in its different guises and the more recent forms of egalitarianism characteristically share a vision of the world in which past history and present-day market-based economic systems are viewed in terms of patterns of oppression and abuses of power. Free markets and capitalism are seen as embodying and furthering male dominance, class oppression, racial intolerance, imperialist coercion and colonialist exploitation. The appeal of this anti-liberal way of thinking seems to have been little affected by the collapse of communism (p. 65).

What is interesting is that Henderson, as an economist, should directly perceive the threat to economic liberalism in terms of "postmodernism," even though he does not really engage with its multiple strands or show any sign of understanding its philosophical roots in Nietzsche, Heidegger and contemporary French philosophy, or its diverse engagements with classical liberal thought. These engagements—for instance, Derrida and Foucault on Kant, or more directly Foucault's governmentality studies—are considerably more sophisticated than Henderson's own brief historical foray. To be sure there are anti-liberal (and anti-modernist) elements in Nietzsche's and Heidegger's thinking and there are strong evaluative critiques of liberalism in both poststructuralism and postmodernism, but this should not be taken to mean that poststructuralists and postmodernist thinkers stand against political freedom. Such a simplistic reduction defies the complexity of the range of philosophical positions that have developed over the last fifty years.

While Henderson believes that neoliberalism has won the battle of ideas and is now the dominant policy story, others have taken up oppositional views. Jan Nederveen Pieterse (2000) maintains:

> As an ideology, neoliberalism is probably past its peak. The trust in the "magic of the marketplace" that characterized the era of Ronald Reagan and Margaret Thatcher has run its course. The criticisms of "the market rules OK," common and widespread, are gradually crystallizing into an alternative perspective…(p. 8).

Although he concedes,

> Institutionally, in the WTO and IMF, neoliberalism remains the conventional wisdom. In development politic, it prevails through the remnants of the "Washington consensus." In NAFTA, it prevails in principle. In Euroland, it prevails through the European Monetary Union (p.9).

He suggests this is a reflection of the hegemony of finance capital and that the global future of a borderless world for capital is a self-fulfilling prophecy achieved through structural reform policies of the IMF and World Bank. At the same time he notes that "Neoliberal futures are being contested on many grounds—labour, the right to development, the environment, local interests, and cultural diversity" (p. 10).[3]

Pieterse (2000) wants to develop a critical approach to global futures which seeks to be inclusive of interests excluded by the mainstream managerial approach based on forecasting and risk analysis, yet seeks to inform futures in utopian and postmodern ways. While I see considerable value in this approach, unlike Pieterse I am less convinced that neoliberalism is exhausted and passed its peak. As a long term historical tendency it will ebb and flow. The Bush administration provided a reversal of the attempted current alignment of neoliberalism and social democracy in Third Way politics back to a neoconservative alignment, especially in foreign policy.

Other international assessments of the recent reform experience of New Zealand are not as compelling or as praiseworthy as David Henderson. John Gray (1999), Professor of European Thought at the London School of Economics, writes:

> The neoliberal experiment in New Zealand is the most ambitious attempt at constructing the free market as a social institution to be implemented anywhere this century. It is a clearer example of the costs and limits of reinventing the free market in a late-twentieth-century context than the Thatcherite experiment in Britain. Among the many novel effects of neoliberal policy in New Zealand has been the creation of an underclass in a country that did not have one before….One of the world's most comprehensive social democracies became a neoliberal state (p. 39).

He continues:

> In New Zealand, the theories of the American New Right achieved a rare and curious feat—self-refutation by their practical application. Contrary to the Right's confident claims, the abolition of nearly all universal social services and the stratification of income groups for the purpose of targeting welfare benefits selectively created a neoliberal poverty trap (p. 42).

He concludes that many of the changes instituted during the neoliberal period are irreversible. In strictly economic terms, neoliberalism achieved many of its objectives—a restructuring of the economy that would have been necessary in any case—yet it could have carried out its policies without the huge social costs. He suggests that while neoliberal reforms will not be overturned they have had the effect of narrowing the scope of future governments to reinstitute social democratic policies, despite the fact that criticism of the excesses of neoliberalism will become part of the new political consensus.

Ramesh Mishra (1999), Professor of Social Policy at York University (Canada) concurs. He remarks:

> New Zealand provides a good example of the role the OECD and IMF in promoting deregulation and privatization in individual countries. The drastic reforms in New Zealand which began in 1984 and continued into the early 1990s changed its economy from being one of the most closed to one of the most open among OECD countries…The OECD evaluated these reforms and the subsequent economic performances of the country in glowing terms and remonstrated with governments for not carrying projected changes far enough…Admitting that these changes involved short-term pain, the report asserts that they are sure to bring long terms gain (p. 10).

He suggests that the OECD plays up the neoliberal reforms, praising their consequences, while the success of the social market economies is glossed over. His assessment is that globalisation is as much a political and ideological project as it is market-driven and he argues that globalisation has "weakened very considerably the influence of domestic national policies on social policy" (p. 3, see Figure 2). In other words, "globalization virtually sounds the death-knell of the classical social democratic strategy of full employment, high levels of public expenditure and progressive taxation" (p. 6).

Robert Cox (1997a), for a long time chief of the International Labour Organisation's (ILO) Program and Planning Division, and later of Columbia and

Toronto Universities, writes:

> The hyperliberal ideology has become entrenched in international institutions,
> backed by American power, overshadowing the residues of the social democrat-
> ic thinking that were more in evidence in the 1960s and 1970s. The key words
> in the currently dominant global ideology are competitiveness, deregulation, pri-
> vatization, and restructuring. Restructuring refers to the reorganisation of glob-
> al production from Fordist economies of scale to post-Fordist economies of
> flexibility. It means fewer reasonably secure high-income core workers and a larg-
> er proportion of precariously employed lower-income peripheral workers, the lat-
> ter weakened by being divided by locations around the world, by ethnicity and
> religion, and by gender. It also means that a large part of the world's population
> exists in deepening poverty, outside the global economy. Privatization and dereg-
> ulation refer to the removal of the state from a substantive role in the national or
> global economy, except as guarantor of free movement for capital and profits.
> Competitiveness is the justification for dismantling the welfare states built up in
> the post-World War period—negating the effort in the more industrialized coun-
> tries to legitimate capitalism by avoiding a recurrence of the immiseration that
> occurred during the Great Depression of the 1930s (p. 31)

Cox (1997b) describes the latest thrust toward globalisation in terms of the internationalisation of production and the internationalisation of the state, with a
changing emphasis from domestic welfare to adapting domestic economies to the
world economy. He also mentions the new international division of labour which
is creating a new pattern of uneven development and, in this regard, talks of the
emergence of a Fourth World, seemingly outside the new developments that characterise the advent of the global economy. His offers his prognosis in the following terms:

> The continuing residue of the Cold War contributes to the progressive decay of
> the old world order. The outlines of a new world order are yet to be perceived.
> Two factors may, in the longer run, be formative of a new order. One is the rival-
> ry among different forms of what Polanyi called "substantive economies," i.e., the
> different ways in which production and distribution are organized. The struggle
> between rival forms of capitalism (hyperliberalism versus social market) in Europe
> may be critical in determining the balance of social and economic power in the
> global economy. At stake are the prospects of subordinating the economy to
> social purpose, and the prospects of redesigning production and consumption so
> as to be compatible with a sustainable biosphere (p. 34)

It is clear that neoliberalism both as a political philosophy and policy mix had taken
deep root by the early 1980s as the world's dominant economic and development

metanarrative. During that decade many governments around the world support-ed the modernising reforms thrust of neoliberalism, particularly the exposure of the state sector to competition and the opportunity to pay off large and accumulating national debts. By contrast many developing countries had "structural adjust-ments policies" imposed upon them as loans conditions from the IMF and WB. The reforming zeal soon ideologised the public sector *per se* and ended by damag-ing key national services (including health and education). By the mid-Nineties, the wheel had turned again—this time towards a realisation that the dogmatism of the neoliberal right had become a serious threat to social justice, to national cohe-sion, and to democracy itself. Large sections of populations had become structural-ly disadvantaged, working and living, on the margins of the labour market; rapidly growing social inequalities had become more evident as the rich had become rich-er and the poor, poorer; companies were failing and under-performing; public ser-vices had been "stripped down" and were unable to deliver even the most basic of services; many communities had become split and endangered by the rise of racism, crime, unemployment and social exclusion. Governments throughout the world looked to a new philosophy and policy mix—one that preserved some of the efficiency and competition gains but did not result in the forms of nation-splitting and social exclusion.

One model advocated by then British Prime Minister Tony Blair and U.S. President Bill Clinton, called the "Third Way," aims to revitalises the concern for social justice and democracy while moving away from traditional policies of redis-tribution, to define freedom in terms of autonomy of action, demanding the involvement and participation of the wider social community. Some commenta-tors see nothing new in the "Third Way," regarding it as a return to the ethical socialism of "old Labour." Other critics see it as a cover for the wholesale adoption of Conservative policies of privatisation and the continued dismantling of the wel-fare state. Still others suggest that the "Third Way" is nothing more than a spin-doctoring exercise designed to brand a political product as different from what went before. Sloganised as "market economy but not market society," advocates of the "Third Way" see it as uniting the two streams of left-of-centre thought: democra-tic socialism and classical liberalism, where the former is said to promote social jus-tice with the state as its main agent and the latter said to assert the primacy of individual liberty in the market economy. Understood in this way, the "Third Way" might be construed as a continuance of classical liberalism, born of the same polit-ical strategy of integrating two streams as the New Right (neoliberalism and neo-conservativism) but this time the "other" stream is "social democracy" rather than conservatism.

Notes

1. This section draws on material from my "*Orthos Logos, Recta Ratio*: Pope John Paul II, Nihilism, and Postmodern Philosophy," *Journal for Christian Theological Research*, available at: [http://apu.edu/~CTRF/articles/2000_articles/peters.html] 5:1 (Peters, 2000).

2. The negative effects of quasi-market choice policies on issues of welfare within the community has been documented by Wylie (1994) who has investigated the broad effects of increasing competition under schemes of choice, citing changes in ethnic and socio-economic composition of schools as well as deterioration in the relations between schools. The Smithfield Project (Lauder, 1994) also documents the negative social effects of choice proposals. Gordon's (1994) research concluded that the status of a neighbourhood was a powerful factor influencing school choice. While poorer parents frequently do not have the option to shift their children from one school to another, more affluent parents do. An implication of this trend, says Gordon "is that within schools, there will be increasingly homogenous class groupings, while between schools differences will be enhanced" (p. 15). Similar patterns of segregation operate in respect to ethnicity.

9

Governmentality, Education and the End of Neoliberalism?

The Birth of Neoliberalism?

THIS CHAPTER UTILIZES FOUCAULT'S NOTION of 'governmentality' to identify and analyse the main forms and characteristics of economic liberalism in its main geopolitical schools—Austrian, German, French and American—that have dominated the economic and policy landscapes of the post-war era, and also laid a template of sorts for the institutional world architecture called 'Bretton Woods' as the monetary system based on liberal conception of the 'open' market with its commitment to 'free' flows of capital and trade, the convertibility of currencies, and the formal apparatus of the IMF and World Bank. Neoliberalism is a popular label for what is commonly understood as the doctrine of political and economic liberalism and set of policies originating in the 1970s that wielded together classical liberal political theory as exemplified by the Mont Pelerin Society after WWII and neoclassical economic theories that became identified with the so-called Chicago school under Milton Friedman in the 1960s.

It is not a unified and coherent doctrine and it has taken on different manifestations at different times and places sometimes with contradictory results. For an ultimately moral doctrine based on a classical account of political and economic freedom—a marriage of the 'free market' and the 'open society'—paradoxically, beginning with Chile in 1973 administrations and policy regimes based on the minimal state and open global market were brutally established with force and coercion, against the rule of law and in an anti-democratic way. This imposition became commonplace during the 1980s with 'structural adjustment' policies of the International Monetary Fund (IMF) and the World Bank (WB) that 'forced' the transitional economies of Latin America and elsewhere to liberalize trade and monetary systems, to open up their economies and to privatize state assets and cut back state welfare.

For analytical purposes, we can postulate several historical stages of neoliberalism:

1. The development of the Austrian, Freiburg and Chicago schools in neoclassical economics as a continuance of classical liberalism in the first part of the twentieth century;

2. The establishment of the Austrian school by Carl Menger with the publication of *Principles of Economics* (*Grundsätze der Volkswirtschaftslehre*) in 1871, his 'subjective theory of value' (theory of marginal utility) and the attack on historicism in the debate over epistemology (*Methodenstreit*) in economics that took place in the 1880s;

3. Menger attracts Eugen von Böhm-Bawerk, Friedrich von Wieser and later Ludwig von Mises who extends marginal utility theory to money in *The Theory of Money and Credit* (1912) and recruits Friedrich von Hayek who develops Mises' business cycle theories and becomes Director of the newly formed Austrian Institute for Business Cycle Research in 1927;

4. On the invitation from Lionel Robbins, Director of the London School of Economics, Hayek shifts to Britain, and in opposition to John Maynard Keynes develops his theory of spontaneous institutions, and engages in debates against socialist planning in the late 1930s;

5. The founding of Freiburg school or the Ordoliberal School in the 1930s at the University of Freiburg in Germany by Walter Eucken, Franz Böhm and Hans Großmann-Doerth;

6. The 'first globalization' of neoliberalism with the establishment of the Mount Pelerin Society in 1947 founded by Hayek who writes *The Road to Serfdom* against big government and totalitarianism;

7. The establishment of the Chicago school by with Frank Knight, Milton Friedman, George Stigler, Ronald Coarse, Gary Becker and others from the 1940s with an emphasis on the assumption of rationality in macroeconomics, monetarism, economics of education and human capital, the economics of information, innovation and political economy of property rights and contracts;

8. The development of the 'Washington consensus' during the 1970s;
9. The coup of Salvador Allende in Chile and the imposition of neoliberal market reforms by General Pinochet during the period 1973–1990;
10. The New Right ascendancy of the Thatcher-Reagan years during the 1980s and the 'export' of neoliberal ideology;
11. The emergence of structural adjustment loans and institutionalization of neoliberalism through a series of world policy agencies such as IMF, WB, OECD (Organisation for Economic Cooperation and Development) and WTO (World Trade Organisation);
12. The transition to 'knowledge economy' and 'knowledge for development' in the 1990s and beyond;
13. The collapse of neoliberal financial infrastructure and ethos and the roll-back of neoliberal policies by Barack Obama's administration during the first term (2009–2013).

This is not the place to detail the growth of neoclassical economics in the Anglo-American and Continental traditions. Suffice to say that standard economic history explains that the Austrian school emerged with Carl Menger in the late nineteenth century with its twin pillars of the subjective theory of value and the political defence of laissez-faire economic policy which became clearer in the hands of Friedrich Wieser, Eugene Böhm-Bawerk, and later, Ludwig von Mises and Friedrich von Hayek.[1] The neoliberalism of the Chicago school really emerged around George Stigler's leadership and Friedman's monetarism in the 1960s that was fiercely anti-Keynesian and against the concept of market failure. This school often referred to as the 'second' Chicago school included work on search theory (Stigler), human capital theory (Becker) and transaction cost analysis (Coarse) which then served as the basis for a series of innovations and new directions often characterized as the 'third' Chicago school including monetarism (Friedman), public choice theory (Buchanan), new classical macroeconomics (Lucas), new institutional economics (Coarse), new economic history (Fogel), new social economics (Becker), and Law-and economics (Posner).[2]

The Freiburg school or the Ordoliberal School was founded in the 1930s at the University of Freiburg in Germany by economist Walter Eucken and two jurists, Franz Böhm and Hans Großmann-Doerth. The founders of the school were united in their common concern for the question of the constitutional foundations of a free economy and society and were anti-naturalist in their conception of the market believing it was a legal-juridical construction.

Foucault's Governmentality

In his governmentality studies in the late 1970s Foucault held a course at the Collège de France on the major forms of neoliberalism, examining the three theoretical schools of German ordoliberalism (including Hayek), France and American neoliberalism in the form of the Chicago school (see Foucault, 2008). Among Foucault's great insights in his work on governmentality was the critical link he observed in liberalism between the governance of the self and government of the state—understood as the exercise of political sovereignty over a territory and its population.

Foucault's approach to governmentality including his analysis of German *ordoliberalism,* a source for the 'social market economy' and the EU's 'social model,' begins with an analysis of the self-limitation of governmentalism reason which he takes to be synonymous with liberalism which he suggests should be understood very broadly as;

1. Acceptance of the principle that somewhere there must be a limitation of government and that this is not just an external right.
2. Liberalism is also a practice: where exactly is the principle of the limitation of government to be found and how are the effects of this limitation to be calculated?
3. In a narrower sense, liberalism is the solution that consists in the maximum limitation of the forms and domains of government action.
4. Finally, liberalism is the organisation of specific methods of transaction for defining the limitation of government practices:
    —constitution, parliament
    —opinion, the press
    —commissions, inquiries (Foucault, 2008, pp. 20–21)

Foucault's lectures on 'The Birth of Biopolitics' could easily have been called 'The Birth of Neoliberalism.' He says, liberalism which in the second half of the twentieth century, 'is a word that comes to use from Germany' (2008, p. 22) and in later chapters he jumps ahead to understand German neoliberalism beginning with Erhard in 1947 to examine contemporary German governmentality: economic freedom, the source of juridical legitimacy and political consensus. What preserves liberalism in its new formation is the way in which neoliberalism picks up on the classical liberal political practice of introducing a self-limitation on governmental reason, while departing from it in terms of a theory of pure competition and the question of how to model the global exercise of political power on the principles of a market economy. Ordoliberalism thus issues in a critique of the protectionist economy according to List, Bismarck's state socialism, the setting up of a planned economy during the First World War, Keynesian interventionism; and the economic policy of National Socialism.

The innovation of American neoliberalism for Foucault is the generalization of the model of *homo economicus* to all forms of behavior representing an extension of economic analysis to domains previously considered to be non-economic and the redefinition of *homo economicus* as entrepreneur of himself with an emphasis on acquired elements and the problem of the formation of human capital in education. Foucault goes on to discuss a resumption of the problem of social and economic innovation and the generalization of the "enterprise" form in the social field.

Foucault (1991) uses the term 'governmentality' to mean *mentalities of rule* and, historically, to signal the emergence of a distinctive mentality of rule that he alleged became the basis for modern liberal politics. He begins to examine the problematic of government by analysing the *series*: security, population, government, maintaining that there was an explosion of interest in the "art of government" in the sixteenth century which was motivated by diverse questions: the government of oneself (personal conduct); the government of souls (pastoral doctrine); the government of children (problematic of pedagogy) (Foucault, 1991). At the intersection of two competing tendencies—state centralisation and a logic of dispersion—Foucault says, the problematic of government can be located; a problematic which poses questions of the *how* of government and seeks "to articulate a kind of rationality which was intrinsic to the art of government without subordinating it to the problematic of the prince and of his relationship to the principality of which he is lord and master" (Foucault, 1991: 89). By the term 'governmentality' Foucault (1991: pp. 102–3) meant three things:

1. The ensemble formed by the institutions, procedures, analyses, and reflections; the calculations and tactics that allow the exercise of this very specific, albeit complex, form of power, which has as its principal form of knowledge political economy and as its essential technical means apparatuses of security.

2. The tendency which, over a long period and throughout the West, has steadily led toward the pre-eminence of this type of power that may be called government over all other forms (sovereignty, discipline, etc.) resulting, on the one hand, in the formation of a whole series of specific governmental apparatuses, and, on the other, in the development of a whole complex of *savoirs*.

3. The process, or rather the result of the process, through which the state of justice of the Middle Ages, transformed into the administrative state during the fifteenth and sixteenth centuries, gradually became 'governmentalized.'

Liberal modes of governing, Foucault tells us, are distinguished in general by the ways in which they utilise the capacities of free acting subjects and, consequently, modes of government differ according to the value and definition accorded the concept of freedom. These different mentalities of rule, thus, turn on whether freedom is seen as a natural attribute as with the philosophers of the Scottish Enlightenment, a product of rational choice making, or, as with Hayek, a civilizational artefact theorised as both negative and anti-naturalist.

Hayek's conception of freedom was one that characterized the market as neither natural nor artificial but rather the product of a spontaneous social order governed by rules selected in a process of cultural evolution. His conception of freedom and 'the constitution of liberty' has special application in the so-called 'knowledge economy' where, as Foucault also acknowledges, following a Kantian critique, the state is strictly limited in its power to know. Hayek argued that the price mechanism of the 'free' market conveys information about supply and demand that is dispersed among many consumers and producers and cannot be coordinated by any central planning mechanism. His early work emphasized that the key to economic growth is 'knowledge' and this insight provided him with the grounds for casting doubt on socialism and state planning, and for advocating that the market was the best way to organize modern society.

For neoliberals inspired by Hayek's insights the commitment to the free market involves two sets of claims: claims for the efficiency of the market as a superior allocative mechanism for the distribution of scarce public resources, and; claims for the market as a morally superior form of political economy. Neoliberalism as a political philosophy, it is often said, involves a return to a primitive form of individualism: an individualism which is 'competitive,' 'possessive' and construed often in terms of the doctrine of 'consumer sovereignty.' It involves an emphasis on freedom over equality where freedom is construed in negative terms and individualistic terms. Negative freedom is freedom from state interference which implies an acceptance of inequalities generated by the market. Neoliberalism is both anti-state and anti-bureaucracy, and its attack on big government is made on the basis of both economic and ethical arguments (see Peters and Marshall, 1996).

Characteristics of Neoliberalism

In *Poststructuralism, Marxism and Neoliberalism* (Peters, 2001), a book written for a U.S. audience and devoted to the proposition that poststructuralism is neither anti-Marxist nor anti-structuralist, I identified twelve features of neoliberalism from a viewpoint heavily influenced by Michel Foucault's (1979) notion of governmentality. Foucault uses the term 'governmentality' to mean the art of government and, historically, to signal the emergence of *distinctive types of rule* that became the basis for modern liberal politics. His starting point for the examination of the problematic of government is the series: security, population, government. He maintains that there is an explosion of interest on the 'art of government' in the sixteenth century which is motivated by diverse questions: the government of oneself (personal conduct); the government of souls (pastoral doctrine); and the government of children (problematic of pedagogy). Foucault says that the problematic of government can be located at the intersection of two competing tendencies: state centralisation and logic of dispersion. This is a problematic that poses questions of the how of government rather than its legitimation and seeks 'to articulate a kind of rationality which was intrinsic to the art of government without subordinating it to the problematic of the prince and of his relationship to the principality of which he is lord and master' (Foucault, 1991: 89). It is only in the late sixteenth and early seventeenth centuries that the art of government crystallises for the first time around the notion of 'reason of state,' understood in a positive sense whereby the state is governed according to rational principles that are seen to be intrinsic to it. In charting this establishment of the art of government Foucault thus details the introduction of 'economy' into political practice (understood as 'the correct manner of managing goods and wealth within the family').

In line with this analysis, Foucault defines governmentality in terms of a specific form of government power based upon the 'science' of political economy, which over a long period, he maintains, has transformed the administrative state into one fully governmentalized, and led to the formation of both governmental apparatuses and knowledges (or *savoirs*). In elaborating these themes Foucault concentrates his analytical energies on understanding the pluralized forms of government, its complexity, and its techniques. Our modernity, he says, is characterized by the 'governmentalization' of the state. He is interested in the question of how power is exercised and, implicitly, he is providing a critique of the contemporary tendencies to overvalue the problem of the state and to reduce it to a unity or singularity based upon a certain functionality. This substantive feature—the rejection of state-centred analyses—has emerged from the governmentality literature as it has become a more explicit problematic. In outlining the main features of neoliberalism it is important to realise that there are both affinities, continuities, and overlapping concepts as well as differences and theoretical innovations with classical liberalism.

I have previously focused on the 'new prudentialism' (O'Malley, 2002) in education based on the entrepreneurial self that 'responsibilizes' the self to make welfare choices based on an actuarial rationality (Peters, 2). The promotion of the entrepreneurial self represents a shift away from a rights-based welfare model of the citizen to a consumer-oriented market individual (based on the rejuvenation of *homo economicus*) willing to calculate the risks and invest in herself at critical points in the life cycle. I have also analysed Foucault's account of German *ordoliberalism,* a configuration based on the theoretical configuration of economics and law developed at the University of Freiberg by W. Eucken and F. Böhm that views the market contingently as developing historically within a judicial-legal framework. The economy is thus based on a concept of the Rule of Law, anchored in a notion of individual rights, property rights and contractual freedom that constitutes, in effect, an economic constitution. German neoliberal economists (Müller-Armack, Röpke, Rüstow) invented the term 'social market economy' which shared certain features with the Freiburg model of law and economics but also differed from it in terms of the 'ethics' of the market (as did Hayek in *The Constitution of Liberty*). This formulation of the "social market economy" proved significant not only in terms of the post-war reconstruction of the (West) German economy but through Erhard, as Minister and Chancellor, became important as the basis of the EEC's and, later, EU's 'social model.'

1. *Classical liberalism as a critique of State reason*: A political doctrine concerning the self-limiting State; the limits of government are related to the limits of State reason, i.e., its power to know; a permanent critique of the activity of rule and government.

2. *Natural versus contrived forms of the market*: Hayek's notion of natural laws based on spontaneously ordered institutions in the physical (crystals, galaxies) and social (morality, language, market) worlds has been replaced with an emphasis on the market as an artefact or culturally derived form and (growing out of the 'catallaxy' approach) a constitutional perspective that focuses on the judicio-legal rules governing the framework within the game of enterprise is played (see Buchanan, 1991).

3. *The Politics-as-exchange innovation of Public Choice theory* ('the marketisation of the State'): The extension of Hayek's spontaneous order conception (callactics) of the institution of the market beyond simple exchange

to complex exchange and finally to all processes of voluntary agreement among persons (see Buchanan & Tullock, 1962).

4. *The relation between government and self-government*: Liberalism as a doctrine which positively requires that individuals be free in order to govern; government as the community of free, autonomous, self-regulating individuals; 'responsibilisation' of individuals as moral agents; the neoliberal revival of homo economicus, based on assumptions of individuality, rationality and self-interest, as an all-embracing redescription of the social as a form of the economic.

5. *A new relation between government and management*: The rise of the new managerialism, 'New Public Management'; the shift from policy and administration to management; emulation of private sector management styles; the emphasis on 'freedom to manage' and the promotion of 'self-managing' (i.e., quasi-autonomous) individuals and entities.

6. *A 'degovernmentalisation' of the State* (considered as a positive technique of government): Government 'through' and by the market, including promotion of consumer-driven forms of social provision (health, education, welfare), 'contracting out,' and privatisation.

7. *The promotion of a new relationship between government and knowledge*: 'Government at a distance' developed through relations of forms of expertise (expert systems) and politics; development of new forms of social accounting; an actuarial rationality; referendums and intensive opinion polling made possible through the new information and computing technologies; privatisation and individualisation of 'risk management'; development of new forms of prudentialism.

8. *An economic theory of democracy* ('the marketisation of democracy'): an emerging structural parallel between economic and political systems—political parties have become entrepreneurs in a vote-seeking political marketplace; professional media consultants use policies to sell candidates as image products; voters have become passive individual consumers. In short, democracy has become commodified at the cost of the project of political liberalism and the state has become subordinated to the market.

9. *The replacement of 'community' for 'the social'*: The decentralisation, 'devolution' and delegation of power/authority/responsibility from the center to the region, the local institution, the 'community'; the emergence of the shadow state; the encouragement of the informal voluntary sector (and an autonomous civil society) as a source of welfare; 'social capital.'

10. *Cultural reconstruction as deliberate policy goal* ('the marketisation of "the

social'") : The development of an 'enterprise society'; privatisation of the public sector; the development of quasi-markets; marketisation of education and health; a curriculum of competition and enterprise

11. *Low ecological consciousness* (Anthony Giddens): 'green capitalism'; 'green consumerism'; linear as opposed to ecological modernisation; 'no limits to growth'; market solutions to ecological problems

12. *Promotion of a neoliberal paradigm of globalisation*: world economic integration based on 'free' trade; no capital controls; International Monetary Fund (IMF), World Bank (WB), World Trade organisation (WTO) as international policy brokers.

This chapter focuses on how neoliberal, third way and neoconservative policies rely on a set of practices that might be termed 'government through the market' to produce 'responsiblized' citizens who harness their own entrepreneurial and self-governing capabilities. This chapter builds upon previous research which has analysed Foucault's approach to governmentality and 'the generalization of an "enterprise form" to all forms of conduct' (Burchell, 1996) and the way in which the promotion of enterprise culture has become a style of governance characteristic of both neoliberalism and Third Way politics.

The aim of the chapter is to consolidate this work and theoretically to distinguish between the different forms neoliberalism in its historical and contemporary complexity in term of actual governmental practices. The collection will focus on philosophical, historical and sociological understandings of 'governmentality' with an accent on *the entrepreneurial and enterprising self* and techniques of governing through the market. The theoretical overview will also trace the centrality of 'law and order,' *ordnung*, and relation of the Rule of Law to economics, in liberal and neoliberal constitutions of 'freedom' and explore the field of constitutional economics, especially in relation to the funding, provision and regulation of public education.

This chapter is based on the theoretical premise of the problematic made explicit by the so-called Anglo-Foucauldians. I am referring mainly to the British and Australian neo-Foucauldians (including for example, Gordon, 1991; Burchell, 1993; Rose, 1993), as distinct from both the French and U.S. neo-Foucauldians, and as exemplified in an edited collection called *Foucault and Political Reason* (Barry et al., 1996). A neo-Foucauldian approach to the sociology of governance avoids interpreting liberalism as an ideology, political philosophy or an economic theory to reconfigure it as a form of governmentality with an emphasis on the question of *how* power is exercised. Such an approach makes central the notion of the self-limiting state, which in contrast to the administrative (or "police") state, brings together in a productive way questions of ethics and technique, through the "responsibilization" of moral agents and the active reconstruction of the relation between government and self-government. It also proposes an investigation of neoliberalism as an intensification of an economy of moral regulation first developed by liberals and not merely or primarily as a political reaction to "big government" or the so-called bureaucratic welfare state of the post-war Keynesian settlement. Indeed, as Andrew Barry et al. (1996) point out, some who adopt this approach the era of post-war view welfarism as an aberrant episode that has little to do with liberalism *per se*. The approach enables an understanding of the distinctive features of neoliberalism. It understands neoliberalism in terms of its replacement of the natural and spontaneous order characteristic of Hayekian liberalism with "*artificially* arranged or contrived forms of the free, *entrepreneurial* and *competitive* conduct of economic-rational individuals" (Burchell, 1996: 23). And, further, it understands neoliberalism through the development of "*a new relation between expertise and politics*" (ibid.), especially in the realm of welfare, where an actuarial rationality and new forms of prudentialism manifest and constitute themselves discursively in the language of "purchaser-provider," audit, performance, and "risk management."

Governmentality Studies and the Challenge of Globalisation

Foucault's concept of governmentality developed in the last years of his life has been developed by a range of thinkers including those who worked with him helping to prepare his famous lecture course, including Jacques Donzelot whose work features prominently in this collection both in a chapter and in interview with Colin Gordon, one of Foucault's English translators and the leading thinker of the Anglo-Foucauldian group that includes Graham Burchell, Peter Miller, Nikolas Rose, Barry Hindess and Mitchell Dean, among others. In Germany the work of Thomas Lemke has been essential reading and his work has been highly influential in governmentality debates around the world. We are fortunate to be able to include a chapter by Lemke. In the development and application of Foucault's work on governmentality we can discern a number of stages: its initial invention and development arising out of Foucault's late political and ethical thought in the late 1970s; the set of sustained reflections on the concept and its relations to biopolitics and neoliberalism in the course entitled 'The Birth of Biopolitics' delivered in 1978–79; the subsequent development of governmentality in a series of courses including 'Du gouvernement des vivants' (1979–1980), 'Subjectivite et verite' (1980–1981), 'Le gouvernment de soi et des autres' (1982–1983), and 'Le gouvernment de soi et des autre: le courage de la verite' (1983–1984) some of which have not yet been transcribed in French or translated into English. The book *The Foucault Effect: Studies in Governmentality* (1991) edited by Graham Burchell, Colin Gordon and Peter Miller combined three essays of Foucault's including the 1978 'Governmentality' with an introduction by Colin Gordon and original essays by Pasquale Pasquino, Graham Burchell, Giovanna Procacci, Jacques Donzelot, Ian Hacking, François Ewald, Daniel Defert and Robert Castel. This was followed by Hunt and Wickham's *Foucault and Law* (1994), the collection by Andrew Barry, Thomas Osborne and Nikolas Rose (1996), *Foucault and Political Reason. Liberalism, neoliberalism and rationalities of government*, and Mitchell Dean's (1999) *Governmentality: Power and rule in modern society*.

Since the end of the 1990s we have seen a flowering of governmentality studies with applications and development across the full range of the social science and humanities: in anthropology[3], politics (Lipschutz & Rowe, 2005); international studies (Larner & Walters, 2004; Sending & Neumann, 2006; Merlingen, 2006); rights and political freedom (Ciccarelli, 2008), cultural studies (Bratich et al., 2003), security (Leander & Rens, 2006) and 'terrorism' (Ventura et al., 2005; Tagma, 2006), development (Watts, 2003; Li, 2007), law (Pavlich & Wickham, 2001), geography (Crampton & Eldon, 2007), education[4] (Masschelein, 2007), everyday life (Nadesan, 2008), European governance (Walters & Haar, 2005) and environment (Death, 2006; Luke, n.d.). This is by no means a comprehensive list or summary.[5] The standard introductions to the concept of governmentality have been provided by Colin Gordon (1991; 2001; this volume), Nikolas Rose et al. (2006) and most recently in a new collection by Ulrich Bröckling, Susanne Krasmann, Thomas Lemke (2009) entitled *Governmentality: Current Issues and Future Challenges* which explores the advantages and limitations of adopting Michel Foucault's concept of governmentality as an analytical framework. The workshop on which the book is based begins:

> The publication of *The Foucault Effect: Studies in Governmentality* in 1991 marked the beginning of a growing interest in the notion of governmentality in the social and political sciences. In the following years, 'governmentality' became a key term that inspired empirical analyses in different subject areas and academic disciplines. The so-called studies of governmentality offered quite a different perspective on state theory and political analysis: They went beyond traditional accounts structured by the opposition between state and civil society, public and private spheres, freedom and constraint by focusing on the interplay between processes of subjectivation and power mechanisms, political rationalities and governmental technolo-

gies. However, the concept of governmentality also engendered serious criticism in recent years which may point to some limitations and shortcomings in this theoretical perspective. Sixteen years after the publication of *The Foucault Effect* the workshop shall provide the opportunity to discuss the theoretical and empirical achievements, future perspectives and persisting problems of an analytics of government. It takes up three major themes that encountered discussions and also critical attention in recent years (http://www.uni konstanz.de/kulturtheorie/Workshop_TheStateofGovernmentality1.pdf).[6]

The brief for the workshop proceeds to highlight the three themes as: 1. Beyond the nation state: Sovereignty, bio-politics and trans-nationalisation; 2. Biological citizenship and the government of life; 3. The economy of government. One of the alleged limitations in Foucault's work, these authors argue, is the focus on the territoriality of the modern state, especially in an increasingly globalized world. Yet a number of authors have begun to apply the governmentality framework systematically beyond the territoriality of the modern state (Perry & Maurer, 2003; Larner & Walters, 2004; Walters & Haar, 2005).

Larner and Walters (2004) emphasized the way in which 'governmentality' has been used in two distinct ways in the literature: (1) 'a form of power whose logic is not the defense of territory or the aggrandizement of the sovereign but the optimization of the health and welfare of the population' and (2) 'an approach that explores how governing always involves particular representations, knowledges, and expertise regarding that which is to be governed' (p. 495). They develop the second sense of the notion as 'the practice of government [which] involves the production of particular "truths" about…the constitution of our societies and ourselves' (ibid.). This 'governmentality' of the international allows Foucault's approach to be used and mapped onto current debates about gloablization where 'the role of nonstate actors in shaping and carrying out global governance-functions is not an instance of transfer of power from the state to nonstate actors but rather an expression of a changing logic or rationality of government (defined as a type of power) by which civil society is redefined from a passive object of government to be acted upon into an entity that is both an object *and* a subject of government' (Sending & Neumann, 2006, p. 651). In a more porous and interconnected world governmentality can shed light on changing practices of political rule that define the identity and functioning of key actors in world politics. Such an understanding is crucial if we are to understand the new economization of the state which depends on networks and the complexity of network effects that challenge the space of pure economic rationality assumed by neoclassical economics and the ideal of rationally calculating economic man. Human capital theory based on this ideal then becomes the focus for an analysis of 'the entrepreneur of oneself' as a technology of indirect government control exercised *across* government policies that traverse national spaces, especially in the field of education and health where these indirect technologies are the substance of biopolitics.

Michael Merlingen (2006) provides a useful discussion of the attempt to extend governmentality beyond the state, reviewing three books: Larner and Walters (2004) collection *Global Governmentality: Governing International Spaces;* Perry and Maurer (2003) collection *Globalization under Construction: Governmentality, Law, and Identity;* and, Walters and Haahr's (2005) *Governing Europe: Discourse, Governmentality and European Integration.* He identifies six strengths of 'governmentality theory,' which, as he argues 'promise to provide some new interpretative purchase upon deterritorialised and de-stated politics' (p. 184). These he lists as: *Networked Governance* that enables governmentality theory with the aid of actor network theory to study policy networks; a *Semiotics of Materiality* that enables 'governmentality theory' to go beyond 'discourse-centred poststructuralist and constructivist approaches in IR and EU studies' (p. 187); the *Denaturalisation of Governance* that helps 'to strip political rule of its self-evident, normal or natural character' (p. 188); *Exploring the European/Global through Micropolitical Sites and Practices* which is the excavation/mapping of all those little knowledges and humble and mundane technologies through which the European/global is articulated' (p. 189); *Resistance and the Fragility of Governance* 'emphasises the likelihood of resistance and the reversibility of power relations' (p. 190). Perhaps most importantly, this feature in

> its peculiar conceptualisation of the linkage between domination and people's capacity for self-control makes the theory well suited for bringing into focus the tensions and opposition between the government of others and self-government and for adding a new perspective on the diverse and often inconspicuous ways in which citizens resist being enrolled in governmental projects of order(liness) (p. 190).

Merlingen (2006) adds *Power and Domination* that understands strategic power as the 'reciprocal attempt of people to shape each other's conduct and the correlated games of control and resistance,' states of domination 'which are asymmetric, institutionalised patterns of interaction, say, between the coloniser and the colonised, man and woman' (p. 190), and 'technologies' as the third concept of power that together provides a toolbox for researchers.

Where researchers only a few years ago were attempting to demonstrate the policy convergence of neoliberalism, its 'export' and institutionalization, and its constitution of globalization (or at least one version), the wheel has turned again with the election of Barack Obama and his instant roll-back of many of Bush's policies, although not all neoliberal policies. Indeed, the crisis of Keynesianism and the welfare state has been followed by the crisis of neoliberalism and free market fundamentalism.

The End of Neoliberalism?

George Soros, the Popperian financier, has warned that this is the age of 'the destruction of capital.' Already conservative estimates indicate that 50 trillion dollars have been wiped off the books worldwide (30 trillion in equity funds, 4 trillion in credit, 3 trillion in lost output, 3 trillion in the sub-prime housing market). The world economy still (at the time of writing in early April 2009) has not showed any consistent signs of improvement or growth. A groundswell of opinion from a variety of scholars point to 'the end of neoliberalism' and the beginning of a new age of state intervention, although there is fierce debate over the extent of further stimulus packages.

In some sense the current series of crises that have rocked Wall Street to its foundations and threatened to destabilize the world financial system and its major banking and insurance institutions is just the latest round of failure for the global justice movement that has coordinated worldwide demonstrations against neoliberalism, 'the American imperialist project,' the Iraq War, and strands referred to since the early 1980s as 'Monetarism,' 'Supply-Side Economics,' 'Reaganism/Thatcherism.' Longtime critics of neoliberalism and its policies of privatization, state non-interference and deregulation summed up in the so-called 'Washington consensus'[11] such as the economists Stiglitz, and Robert Pollin (2003), sociologist Pierre Bourdieu (1998), geographer David Harvey (2005), philosopher/linguist Noam Chomsky (1999), as well as the anti-globalization movement in general,[12] have consistently argued that neoliberalism is a class project that benefits the rich and leads to ever-increasing inequalities both within and between states.

A major overhaul of the financial system is almost certainly required and government regulation needs to be established, minimally, to ensure transparency and full disclosure, to spell out capital requirements and to avoid conflicts of interest. Timothy Geitner as Obama Treasury Secretary is currently implementing a plan to buy over $1 trillion in troubled assets and mortgages and the G20 under Gordon Brown is pushing for a new global framework for tighter regulation, spelling the end of global financial laissez-faire. The move to state-centric policies and to forms of regulation in the U.S. and elsewhere seems almost inevitable. Government intervention and (neo)Keynesianism is now suddenly back in fashion. The move to Federal regulation and a reform of the financial system seems to chime with the development of state capitalism elsewhere, especially in East Asia.[13]

As the centre of economic gravity shifts to East Asia it is not clear whether new Keynesianism will be embraced or whether in face of such intensive global competition and fierce economic nationalism whether Western economies can ever afford it. There is never the option of an innocent return historically and a return to the golden days of the welfare state in Scandinavia or New Zealand, or to the 'social model' in Europe, especially as new costly environmental and energy contingencies begins to bite. Some argue that what is required is a change of *ethos*—not 'confidence' and 'trust' of the market but rather the development of trust that comes with the radically decentred democratic collaboration that epitomizes distributed knowledge, political and energy systems. Yet all these explanations seem to be predicated upon understanding neoliberalism as a doctrine, ideology or set of policies and none have benefited from Foucault's notion of generality as a mentality of rule.

President Barack Obama has a strong vision for America, for reclaiming the American dream, and for a political and economic philosophy based on a combination of American pragmatism with a strong emphasis on 'what works' and an interventionist government-led emphasis on ethics and responsibility to change the culture of corruption in Washington. Obama's political philosophy is based on the notions of unity, community, equality and hope. He wants to transcend all divisions, to provide a new universalism of provision and encourage a greater inclusiveness that moves beyond the dualism and dichotomies that haunt the U.S. going back to the 1960s—white-black, male-female, Democrat-Republican—in order to assert the American moment and to provide global leadership.[14] Obama's administration is attempting to implement a progressivist egalitarian economic philosophy that is a managed form of capitalism oriented to crisis management in the short term with massive government assistance to banks, tax cuts to the middle class, and huge infrastructure investment aimed at economic recovery. In the longer term Obama is pursuing market-friendly innovation policies based on the reform of science and technology and structural reforms in green energy and universal health care.

The question is whether this really does mean the end of neoliberalism. Clearly, the IMF and World Bank are still pursuing their old structural adjustment policies especially in bankrupt states like the Ukraine and Latvia. Both internationally and within the U.S. the neoliberal mantra against big government has been given short shrift as governments world-wide have embarked on interventionist policies consisting in bail-outs, stimulus packages and in some cases wholesale nationalization of banking and insurance institutions or partnership with private interests. At the same time there is a clear set of policy intentions from Obama's administration to intervene directly in the economy by socializing and universalizing health as well as investing heavily in education, energy, science and technology. This means that the state under Obama has begun to move toward a model of greater collective responsibility reversing the earlier neoliberal strategy of making individuals responsible for social risks while at the same time resisting the move to Keynesian policies of full employment. The question is whether the concept of governmentality now provides the means to understand the constitution of new political forms and the reshaping of identities and subjectivities that follow from a community model.

Contemporary social theory, strongly influenced by Foucault focusing on identity studies seeks the constitution and manufacture of consciousness and subjectivity in more nuanced ways, emphasizing cultural processes of formation within larger shifts concerning globalization, the 'knowledge economy,' and the mobility of peoples across national boundaries and frontiers. Economists have given greater attention to the world of social media and new technologies in relation to identity formation and the transformation of patterns of work and its definition in a postindustrial society. In economics there has developed an entire new field called 'behavioral economics' that repudiates aspects of neoclassical theory based on the simplifying assumptions of *Homo economicus*, importing and basing its insights on psychology.

At one time, at the very beginning of its disciplinary formation in the heyday of 'political economy,' economics had a strong relationship to the other social sciences and, particularly, to questions of psychology. In *The Theory of Moral Sentiments* Adam Smith (1759) commented upon the psychological principles guiding human behavior providing the ethical and methodological principles for his later works. Broadly speaking, Smith followed his mentor, Francis Hutcheson, in dividing moral systems into two: nature (Propriety, Prudence, and Benevolence) and motive (Self- Love, Reason, and Sentiment). Smith, in contrast to Hutcheson, provides us with a psychological account of morality, beginning *Moral Sentiments* with the observation that however selfish a man may be supposed to be there are 'some principles in his nature, which interest him in the fortunes of others, and render their happiness necessary to him, though he derives nothing from it, except the pleasure of seeing it.' As the discipline developed, especially during the neoclassical phase, economists began to distance themselves from psychology as they sought to base their explanations on the hypothesis of rational agents, especially with the development of the concept of *Homo economicus* that appeared for the first time in the work of John Stuart Mill where the psychology of the postulated entity was defined as fundamentally rational. In 'On the Definition of Political Economy, and on the Method of Investigation Proper to It,' Mill (1836) suggests that 'political economy is concerned with . . . [Man] solely as a being who desires to possess wealth, and who is capable of judging the comparative efficacy of means for obtaining that end.'

The essential aspect of *Homo economicus* is the 'rational' element in the sense that well-being is defined by the optimization of the utility function and is normally described in terms of three governing assumptions: individuality (all choices are made by individuals); rationality (these are conscious deliberative choices); and self-interest (they are made in the interest of the choicemaker). The rationality of Economic Man has been called into question by other disciplines that emphasize the cultural and gendered nature of rationality or point to the way in which economic agents act irrationally or in not rationally optimal ways. The rejuvenation of *Homo economicus* as a basis for addressing public policy came during the decades of neoliberalism beginning under Thatcher and Reagan that so drastically restructured the public sector, reducing the number of public servants, commercializing and privatizing state enterprises, and selling off state assets. It also reshaped the global labor marketplace and restructured higher education in accord with its own globalization ideals. The building of 'enterprise culture' was as much a moral crusade to redefine the nature of society through a redefinition of work as were the first attempts to theorize the economic nature of humankind.

A new generation of social theorists and researchers now look for approaches that link discourse, power, psychology and the self with economics to explain the failings of assumptions of *Homo economicus*. Nowhere is this confluence of psychology and economics more important than in the newly emerging field of behavioral economics and finance. Robert J. Shiller, one of its ablest practitioners, writes, 'Behavioral economics incorporates insights from other social sciences, such as psychology and sociology, into economic models, and attempts to explain anomalies that defy standard economic analysis.' He treats behavioral economics alongside institutional economics as 'the study of the evolution of economic organisations, laws, contracts, and customs as part of a historical and continuing process of economic development' and notes that 'topics include economic fluctuations and speculation, herd behavior, attitudes towards risk, money illusion, involuntary unemployment, saving, investment, poverty, identity, religion, trust, risk management and social welfare institutions.'[15]

The fact is that the question of identity strongly influences economic thinking and behavior and people do not behave in the way that the strong rationality model of neoclassical economics has taught us to believe in the basis of *Homo economicus*. In this vein I am reminded of Foucault's (2008) lectures on the birth of neoliberalism and in particular lectures nine to twelve where he analyses Amercian neoliberalism and the theory of human capital—the application of economics to the domain of social life (law and criminality) and the redefinition of *Homo economicus* as entrepreneur of himself, in effects, its generalization to every form of behavior. Foucault comments how *Homo economicus* emerged as the basic element of the new governmental reason in the eighteenth century as a correlate of the liberal art of government with its focus on civil society which he traces to Ferguson's (1787) *A History of Civil Society*.

When Obama (2009) asserts that 'ours is a market society' in a strong sense he is also adverting to the deep institutionalization of *Homo economicus* in American society, the bi-partisan acceptance of human capital theory in economics and all spheres of life, especially in terms of a generalization of the form 'entrepreneur of himself' chiming with an embedded American ethos, even if under Obama this might come to mean a greater socialization of entrepreneurship and corresponding a greater personalization of services through social networks and social media.

Foucault (2008: 407) ends his lectures with the statement:

> You can see that in the modern world, in the world we have known since the nineteenth century, a series of governmental rationalities overlap, lean on each other, challenge each other, and struggle with each other: art of government according to truth, art of government according to the rationality of the sovereign state, and art of government according to the rationality of economic agents, and more generally, according to the rationality of the governed themselves. And it is all these different arts of government, all these different types of ways of calculating, rationalizing, and regulating the art of government which, overlapping each other, broadly speaking constitute the object of political debate from the nineteenth century. What is politics, in the end, if not both the interplay of these different arts of government with their different reference points and the debate to which these different arts of government give rise?

It is useful to project the concept of 'art of government' into the twenty-first century and in relation to the U.S. under Obama especially after the midterm elections after the Republicans have retaken the House. In this case the art of government is more than ever locked into interests of big business and the manipulation of the American Dream by a form of political media that is increasingly partisan. For Obama the art of government is still above all related to an economic rationality of deficit financing in the age of a declining hegemony that seek to balance its debt at home and abroad,while fighting two wars and adjusting to the rise of Asia.

Notes

1. This description is drawn from 'Schools of [Economic] Thought' at http://cepa.newschool.edu/het/.

2. See the Chicago Department of Economics website at, http://economics.uchicago.edu/index.shtml, where it makes the following description: 'Any definition of the "Chicago School" would have to find room for the following ideas (in chronological order from the 1940s to the present): the economic theory of socialism, general equilibrium models of foreign trade, simultaneous equation methods in econometrics, consumption as a function of permanent income, the economics of the household, the rationality of peasants in poor countries, the economics of education and other acquired skills (human capital), applied welfare economics, monetarism, sociological economics (entrepreneurship, racial discrimination, crime), the economics of invention and innovation, quantitative economic history, the economics of information, political economy (externalities, property rights, liability, contracts), the monetary approach to international finance, and rational expectations in macroeconomics.'

3. See the work that originates with Paul Rabinow and others 'Critical Ethnographies of Globalization and Governmentality' http://ls.berkeley.edu/dept/anth/gandg.html.

4. See also the website 'Contemporary Theory, Poststructuralism and Governmentality' at http://edtheory.ning.com/.

5. For a more comprehensive summary see the journal *Foucault Studies* at http://rauli.cbs.dk/foucault_splash.html and the special issue on *Neoliberal Governmentality* (Issue No. 6, February, 2009) edited by Sverre Raffnsøe, Alan Rosenberg, Alain Beaulieu, Sam Binkley, Jens Erik Kristensen, Sven Opitz, Morris Rabinowitz, Ditte Vilstrup Holm.

6. The workshop was held at the University of Leipzig, Dept. of Political Sciences, September 14–15, 2007.

7. See Stiglitz's commentary at http://www.project-syndicate.org/commentary/stiglitz 101.

8. It seems almost inevitable that both Morgan Stanley and Goldman Sachs will also disappear. Morgan Stanley is in talks with the China Investment Corp. In the UK the Government rescued Northern Rock and Lloyds has bought out HBOS. Central banks around the world offered $180 billion to banks outside the US to weather the financial storm.

9. See Lance Freeman's blog of March 2008 at http://www.planetizen.com/node/30187 and Robert Reich's Blog at http://robertreich.blogspot.com/. Both talk of the end of neoliberalism; see also Wallerstein's (2008) 'The Demise of Neoliberal Globalization' who argues the end of neoliberalism is a cyclical swing in the history of the capitalist world-economy, at http://www.monthlyreview.org/mrzine/wallerstein010208 .html.

10. See his blog at http://johnquiggin.com/index.php/archives/2008/09/08/the-end-of-neoliberalism/.

11. The original consensus was based around the following tenants: 1. Fiscal discipline; 2. Reorientation of public expenditures; 3. Tax reform; 4. Financial liberalization; 5. Unified and competitive exchange rates; 6. Trade liberalization; 7. Openness to DFI; 8. Privatization; 9. Deregulation; 10.Secure Property Rights.

12. I take Susan George's 'A Short History of Neoliberalism' as emblematic of this movement, see http://www.zmag.org/CrisesCurEvts/Globalism/george.htm.

13. In this regard see, in particular, Parag Khanna's (2008) *The Second World: Empires and Influence in the New Global Order.*

14. Barack Obama, 'Renewing American Leadership' *Foreign Affairs*, July-August, 2007, at http://www.foreignaffairs.org/20070701faessay86401/barack-obama/renewing-american-leadership.html.

15. See his course description of 'Behavioral and Institutional Economics' at http://www.econ.yale.edu/~shiller/course/527/ec52704.rl.htm.

10

The Global Recession, Education and the Changing Economics of the Self

Privatize Profits; Socialize Losses

A GROUNDSWELL DISCOURSE OF 'THE END OF NEOLIBERALISM' is jamming the Left blogosphere. It has been building for some time. The Nobel prize-winning economist Joseph Stiglitz (2008, July 7) in *Project Syndicate* began his column with the assertion that the ideology of 'market fundamentalism' has failed:

> The world has not been kind to neoliberalism, that grab-bag of ideas based on the fundamentalist notion that markets are self-correcting, allocate resources efficiently, and serve the public interest well. It was this market fundamentalism that underlay Thatcherism, Reaganomics, and the so-called "Washington Consensus" in favor of privatization, liberalization, and independent central banks focusing single-mindedly on inflation.[1]

Writing before the collapse of Wall Street's investment banks—the bankruptcy of Lehman Brothers, the sell-off of Merrill Lynch, the Federal bridging loan of $85 billion to AIG, and the massive $700 billion assistance to the U.S. financial sector—Stiglitz criticized neoliberal policies and their costs to developing economies.[2] He faulted the financial market allocation of resources to housing in the 1990s and the sub-prime crisis that has precipitated a global financial crisis and credit squeeze he thinks will be prolonged and widespread. He criticized the selective use of free-market rhetoric used to support special interests and the way that Bush's policies have served the military-industrial complex. He concluded:

> Neoliberal market fundamentalism was always a political doctrine serving certain interests. It was never supported by economic theory. Nor, it should now be clear, is it supported by historical experience. Learning this lesson may be the silver lining in the cloud now hanging over the global economy.

John Quiggin[3] (September 8, 2008), the Australian social-democrat, following Stiglitz's lead and spurred by the nationalization of Fannie Mae and Freddy Mac (that between them held some $5 trillion of mortgages), under the same banner 'The End of Neoliberalism?' remarks:

> The fact that the credit crisis has reached this point marks the failure of the central claim of the neoliberal program, namely that private capital markets, free from intrusive government regulation, can enable individuals and households to handle the risks they face more flexibly and efficiently than a social-democratic welfare state.

Others made similar claims and raised similar doubts concerning the march of neoliberalism after the Federal Reserve's bailout of Bear Stearns. Thus, Lance Freeman (18 March, 2008), for instance, comments:

> The Federal Reserve's bailout (arranged liquidation to some) of Bear Stearns over the weekend seriously calls into question the headlong march toward neoliberalism that has been ascendant for the past few decades. Roughly speaking, neoliberalism called for a retrenchment of the state in favor of deregulated markets. As an ideological force neoliberalism held great sway in trade policy, the overall management of the economy and even at the local level where most planners operate.[4]

He continues:

> Once a government lifeline is thrown to Wall Street the whole philosophical underpinnings of neoliberalism would have to be called into question, even among the most faithful adherents of neoliberalism. The question of government intervention becomes a matter of degree rather than kind. That is, a strong central authority is needed to guide the economy. Left to its own devices the "free market" can run off the rails. Critics of neoliberalism have pointed this out for years. But as long as most of the pain was confined to the more disadvantaged members of the world proponents of neoliberalism could wave the misfortunes off as

the forces of creative destruction, etc. With the whole system under strain, that is no longer the case. The notion that reducing government and deregulation is the answer to all our problems seems laughable now.

In some sense the current series of crises that have rocked Wall Street to its foundations and threatened to destabilize the world financial system and its major banking and insurance institutions is just the latest round of failure for the global justice movement that has coordinated worldwide demonstrations against neoliberalism—including 'the American imperialist project,' the Iraq War, and strands referred to since the early 1980s as 'Monetarism,' 'Supply-Side Economics,' 'Reaganism/Thatcherism.' Longtime critics of neoliberalism and its policies of privatization, state non-interference and deregulation summed up in the so-called 'Washington consensus'[5] such as the economists Stiglitz, and Robert Pollin (2003), sociologist Pierre Bourdieu (1998), geographer David Harvey (2005), philosopher/linguist Noam Chomsky (1999), as well as the anti-globalization movement[6] in general, have consistently argued that neoliberalism is a class project that benefits the rich and leads to ever-increasing inequalities both within and between states.

One of the most objectionable and inconsistent aspects of the neoliberal doctrine was the way in which market fundamentalism was *imposed* on developing nations as part of structural adjustment loans or simply forced through political and military measures, starting with the CIA-backed coup against a democratically elected government in Chile in 1973 (supported strongly by Milton Friedman) and becoming the policy stable for World Bank loans and prescriptions especially in Latin America during the 1980s. The imposition of market fundamentalism runs in complete opposition to neoliberalism's own libertarian premises and emphasis on negative freedom.

The U.S. economy's plight driven by the insurance and banking failures on Wall Street excited the Obama-McCain debate for the U.S. presidency with McCain glossing over his support of Bush's policies and trying to play down the statement that the 'fundamentals of the economy are strong' while Obama planned to strengthen the economy through tax breaks to the middle classes, emphasis on 'fair trade,' job creation through investment in manufacturing and protection of home ownership. The issue of the economy took pride of place in the election and dislodged the Republican emphasis on 'character' and 'leadership' that degenerated into a series of scurrilous attacks on Obama as 'terrorist,' 'secret Muslim,' and 'Marxist.'

The Wall Street fiasco adversely affected world stock markets in Asia, Europe and Russia (which experienced the largest one-day fall in ten years). There are network effects in terms of the global economy. Robert Reich[7] (15 September, 2008), former Secretary of Labor under Clinton, remarked that

> Ironically, a free-market-loving Republican administration is presiding over the most ambitious intrusion of government into the market in almost anyone's memory.

And he added that although 'The sub-prime mortgage mess triggered it, but the problem lies much deeper.' He argued Wall Street is facing a crisis of trust based on promises that weren't worth the paper they were written on and he concluded:

> If what's lacking is trust rather than capital, the most important steps policymakers can take are to rebuild trust. And the best way to rebuild trust is through regulations that require financial players to stand behind their promises and tell the truth, along with strict oversight to make sure they do.

It seems clear that some major overhaul of the international financial system is required; that government regulation needs to be established, minimally, to ensure transparency and full disclosure, to spell out capital requirements and to avoid conflicts of interest; and that some new order is required with the participation of both China and India.

The move to state-centric policies and to forms of Federal regulation in the U.S. and elsewhere now seem almost inevitable. Government intervention is now suddenly back in fashion and on the books at the IMF and World Bank. The move to Federal regulation and a reform of the financial system seems to chime with the development of state capitalism elsewhere, especially in East Asia,[8] and other forms of state-centrism seen as necessary for job creation and national reinvestment in infrastructure.

Immanuel Wallerstein (2008)[9], the prominent world-systems theorist, also talked of the 'demise' of neoliberalism. He explained that 'non-interference' is actually an old idea that cyclically comes into fashion and that its counterview summed up in Keynesianism (mixed economies, protection of citizens from foreign monopolies, equalization and redistribution through taxation) has also prevailed in most western countries. He suggested that:

> The political balance is swinging back. Neoliberal globalization will be written about ten years from now as a cyclical swing in the history of the capitalist world-economy. The real question is not whether this phase is over but whether the swing back will be able, as in the past, to restore a state of relative equilibrium in the world-system. Or has too much damage been done? And are we now in for more violent chaos in the world-economy and therefore in the world-system as a whole?

As the center of economic gravity shifts to East Asia and to the BRIC (Brazil, Russia, India and China) it is not clear whether new Keynesianism will be embraced or whether in face of such intensive global competition and fierce economic nationalism whether Western economies can ever afford to reestablish it. There is no option of an innocent return historically or a return to the golden days of the welfare state in Scandinavia or New Zealand, or to the 'social model' in Europe, especially as new costly environmental and energy contingencies begin to bite. What is required is a change of *ethos*—not 'confidence' and 'trust' of the market but rather the development of trust that comes with the radically decentered democratic participation, collaboration and co-production that epitomizes the creation of public goods and distributed political, knowledge, and energy systems.

The Economic Report of the President (2010: 4) made to Congress in February 2010 focused on lost jobs and the process of economic rebuilding. The President's own message that prefaces the report emphasized a low starting point when he took office: the way 'irresponsible risk-taking and debt-fueled speculation . . . led to the near-collapse of our financial system,' the loss of 'an average of 700,000 jobs each month,' '$13 trillion of Americans' household wealth had evaporated as stocks, pensions, and home values plummeted' in the course of one year, the sharp fall in GDP, and the halt to credit flows. It is clear that the administration believed they faced economic collapse that could have led to a second Great Depression. Obama recounts the attempts in the ensuing months after taking office to address crises in the banking sector, the housing market, and the auto industry and he mentions the American Recovery and Reinvestment Act of 2009 with tax cuts to small businesses, and investments in health care, education, infrastructure, and clean energy as a basis for transforming the US. Indeed, the Stimulus Act which followed Bush's economic recovery legislation, nominally worth $787 billion included $100 billion investment in education with $53.6 billion in aid to local school districts to prevent layoffs and cutbacks, $15.6 billion to increase Pell grants, $13 billion for low-income public schoolchildren, $12.2 billion for special education and smaller amounts dedicated to Head Start, childcare services, educational technology, increased teacher salaries, and funds to analyse student performance, support working college students and provide education of homeless children.

Two major shifts of wealth are occurring: first, internally the U.S. has experienced a shift of wealth more than any time in the past where there is increasing concentration of wealth and greater inequalities; second, the centre of economic gravity is moving from West to East, from the industrialized economies to the large developing BRIC economies, particularly China, India and Brazil. This trend is set to continue with emerging and developing economies accounting for nearly 60%

of world GDP by 2030. Both of these developments will impact upon education increasing educational inequalities at home and significantly decreasing the demand for U.S. higher education abroad, especially at the undergraduate level.

Increasingly education must be seen in a global context where the existing global order has been disrupted by the growth of 'state capitalism' which Ian Bremmer (2010) in *The End of the Free Market: Who Wins the War Between States and Corporations?* argues constitutes a new threat to the free market. State capitalism, Bremmer explains, is a system in which governments use markets to create wealth and advance their political interests. In China, Russia and Saudi Arabia the state controls key industries and regularly favors domestic firms. In particular, state power can be seen in the global oil and gas markets, three-quarters of which is controlled by governments. It also appears that state capitalism will increasingly defend, protect and regulate higher education as a source of postindustrial growth in the era of knowledge capitalism, developing a massive monopolization and privatization of knowledge. Much of this development is happening under the radar with the development of national corporations, the encouragement of privately owned national champions linked to the state in preferential arrangements, and strategic deployment of sovereign wealth funds.

Global Recession and the Changing Economics of the Self

The dimensions of global recession of the world economy are now well established: the IMF's (2008) *World Economic Outlook* warned that the world economy is 'entering a major downturn,' the worst since the 1930s. While there is no commonly accepted definition of a global recession the IMF estimates global growth to be less than 3% for 2009[10]. One of the consequences of this downturn is the massive loss of jobs: almost 80,000 jobs in the U.S. were lost in just one day (Monday, 26 January 2010) as giants such as Caterpillar, Phillips, Corus (UK steelmaker), Spring Nextel and Pfizer, among others laid-off workers. The U.S. Bureau of Labor Statistics released statistics for December 2008 indicating that regional and state unemployment rates were universally higher in December, with all 50 states and the District of Columbia recorded both over-the-month and over-the-year unemployment rate increases and large regional differences from 2.2% in Wyoming to - 4.5% in Rhode Island.[11] One of the goals of the Obama administration is the creation of 3 million jobs in fixing America's infrastructure and in the green energy sector which falls considerable short of the commitment to full employment.[13] In this climate closer attention needs to be paid to the relationship between unemployment, education and the changing economics of the self. Unemployment is the new global reality for the developed world and also increasingly for developing economies like China and India that have experienced spectacular growth rates over the last five years. The relationship between education, work, and identity is often the basis for meaningful participation in society and investment in quality education is indeed of the essence (ILO, 2007).

Contemporary social theory, including economics, in the form of identity studies seek the constitution and manufacture of consciousness and subjectivity in more nuanced ways emphasizing cultural processes of formation within larger shifts concerning globalization, the 'knowledge economy,' and the mobility of peoples across national boundaries and frontiers. Accordingly, very often social theorists have given greater attention to the world of social media and new technologies in relation to identity formation and the transformation of patterns of work and its definition in a postindustrial society.

In economics there has developed an entire new field called 'behavioral economics' that repudiates aspects of neoclassical theory based on the simplifying of *Homo economicus*, importing and basing its insights on psychology.

As the discipline developed especially during the neoclassical phase economists began to distance themselves from psychology as they sought to base their explanations on the hypothesis of rational agents especially with the development of the concept of *Homo economicus* that appeared for the first time in the work of John Stuart Mill where the psychology of the postulated entity was defined as fundamentally rational. In 'On the Definition of Political Economy, and on the Method of Investigation Proper to It,' Mill (1836) suggests

> [Political economy] does not treat the whole of man's nature as modified by the
> social state, nor of the whole conduct of man in society. It is concerned with him
> solely as a being who desires to possess wealth, and who is capable of judging the
> comparative efficacy of means for obtaining that end.

The essential aspect of *Homo economicus* is the 'rational' element in the sense that well-being is defined by the optimization of the utility function and is normally described in terms of three governing assumptions: individuality (all choices are made by individuals); rationality (these are conscious deliberative choices) and self-interest (they are made in the interest of the choice-maker). The rationality of Economic Man has been called into question by other disciplines that emphasize the cultural and gendered nature of rationality or point to the way in which economic agents act irrationally or in not rational optimal ways.

The rejuvenation of *Homo economicus* as a basis for addressing public policy came during the decades of neoliberalism beginning under Thatcher-Reagan that so drastically restructured the public sector reducing the number of public servants, commercializing and privatizing state enterprises, and selling off state assets. Part of the international creed of neoliberalism has been to critique big government, especially the so-called welfare state by attacking welfare dependents, highlighting benefit fraud, and tightening up eligibility criteria. These reforms aimed to reduce welfare dependency by introducing a workfare state defined through a new work ethic dressed up in moral terms. At the same time neoliberalism was committed to a form of globalization advertized in terms of 'free trade' and the free flow of capital across national borders. This massive reprivatization of the public sphere and commitment to a deregulated finance capitalism permitting the free flow of capital fundamentally disrupted traditional identities, impacting on women, especially solo parents, cultural minorities and male middle-management. It also reshaped the global labor marketplace and restructured higher education in accord with its own globalization ideals. The building of 'enterprise culture' was as much a moral crusade to redefine the nature of society through a redefinition of work as was the first attempts to theorize the economic nature of humankind.

In early 2009 immediately after the U.S. November elections the world now seems poised between the old rationality model of the individual and the possibility of the new community view. The 'Washington consensus' now seems laughable as America struggles with its own economy having experienced the triple whammy of the sub-prime crisis, the instability of its major financial institutions, and brief but volatile hike in oil prices. The U.S. Democrats have ushered in a U.S.-style emphasis on gender and race for the first time since the civil rights era and Barrack Obama, representing new hope to America's youth, fought neck-and-neck with the Bush neocon surrogate John McCain to outline a new philosophy of hope, inclusiveness and community that will define the next decade. Yet Obama's administration pulls back from a commitment to full employment.

Economists now no longer debate whether the U.S. has technically entered into a recession (defined as two quarters of negative growth) as the number of foreclosures and unemployed mushroom. Over two million Americans have had their mortgages foreclosed and unemployment has now reached over three and a half million (7.5%) with economists predicting 10% by the end of the year. New discourses are appearing on the horizon concerning questions of power and identity, especially in relation to rising unemployment, to social media, to globalization, and to new forms of work. A new generation of social theorists and researchers look for approaches that link discourse, power, psychology and the self.[15]

Nowhere is this confluence of psychology and economics more important than the newly emerging field of behavioral economics and finance.

Shiller's (2006) *The Subprime Solution: How Today's Global Financial Crisis Happened, and What to Do about It* correctly foretold and analysed the subprime housing market crisis and also how it led to the current credit squeeze and financial meltdown. Shiller is Professor of Economics at Yale and Fellow in the Yale International Centre for Finance. His work has demonstrated through detailed analysis of the U.S. stock market since the 1920s that its huge variation and volatility is greater than can be explained plausibly by a rational view of the future. This has led him to challenge the efficient markets model and to hypothesize that decisions are often driven by psychological factors rather than being the result of rational calculation. As one website makes clear 'The standard (neoclassical) economic analysis assumes that humans are rational and behave in a way to maximize their individual self-interest. Whilst this "rational man" assumption yields a powerful tool for analysis, it has many shortfalls that can lead to unrealistic economic analysis and policy-making.'[16] For instance, as the website for 'new economics' indicates people emulate other people's behavior and 'are encouraged to continue to do things when they feel other people approve of their behavior.' Furthermore, habits are important so that often people do things without consciously thinking. Often, people are motivated to 'do the right thing,' are 'loss-averse' or are unduly influenced by their own self-expectations and 'want their actions to be in line with their values and their commitments.' Also 'people are bad at computation when making decisions: they put undue weight on recent events and too little on far-off ones; they cannot calculate probabilities well and worry too much about unlikely events; and they are strongly influenced by how the problem/information is presented to them.' Finally, 'People need to feel involved and effective to make a change: just giving people the incentives and information is not necessarily enough.' The fact is that the question of identity strongly influences economic thinking and behavior and people do not behave in the way that the strong rationality model of neoclassical economics has taught us to believe on the basis of *Homo economicus.*[17] This has important implications for public policy and for the promotion of full employment policy.

In the blurb to their book *Animal Spirits* George A. Akerlof and Robert J. Shiller (2007) describe (as they put in their subtitle) *How Human Psychology Drives the Economy, and Why It Matters for Global Capitalism;*

> The global financial crisis has made it painfully clear that powerful psychological forces are imperiling the wealth of nations today. From blind faith in ever-ris-

ing housing prices to plummeting confidence in capital markets, 'animal spirits' are driving financial events worldwide.

The blurb continues:

> Akerlof and Shiller reassert the necessity of an active government role in econom-
> ic policymaking by recovering the idea of animal spirits, a term John Maynard
> Keynes used to describe the gloom and despondence that led to the Great
> Depression and the changing psychology that accompanied recovery. Like Keynes,
> Akerlof and Shiller know that managing these animal spirits requires the steady
> hand of government—simply allowing markets to work won't do it. In rebuild-
> ing the case for a more robust, behaviorally informed Keynesianism, they detail
> the most pervasive effects of animal spirits in contemporary economic life—
> such as confidence, fear, bad faith, corruption, a concern for fairness, and the sto-
> ries we tell ourselves about our economic fortunes—and show how Reaganomics,
> Thatcherism, and the rational expectations revolution failed to account for them.

The significance of psychological factors is perhaps even more evident in finance markets than in other markets for it is in this context that fear and herd mentali-ty become a heady mixture. One might argue, following Shiller that such consid-erations are also operative in labor markets and militate in favor of the commitment to a policy of full employment on grounds of generating greater public confidence alone. Providing a job for everyone who is willing to work is not just an important part of moral economy, the basis of the fair society and participation in one's community, it is also a policy imperative in these unsettled times. Yet job growth is the elusive target for the Obama administration and the relationship between investment in education and job creation does not look good following the reces-sion.

With less than a couple of years to go before the next elections and Obama hav-ing to face a roll-back in the mid-term elections it is not clear whether his man-date for education can be achieved or that he is able to turn around the economy and create enough jobs to stave off electoral defeat. In the meantime neoliberalism is back with conservative governments in Europe pursuing cuts across the board and in particular universities facing cuts of up to twenty-five percent in the UK. In the US the Republican mantra of less government, tax cuts and cuts in services to finance the growing deficit has found favor with an American public. Should the Republicans win, or indeed, even if the Tea Party manages to sustain its momentum and actually win seats in Congress to help steer the Republican Party further to the right the hope for greater education equality and provision seem des-tined to disappear.

In the next two to three years education will generate contention through the doubling and tripling of student fees. In this environment cuts to programs and to faculty will be common, leading to protests in the streets demonstrating against government mandated increases in student fees.

Notes

1. See Stiglitz's commentary at http://www.project-syndicate.org/commentary/ stiglitz101.
2. The global credit crunch started with the subprime mortgage problems in the U.S. in the three year lead-up to 2007 and the faltering of Bear Sterns which was acquired by JP Morgan Chase for $240m backed by $30b of central bank loans (March, 2008). In the UK the Government rescued Northern Rock (Feb, 2008) and Lloyds buys out HBOS. IMF warns that the credit crunch could be higher than 1 trillion dollars (April). Indymac collapses in July and U.S. government steps in to assist Fannie Mae and Freddie Mac (guarantors of $5 trillion in mortgages) and later provides the largest bailout in U.S. history. Major European banks falter. UK nationalizes much of its banking sector; other countries follow suit. U.S. passes $700b financial rescue plan (3rd October). World stock markets volatility with largest one-day gains and losses. See the BBC credit crunch timeline: http://news.bbc.co.uk/2/hi/business /7521250.stm. World-wide network effects of credit crunch become evident, not well understood by economists because of the unregulated financial derivatives and complexity of credit default-swaps. Decoupling hypothesis (e.g., China and India insulated) seems disproven. Bank of England estimates 25% decline in value of global stock markets and $2.7 trillion in credit crunch.
3. See his blog at http://johnquiggin.com/index.php/archives/2008/09/08/the-end-of-neoliberalism/.
4. See his blog at http://www.planetizen.com/node/30187.
5. The original consensus was based around the following tenants: 1. Fiscal discipline; 2. Reorientation of public expenditures; 3. Tax reform; 4. Financial liberalization; 5. Unified and competitive exchange rates; 6. Trade liberalization; 7. Openness to DFI; 8. Privatization; 9. Deregulation; 10.Secure Property Rights.
6. I take Susan George's 'A Short History of Neoliberalism' as emblematic of this movement, see http://www.zmag.org/CrisesCurEvts/Globalism/george.htm.
7. See Robert Reich's Blog at http://robertreich.blogspot.com/.
8. In this regard see, in particular, Parag Khanna's (2008) *The Second World: Empires and Influence in the New Global Order.*
9, See Wallerstein (2008) 'The Demise of Neoliberal Globalization' at http://www. monthlyreview.org/mrzine/wallerstein010208.html.

10. This is part of the IMF technical definition of global recession. The IMF estimates that global recessions seem to occur over a cycle lasting between 8 and 10 years and by their definition there have been three global recessions: 1990–1993, 1998 and 2001–2002. For the geopolitical consequences of 'The Great Crash, 2008' see Roger C. Altman, *Foreign Affairs*, 88, 1: 2–14.

11. See the Newsletter of the Bureau and maps of regional differences at http://www.bls.gov/news.release/archives/laus_01272009.pdf .

12. See Robert Shiller, 'To Build Confidence, Aim for Full Employment' At http://www.nytimes.com/2008/12/14/business/economy/14view.html?_r=1&scp=3 &sq=economic+view+and+shiller&st=nyt.

13. See e.g. my work on the 'new prudentialism and entrepreneurial self' (Peters, 2005) and related work on the knowledge and creative economy: Besley & Peters (2005), Olssen & Peters (2005) and Peters & Besley (2008).

14. See the online text at http://www.ibiblio.org/ml/libri/s/SmithA_Moral Sentiments_p.pdf.

15. See his course description of 'Behavioral and Institutional Economics' at http://www.econ.yale.edu/~shiller/course/527/ec52704.rl.htm.

16. See http://www.neweconomics.org/gen/uploads/tfi0ypn1141p45zoi0mrrgf2220 92005201739.pdf.

17. See e.g., 'Identity Economics' at http://www.staff.u-szeged.hu/~garai/Identity_ Economics.htm.

References

Abercrombie, N., Hill, S. and Turner, B. (1986) *Sovereign Individuals of Capitalism*. London, Allen and Unwin.

Akerlof, G. A. and Shiller, R. J. (2009) *Animal Spirits: How Human Psychology Drives the Economy, and Why It Matters for Global Capitalism* Princeton, Princeton University Press.

Alcorn, N. (1999) *To the Fullest Extent of His Powers: C. E. Beeby's Life in Education*, Wellington, Victoria University Press.

Alston, P. (1999) (ed. with the assistance of Mara Bustelo and James Heenan) *The EU and Human Rights*, Oxford, Oxford University Press.

Althaus, C. (1997) The Application of Agency Theory to Public Sector Management. In G. Davis, B. Sullivan and A. Yeatman (eds) *The New Contractualism*? Melbourne, Macmillan Education, 137–153.

Altman, R. C. (2009) The Great Crash, 2008: A Geopolitical Setback for the West. *Foreign Affairs* at http://tomweston.net/TheGreatCrash.pdf.

Appadurai, A. (2001) (ed.) *Globalization*. Durham, Duke University Press.

Baker, B. (2001) *In Perpetual Motion: Theories of Power, Educational History and the Child*, New York, Peter Lang.

Ball, S. (1994) *Education Reform: A Critical and Post-structural Approach*. Buckingham, Philadelphia, Open University Press.

Ball, S. (ed.) (1990) *Foucault and Education: Disciplines and Knowledge*. London, Routledge.

Ball, S., Maguire, M. and Macrae, S. (2000) *Choice, Pathways, and Transitions Post-16: New Youth, New Economies in the Global City*. London, New York, Falmer Press.

Barnett, C. (2005) The Consolations of Neoliberalism, *Geoforum* 36(1), 7–12.

Barnett, R. (2000) *Realising the University in an Age of Supercomplexity*, Ballmoor, Bucks, Open University Press.

Barry, A., Osborne, T. and Rose, N. (1996) (eds.) *Foucault and Political Reason: Liberalism, Neoliberalism and Rationalities of Government*, London, UCL Press.

Becher, T. and Kogan, M. (1994) *Graduate Education in Britain*. London, Jessica Kingsley.

Becker, G. (1964) *Human Capital; A Theoretical and Empirical Analysis, with Special Reference to Education*, New York, National Bureau of Economic Research; distributed by Columbia University Press.

Bell, D. (1973) *The Coming of Postindustrial Society: A Venture in Social Forecasting*, New York, Basic Books.

Bell, D. (1966) *The Reforming of General Education; The Columbia College Experience in Its National Setting*. With a foreword by David B. Truman. New York, Columbia University Press.

Bell, W. (2001) *Future in the Balance: Essays on Globalization and Resistance*. Oakland, Food First Books.

Berlin, I. (1969) Two Concepts of Liberty in his *Four Essays on Liberty*. Oxford, Oxford University Press, 118–72.

Bertram, G. (1988) Middle Class Capture: A Brief Survey. In *Future Directions*, Vol. III, Part II of the *April Report of the Royal Commission on Social Policy*. Wellington, Government Printer, 109–70.

Besley, A. C. (2000) *Self, Identity, Adolescence and the Professionalisation of School Counselling in New Zealand: Some Foucauldian Perspectives*. Unpublished PhD thesis, University of Auckland, NZ.

Besley, T. and Peters, M. A. (2005) Performative Epistemologies: The Theatre of Fast Knowledge, *The Review of Education, Pedagogy and Cultural Studies,* 27 (2) April-June, 111–126.

Bobbio, N. (1995) *The Age of Rights*, London, Polity Press.

Boisot, M. (1998) *Knowledge Assets: Securing Competitive Advantage in the Information Economy*, Oxford, Oxford University Press.

Boston, J. (1991) The Theoretical Underpinnings of Public Sector Restructuring. In J. Boston, J. Martin, J. Pallot and P. Walsh (eds.), *Reshaping the State: New Zealand's Bureaucratic Revolution*, Auckland, Oxford University Press, 1–26.

Boston, J. and Cooper, F. (1989) The Treasury: Advice, Co-ordination and Control. In H. Gold (ed.), *New Zealand Politics in Perspective*, 2nd Edition. Auckland, Longman Paul.

Boston, J. and Paul, D. (1992) *The Decent Society? Essays in Response to National Economic and Social Policies* . Auckland, Oxford University Press.

Bourdieu, P. (1998) L'essence du néolibéralisme, *Le Monde diplomatique* Mars 1998, http://www.monde-diplomatique.fr/1998/03/BOURDIEU/10167.

Bourner, T., Bowden, R. and Laing, S. (2000) The Adoption of Professional Doctorates in English Universities: Why Here? Why Now? Presentation for the Professional

Doctorates 3rd Biennial International Conference, Doctoral Education and Professional Practice: The Next Generation. University of New England, Armidale, NSW, Australia, 10–12 September.

Bratich, J. Z., Packer, J. and McCarthy, C. (2003) *Foucault, Cultural Studies, and Governmentality*, New York, State University of New York Press.

Bremmer, I. (2010) *The End of the Free Market: Who Wins the Way Between States and Corporations?*, New York, Viking.

Brennan, J. and Little, B. (1996) *A Review of Work-Based Learning in Higher Education.* London, Department of Education and Employment.

Britton, S., Le Heron, R. and Pawson, E. (1992) *Changing Places in New Zealand: A Geography of Restructuring.* Christchurch, New Zealand, New Zealand Geographical Society.

Bröckling, U., Krasmann, S. and Lemke, T. (2009) *Governmentality: Current Issues and Future Challenges*, London, Routledge.

Broyer, S. (1996) The Social Market Economy: Birth of An Economic Style, Discussion paper FS I 96–318, Social Science Research Center, Berlin.

Buchanan, J. (1975) *The Limits of Liberty: Between Anarchy and Leviathan.* Chicago, University of Chicago Press.

Buchanan, J. (1991) *Constitutional Economics,* Oxford, UK ; Cambridge, MA, Blackwell, 1991.

Buchanan, J.M. (1986) *Liberty, Market and the State: Political Economy in the 1980s*, Brighton, Wheatsheaf Books.

Buchanan, J. and Tullock, G. (1962) *The Calculus of Consent, Logical Foundations of Constitutional Democracy*, Ann Arbor, University of Michigan Press.

Burchell, D. (1997) "Liberalism" and Government: Political Philosophy and the Liberal Art of Rule. In C. O'Farrell (ed.), *Foucault, the Legacy.* Brisbane, Queensland University of Technology.

Burchell, G. (1993) Liberal Government and Techniques of the Self. *Economy and Society*, 22 (3), 267–282. Also in A. Barry, T. Osborne, N. Rose (Eds.), *Foucault and Political Reason,* 19–36. London, UCL Press.

Burchell, G., Gordon, C. and Miller, P. (Eds.) (1991) *The Foucault Effect: Studies in Governmentality.* Hemel Hempstead, England, Harvester Press.

Burton-Jones, A. (1999) *Knowledge Capitalism: Business, Work and Learning in the New Economy*, Oxford, Oxford University Press.

Bushnell, P. and G. Scott (1988) An Economic Perspective. In J. Martin & J. Harper (eds.) *Devolution and Accountability.* Wellington, G. P. Books.

Capper, P. (1992) Curriculum 1991. *New Zealand Annual Review of Education*, 1, 15–27.

Carnoy, M. (1995) Structural Adjustment and the Changing Face of Education. *International Labour Review*, 653–673.

Carnoy, M. and Rhoten, D. (2002) What Does Globalization Mean for Educational Change? A Comparative Approach, *Comparative Education Review*, 46 (1), 1–9.

Carnoy, M. (2000) *Globalization and Educational Restructuring*, Paris, International Institute of Educational Planning.

Carpinter, A. (1991) *Managing Data, Knowledge and Know-how: Information Policy Issues for the 1990s*. Wellington, National Library of New Zealand.

Carter, I. (1993) *Gadfly: The Life and Times of James Shelley*, Auckland, Auckland University Press, in association with Broadcasting History Trust.

Castles, F. (1985) *The Working Class and Welfare*. Sydney, Allen & Unwin.

Castles, F. and Mitchell, D. (1992) Identifying Welfare State Regimes: The Link between Politics, Instruments and Outcomes, *Governance*, 5 (1), 12–18.

Chomsky, N. (1999) *Profit over People—Neoliberalism and Global Order*. New York, Seven Stories Press.

Choo, C. W. (1998) *The Knowing Organization: How Organizations Use Information to Construct Meaning, Create Knowledge, and Make Decisions*, Oxford, Oxford University Press.

Chorev, N. (2010) *On the Origins of Neoliberalism: Political Shifts and Analytical Challenges*. New York, Springer.

Ciccarelli, R. (2008) Reframing Political Freedom: An Analysis of Governmentality, *European Journal of Legal Studies*, 2008, 1, 3, 307–327. Special conference issue.

Clark, M. (1998) (ed.) *Peter Fraser, Master Politician*, Palmerston North, NZ, Dunmore Press.

Clarke, C. (1998) Resurrecting Research to Raise Standards, *ESRC Updates ESRC Corporate News*, *http://www.esrc.ac.uk*.

Cox, R. W. (1997a) Influences and Commitments, in *Approaches to World Order*, New York, Cambridge University Press.

Cox, R. W. (1997b) The Global Political Economy and Social Choice, in *Approaches to World Order*, New York, Cambridge University Press.

Crampton, J.W. and Eldon, S. (2007) *Space, Knowledge and Power: Foucault and Geography*, London, Ashgate.

Crocombe, G.T., Enright, M. and Porter, M. (1991) *Upgrading New Zealand's Competitive Advantage*. Auckland, Oxford University Press.

Cullenberg, S., Amariglio, J., and Ruccio, D. (2001) *Postmodernism, Economics and Knowledge*. New York, Routledge.

Curtis, B. (2002) Foucault on Governmentality and Population: The Impossible Discovery, *Canadian Journal of Sociology*, Fall, 27, 4, 505–35.

Dahlman, C. and Aubert, J-E (2001) *China and the Knowledge Economy: Seizing the 21st Century*, Washington, The World Bank.

Dale, R. (1994) The State and Education, in A. Sharp (ed.), *Leap into the Dark: The Changing Role of the State in New Zealand since 1984*, 68–87. Auckland, Auckland University Press.

Dale, R. and Jesson, J. (1992) Mainstreaming Education: The Role of the State Services Commission. *Annual Review of Education*, 2, 7–34.

Dalziel, P. (1992) 'Policies for a Just Society.' In J. Boston and P. Dalziel (eds.) *The Decent Society?* Auckland, Oxford University Press: 208–223.

Davenport, T. H. and Prusak, L. (1997) *Working Knowledge: How Organizations Manage What They Know*, Boston, Harvard Business School Press.

Davis, J. B. (2003) *The Theory of the Individual in Economics*. London, Routledge.

Day, R. B. (2002) History, Reason and Hope: A Comparative Study of Kant, Hayek and Habermas, *Humanitas*, XV, No 2. 4–24.

Dean, M. (1991) *The Constitution of Poverty: Toward a Genealogy of Liberal Governance*. London, Routledge.

Dean, M. (1999) *Governmentality: Power and Rule in Modern Society*. London, Sage.

Dean, M. and B. Hindess (eds.) (1998) *Governing Australia: Studies in Contemporary Rationalities of Government*. Cambridge, Cambridge University Press.

Deane, R. (1989) *Corporatisation and privatisation: A discussion of the issues*. Wellington, Electrocorp.

Death, C. (2006) Resisting (Nuclear) Power? Environmental Regulation and Eco-governmentality in South Africa, *Review of African Political Economy*, 33 (109) 407–424.

Defert, D. (1991) Popular Life" and Insurance Technology. In G. Burchell, C. Gordon, P. Miller (eds.), *The Foucault Effect: Studies in Governmentality*, 211–237. Hemel Hempstead, England, Harvester Wheatsheaf.

Deleuze, G. (1995) Postscript on Control Societies. *Negotiations 1972–1990*, trans. M. Joughin. New York, Columbia University Press.

Department for Trade and Industry, UK (1998a) *Our Competitive Future: Building the Knowledge-Driven Economy*. London, Cm4176.

Department for Trade and Industry, UK (1998b) *Our Competitive Future: Building the Knowledge-Driven Economy: Analytical Background*. http://www.dti.gov.uk/comp/competitive/an_reprt.htm

Department of Education (NZ) (1988a) *Administering for Excellence: Effective Administration in Education* (The Picot Report), Wellington, Government Printer.

Department of Education, (NZ) (1988b) *Report of the Early Childhood Care and Education Working Group* (The Meade Report), Wellington, Government Printer.

Department of Education, (NZ) (1988c) *Report of the Working Group on Post-Compulsory Education and Training* (The Hawke Report), Wellington, Government Printer.

Department of Education, (NZ) (1988d) *Tomorrow's Schools: The Reform of Educational Administration in New Zealand*, Wellington, Government Printer.

Department of Education, (NZ) (1988, 1989) *Learning for Life*, and *Learning for Life Two*, Wellington, Government Printer.

Department of Education & Employment (DfEE) (UK) (1999) Baroness Blackstone Welcomes Boost to University Teaching Standards, *DfEE Press Release 287/99*, 23 June.

Derrida, J. (1982) The Ends of Man. In J. Derrida, *Margins of Philosophy*, trans. A Bass, Chicago, Chicago University Press.

Dewey, J. (1916) *Democracy and Education*. New York, Macmillan.

DiZerega, G. (1989) Democracy as Spontaneous Order, *Critical Review*. (Spring), 206–240.

Donnelly, J. (1989) *Universal Human Rights in Theory and Practice*, Ithaca, Cornell University Press.

Donzelot, J. (1979) *The Policing of Families*. Trans. R. Hurley, Foreword by G. Deleuze. New York, Pantheon Books.

Donzelot, J. (1991) The Mobilization of Society. In G. Burchell, C. Gordon, P. Miller (Eds.), *The Foucault Effect: Studies in Governmentality*, 169–180. Hemel Hempstead, England, Harvester Wheatsheaf.

Douglas, R. (1989) The Politics of Successful Reform, speech to the Mont Pelerin Society, Australia. In R. Douglas *Unfinished Business*. Auckland, Random House.

Douglas, R. (1993) *Unfinished Business*. Auckland, Random House.

Drucker, P. (1959) *Landmarks of Tomorrow: A Report on the New 'Post-Modern.'* New York, Transaction.

Drucker, P. (1994) The Age of Social Transformation, *The Atlantic Monthly*, Nov., 274, 5, 53(18).

Du Gay, P. (1996) *Consumption and Identity at Work*. London, Sage.

Duncan, I. and Bollard, A. (1992) *Corporatisation & Privatisation: Lessons from New Zealand*. Auckland, Oxford University Press.

During, S. (1990) Postmodernism or Post-Colonialism Today. In A. Milner, P. Thomson and C. Worth (Eds.) *Postmodern Conditions*. Providence, R.I., Berg Publishers, 113–131.

Dworkin, R. (1977) *Taking Rights Seriously*, Cambridge, Harvard University Press.

Easton, B. (1990) Policy as Revolution: Two Case Studies. Paper presented at the New Zealand Political Studies Association Annual Conference, Dunedin.

Ebenstein, A. (2003) *Hayek's Journey*. New York, Palgrave Macmillan.

Economy, E. C. and Segal, A. (2009) The G-2 Mirage: Why the United States and China Are Not Ready to Upgrade Ties, *Foreign Affairs*, May/June: 14–23.

Edvinnson, L. and Malone, M. S. (1997) *Intellectual Capital*, London, Piatkus.

Esping-Anderson, G. (1990) *The Three Worlds of Welfare Capitalism*. Princeton, Princeton University Press.

Fairburn, M. (1989) *The Ideal Society and Its Enemies: The Foundations of Modern New Zealand Society, 1850–1900*, Auckland, Auckland University Press.

Ferge, S. (1997) The Changed Welfare Paradigm: The Individualization of the Social. *Social Policy and Administration*, 31(1), 20–44.

Ferguson, A. (1996) An Essay on the History of Civil Society 1767, edited with Introduction by Duncan Forbes, Edinburgh, Edinburgh University Press.

Foray, D. and Lundvall, B. (1996) The Knowledge-based Economy: From the Economics of Knowledge to the Learning Economy. In OECD, *Employment and Growth in the Knowledge-based Economy*. Paris, OECD.

Forrester, I. (1991) *New Zealand, Repositioning for the Information Age: 'A World Communications Laboratory': The Vision and the Reality*. Wellington, the Ministry of Research, Science and Technology.

Foucault, M. (1973) *The Order of Things: An Archaeology of the Human Sciences*. New York, Vintage Books.

Foucault, M. (1977) *Discipline and Punish: The Birth of the Prison*. Trans. Alan Sheridan. London, Penguin, 195–228.

Foucault, M. (1977) *Language, Counter-Memory, Practice: Selected Essays and Interviews,* ed. Donald Bouchard. Oxford, Blackwell, 204–217.

Foucault, M. (1982) The Subject and Power. In H. Dreyfus and P. Rabinow (eds.), *Michel Foucault: Beyond Structuralism and Hermeneutics*, Brighton, Harvester Press, 208–226.

Foucault, M. (1982) Space, Knowledge and Power: Interview. *Skyline*, March. (PAGES?)

Foucault, M. (1984) "What Is Enlightenment?" *The Foucault Reader,* ed. Paul Rabinow. New York, Pantheon, 32–50.

Foucault, M. (1985) *The Use of Pleasure: The History of Sexuality,* Volume 2. Trans. Robert Hurley. New York, Pantheon, 29–30.

Foucault, M. (1986) *Kant on Enlightenment and Revolution.* Trans. Colin Gordon. *Economy and Society* 15.1: 88–96.

Foucault, M. (1988a) 'The Political Technology of Individuals'. In *Technoogies of the Self: A Seminar with Michel Foucault*, Martin L. H. et al. (eds.), London: Tavistock.

Foucault, M. (1988b) *Technologies of the Self: A seminar with Michel Foucault*. Luther H. Martin, Huck Gutman, Patrick H, Hutton (eds), Amherst, University of Massachusetts Press.

Foucault, M. (1989) Résumé des cours 1970–1982, Paris: conferencs, essais et lecons du Collège de France, Paris, Julliard.

Foucault, M. (1989) An Aesthetics of Existence. In *Foucault Live*, New York, Semiotext(e):309–316.

Foucault, M. (1991a) Governmentality in Graham Burchell, Colin Gordon, Peter Miller (eds.) *The Foucault Effect: Studies in Governmentality,* pp. 87–104. Hemel Hempstead, England, Harvester Press

Foucault, M. (1991b) *Remarks on Marx: Conversations with Duccio Trombadori,* trans. R. James Goldstein and James Cascaito, New York, Semiotext(e).

Foucault, M. (1997) The Ethics of the Concern for the Self as a Practice of Freedom. *Ethics: Subjectivity and Truth. Essential Works of Michel Foucault, 1954–1984*, ed. Paul Rabinow. Trans. Robert J. Hurley. Vol. 1. London, Penguin, 281–301.

Foucault, M. (2001) *Power: Michel Foucault: The Essential Works 1954–1984*, 3, ed. J.D. Faubion, trans. R. Hurley and others, London, Allen Lane & The Penguin Press.

Foucault, M. (2003) *Society Must Be Defended*. Trans. D. Macey. New York, Picador.

Foucault, M. (2004a) *Sécurité, Territoire, Population: Cours au collège de France (1977–1978)*, Édition établie sous la direction de Francois Ewald et Alessandro Fontana, par Michel Senellart, Paris, Éditions Gallimand et des Éditions du Seuill.

Foucault, M. (2004b) *Naissance de la biopolitique: Cours au collège de France* (1978–1979), Édition établie sous la direction de Francois Ewald et Alessandro Fontana, par Michel Senellart, Paris, Éditions Gallimand et des Éditions du Seuill.

Freeman, M. (1994) The Philosophical Foundations of Human Rights," *Human Rights Quarterly*, August 16, 3, 491–514.

Friedland, R. and Robertson, A. F. (1990) Rethinking the Marketplace. In R. Friedland and A. Robertson (eds.), *Beyond the Marketplace: Rethinking Economy and Society*. New York, Walter de Gruyter, 3–52.

Friedman, M. (1962) *Capitalism and Freedom*, with the assistance of Rose D. Friedman. Chicago, University of Chicago Press.

Friedman, M. (1989) Feminism and Modern Friendship: Dislocating the Community, *Ethics*, 99, 275–290.

Friedman, M. (1994) *Introduction to the 50th anniversary edition of F.A. Hayek's* Road to Serfdom. *Booknotes*. Retrieved from http://www.booknotes.org/Transcript/?Program ID=1226.

Garret, E. M. and Bates, R.J. (1977) Education: Socialisation, Social Welfare and Social Control. In A. D. Trlin, ed., *Social Welfare and New Zealand Society*. Wellington, Methuen, 61–77.

Gaus, G. F. (1996) *Justificatory Liberalism: An Essay on Epistemology and Political Theory*. New York, Oxford University Press

Gewirth, A. (1982) *Human Rights: Essays on Justification and Application*, Chicago, University of Chicago Press.

Gillborn, D. and Youdell, D. (2000) *Rationing Education: Policy, Practice, Reform, and Equity*. Buckingham [England] Philadelphia, Open University Press.

Gokay, B. (2009) The 2008 World Economic Crisis: Global Shifts and Faultlines, *Global Research*, at http://www.globalresearch.ca/index.php?context=va&aid=12283.

Gordon, C. (1991) Governmental Rationality: An Introduction. In G. Burchell, C. Gordon, P. Miller (eds.), *The Foucault Effect: Studies in Governmentality*. Hemel Hempstead, England, Harvester Wheatsheaf.

Gordon, C. (1996) Foucault in Britain. In A. Barry, T. Osborne, N. Rose (eds.), *Foucault and Political Reason*, London, UCL Press, 253–270.

Gordon, C. (2001) Introduction to *Power: Michel Foucault The Essential Works 1954–1984*, 3, ed. J.D. Faubion, trans. R. Hurley and others, London, Allen Lane & The Penguin Press, xi-xli.

Gordon, L. (1992) The State, Devolution and Educational Reform in New Zealand. *Journal of Education Policy*, 7(2), 187–203.

Gordon, L. (1994) Is School Choice a Sustainable Policy for New Zealand? A Review of Recent Research Findings and a Look to the Future. *New Zealand Annual Review of Education*, 4, 9–24.

Gray, J. (1982) F. A. Hayek and the Rebirth of Classical Liberalism, Literature of Liberty, vol. v, no. 4, Winter, at: http://www.econlib.org/library/Essays/LtrLbrty/gryHRC.html

Gray, J. (1984) *Hayek on Liberty*. Oxford, Blackwell.

Gray, J. (1999) *False Dawn: The Delusions of Global Capitalism*. London , Granta Books.

Green, D. (1987) *The New Right: The Counter-Revolution in Political and Economic Thought*, Brighton, Wheatsheaf Books.

Greer, P. (1992) The Next Steps Initiative: The Transformation of Britain's Civil Service. *The Political Quarterly*, 63, April/June, 222–227.

Gruber, D. (1989) Foucault's Critique of the Liberal Individual, *The Journal of Philosophy*, LXXXVI (11), 615–621.

Hale, S. (2000) Professor Macmurray and Mr. Blair: The Strange Case of the Communitarian Guru That Never Was. Available at http://www.sussex.ac.uk/Units /CST/for/3rdway/ (last accessed 27/02/04).

Halford, S. and Leonard, P. (1999) New Identities? Professionalism, Managerialism and the Construction of Self, in M. Exworthy and S. Halford (eds.), *Professionals and the New Managerialism in the Public Sector.* Buckingham, Open University Press.

Hall, S. (1991) Old and New Identities, Old and New Ethnicities in A. King (ed.) *Culture, Globalisation and the World System: Contemporary Conditions for the Representation of Identity.* London, Macmillan, 41–68.

Hall, S. (1992) New Ethnicities in J. Donald and A. Rattansi (eds.) *'Race,' Culture and Difference.* London, Sage, 252–259.

Hanson, E.A. (1975) The Social Security Story: A Study of the Political Origins of the 1938 Social Security Act. MA thesis, University of Auckland, NZ.

Harris, M (1996) *Report of the HEFCE, CVCP, SCOP Review of Postgraduate Education.* Bristol, HEFCE.

Hartwell, R. M. (1955) *A History of the Mont Pelerin Society.* Indianapolis, Liberty Fund.

Hartwich, O. M. (2009) Neoliberalism: The Genesis of a Political Swearword, CIS Occasional Paper 114, http://www.cis.org.au/temp/op114_neoliberalism.pdf.

Harvey, D. (2005) *A Brief History of Neoliberalism.* New York, Oxford University Press.

Hayek, F. A. (1937) Economics and Knowledge, Economica IV. Available at: (http://www.hayekcenter.org/friedrichhayek/hayek.html).

Hayek, F. A. (1944) *The Road to Serfdom.* London, Routledge & Kegan Paul.

Hayek, F. A. (1945) The Use of Knowledge in Society, *American Economic Review* XXXV, 4: 519–30. (http://www.hayekcenter.org/friedrichhayek/hayek.html).

Hayek, F. A. (1948) *Individualism and Economic Order.* Chicago, University of Chicago Press.

Hayek, F. A. (1952) *The Sensory Order.* London, Routledge & Kegan Paul.

Hayek, F. A. (1960) *The Constitution of Liberty.* London, Routledge & Kegan Paul.

Hayek, F. A. (1967) *Studies in Philosophy, Politics and Economics.* London, Routledge & Kegan Paul.

Hayek, F. A. (1973) *Law, Legislation & Liberty, Vol.1.* London, Routledge & Kegan Paul.

Hayek, F. A. (1976) *Law, Legislation and Liberty, Vol.II: The Mirage of Social Justice.* London, Routledge & Kegan Paul.

Hayek, F. A. (1978) *New Studies in Philosophy, Politics, Economics and the History of Ideas.* Chicago, University of Chicago Press.

Hayek, F. A. (1992) *The Fortunes of Liberalism: Essays on Austrian Economics and the Ideal of Freedom*, The Collected Works of F.A. Hayek, Vol 4, ed. Peter G. Klein, Chicago, University of Chicago Press.

Hayek, F. A. (2007) *The Road to Serfdom: Text and Documents—The Definitive Edition* by F. A. Hayek, ed. Bruce Caldwell, Chicago, University of Chicago Press.

Hayes, C. (2009) *Popper, Hayek and the Open Society*. London, Routledge.

Hede, A. (1991) The Next Steps Initiative for Civil Service Reform in Britain: The Emergence of Managerialism in Whitehall? *Canberra Bulletin of Public Administration*, 65, 32–40.

Hega, G.M. and Hokenmaier,K. A. (2002) The Welfare State and Education: A Comparison of Social and Educational Policy in Advanced Industrial Societies, *German Policy Studies*, Vol. 2, No. 1. (PAGES?)

Henderson, D. (1999) *The Changing Fortunes of Economic Liberalism: Yesterday, Today and Tomorrow* with an Introduction by Nigel Lawson and an excerpt from Milton and Rose Friedman, Wellington, the Institute of Public Affairs & New Zealand Business Roundtable.

Henig, J., Hamnett, C. and Feigenbaum, H. (1988) The Politics of Privatisation: A Comparative Perspective, *Governance*, 1, (4), 442–68.

Hindess, B. (1996) *Discourses of Power: From Hobbes to Foucault*. Oxford, Blackwell.

Hindess, B. (1997) Politics and Governmentality. *Economy and Society*, 26 (2), 252–272.

Hood, C. (1991) A Public Management for All Seasons?, *Public Administration*, 69 (Spring): 3–19.

Howard, R. E. (1993) Cultural Absolutism and the Nostalgia for Community, *Human Rights Quarterly*, May 1993 15, 2, 315–338.

Hull, R. (2003) *The Great Lie: Markets, Freedom and Knowledge*. Retrieved from http://homepages.3-c.coop/richard/MyChapter.pdf.

Illich, I. (1971) *Deschooling Society*, London, Calder & Boyars.

International Labour Organisation (ILO) 2007. *Equality at Work: Tackling the Challenges*. Report 1(B). Geneva, International Labour Office.

Jackson, B. (2010) At the Origins of Neo-Liberalism: The Free Economy and the Strong State, 1930–1947, *The Historical Journal*, 53, 1: 129–151.

James, H. (2009) The Making of a Mess: Who Broke Global Finance, and Who Should Pay for It?, *Foreign Affairs*, January/February. (PAGES?)

Jameson, F. (1985) Postmodernism and Consumer Society. In H. Foster (ed.), *Postmodern Culture*, London, Pluto Press: 111–125.

Jesson, B. (1992) The Disintegration of a Labour Tradition: New Zealand Politics in the 1980s, *New Left Review*, 1/192, 37–54.

Joerges, C. and Rödl, F. (2004) "Social Market Economy" as Europe's Social Model?, European University Institute (Florence) Working paper LAW No. 2004/8 at www.iut.it.

Joppke, C. (1987) The Crisis of the Welfare State, Collective Consumption, and the Rise of New Social Actors, *Berkeley Journal of Sociology*, XXXII, 237–260.

Kamenka, E. (1978) The Anatomy of an Idea in Kamenka, Eugene and Alice Erh-Soon Tay, (eds.) *Human Rights*, New York, St. Martin's Press.

Kelsey, J. (1993) *Rolling Back the State: Privatisation of Power in Aotearoa/New Zealand.* Wellington, Bridget Williams Books.

Kelsey, J. (1997) *The New Zealand Experiment: A World Model for Structural Adjustment?* Auckland, Auckland University Press/ Bridget Williams Books.

Khanna, P. (2008) *The Second World: Empires and Influence in the New Global Order.* New York, Random House.

King, D. (1987) *The New Right: Politics, Markets and Citizenship*, London, Macmillan Press.

King, M. (1998) The Origins of Peter Fraser's Early Radicalism in Clark, Margaret (1998) ed. *Peter Fraser Master Politician*, Palmerston North, NZ, Dunmore Press.

Klaes, M. (2008) Postmodernism, *New Palgrave Dictionary of Economics.* S. Durlauf and L. Blume (eds.) New York, Palgrave Macmillan. Retrieved from http://e-notes.co.uk/pdf/2008-Klaes-Pomo-preprint.pdf.

Krogh, G. von, Ichijo, K.and Nonaka, I.(2000) *Enabling Knowledge Creation: How to Unlock the Mystery of Tacit Knowledge and Release the Power of Innovation*, Oxford, Oxford University Press.

Laclau, E. and Mouffe, C. (1985) *Hegemony and Socialist Strategy :Towards a Radical Democratic Politics*, trans. Winston Moore and Paul Cammack, London, Verso, (esp. pp. 153–155).

Lankshear, C., Peters, M.A., and Knobel, M. (2000) Information, Knowledge, and Learning: Some Issues Facing Epistemology and Education in a Digital Age, *Enquiries at the Interface: Philosophical Problems of On-line Education*, Nigel Blake and Paul Standish (eds.), special issue, *Journal of Philosophy of Education*, 34 (1), 17–39.

Larner, W. and Walters, W. (2004) Globalization as Governmentality, *Alternatives: Global, Local, Political*, Vol 29, Special Issue—*Governing Society Today*, ed. Mitchell Dean and Paul Henman, 495–514.

Larner, W. (2000) Neo-liberalism: Policy, Ideology, Governmentality, *Studies in Political Economy* 63 (Autumn), 5–25.

Larner,W. and Walters, W. (2004) *Global Governmentality*, London, Routledge.

Lauder, H. (1994) *The Creation of Market Connections for Education in New Zealand: An Empirical Analysis of a New Zealand Secondary School Market 1990–1993.* Wellington, Ministry of Education.

Le Grand, J. (1982) *The Strategy of Equality.* London, Allen and Unwin.

Le Grand, J. (1987) The Middle Class and the Use of British Social Services. In R. Goodin and J. Le Grand (eds.), *Not Only the Poor.* London, Allen and Unwin.

Le Grand, J. and Robinson, R. (1984) Privatisation and the Welfare State: An Introduction, in J. Le Grand and R. Robinson (eds.), *Privatisation and the Welfare State*, London, Allen and Unwin.

Le Heron, R. and E. Pawson (1996) *Changing Places: New Zealand in the Nineties.* Auckland, New Zealand, Longman Paul.

Le Heron, R. (2007) Globalisation, Governance and Poststructural Political Economy: Perspectives from Australasia, *Asia Pacific Viewpoint* 48 (1), 26–40.

Leander, A. and van Munster, R. (2006) Neo-Liberal Governmentality of Contemporary Security: Understanding Private Security Contractors in Darfur and EU Immigration Control. Paper presented at the annual meeting of the International Studies Association, Town & Country Resort and Convention Center, San Diego, California, Mar. 22, 2006 at http://www.allacademic.com/meta/p98828_index.html.

Li, T. M. (2007) *The Will to Improve: Governmentality, Development, and the Practice of Politics.* Durham, Duke University Press.

Li, X. (1998) Postmodernism and Universal Human Rights: Why Theory and Reality Don't Mix, *Free Inquiry,* Fall 1998, 18, 4, 28(4). At: http://www.secularhumanism .org.library/fi/li_18_4.html

Lipschutz, R.D. and Rowe, J.K. (2005) *Globalization, Governmentality and Global Politics: Regulation for the Rest of Us?* London, Routledge.

Lucas, R.E. (1988) On the Mechanisms of Economic Development, *Journal of Monetary Economics,* 22, 3–22.

Luke, T.W. (n.d.) Generating Green Governmentality: A Cultural Critique of Environmental Studies as a Power/Knowledge Formation at http://www.cddc.vt. edu/tim/tims/Tim514a.PDF.

Lyotard, J.-F. (1993) The Other's Rights, in Stephen Shute and Susan Hurley (eds.) *On Human Rights*, The Oxford Amnesty Lectures, New York, Basic Books, 135–148.

Lyotard, J.-F.(1984) *The Postmodern Condition: A Report on Knowledge*, trans. G. Bennington and B. Massumi, Manchester, Manchester University Press.

Macdonald, L. and Ruckert, A. (2009) (eds.) *Post-Neoliberalism in the Americas.* New York, Palgrave Macmillan.

Machlup, F. (1962) *The Production and Distribution of Knowledge in the United States,* Princeton, NJ, Princeton University Press.

Machlup, F. (1970) *Education and Economic Growth*, Lincoln, University of Nebraska Press.

Machlup, F. (1980) *Knowledge and Knowledge Production.* Princeton Guildford, Princeton University Press.

Machlup, F. (1980) *Knowledge, Its creation, Distribution, and Economic Significance*, Princeton, NJ, Princeton University Press.

MacIntyre, A. (1981) *After Virtue: A Study in Moral Theory*, London, Duckworth

Macpherson, C.B. (1962) *The Political Theory of Possessive Individualism: Hobbes to Locke.* Oxford, Clarendon Press.

Mandle, J. (2001) *Globalization and the Poor.* Cambridge, Cambridge University Press.

Marginson, S. (1997) Competition and Contestability in Australian Higher Education, 1987–1997. *Australian Universities Review*, 40 (1), 5–14.

Marginson, S. (1999) Harvards of the Antipodes? Nation Building Universities in a Global Environment. *Access: Critical Perspectives on Cultural and Policy Studies in Education.* 18 (2), 1–20.

Marginson, S. and Considine, M. (2000) *The Enterprise University: Governance, Strategy, Reinvention.* Melbourne, Cambridge University Press.

Marion, M. (2005) Louis Rougier, the Vienna Circle and the Unity of Science, *Veröffentlichungen des Instituts Wiener Kreis*, Vol 13, Vienna, Springer.

Marshall, J. (1996) *Michel Foucault: Personal Autonomy and Education.* Dordrecht, Kluewer.

Marshall, J.D., Peters, M.A. and Smith, G. (1991) The Business Roundtable and the Privatisation of Education: Individualism and the Attack on Maori. In L. Gordon and J. Codd (eds.), *Education Policy and the Changing Role of the State*, Massey University, Delta,81–98.

Marshall, T. H. (1950) *Citizenship and Social Class and Other Essays.* Cambridge, Cambridge University Press.

Masschelein, J. Simons, M., Brockling, U. and Pongratz, L. (2007) *The Learning Society from the Perspective of Governmentality, Educational Philosophy and Theory* Monograph series, Oxford, Blackwell.

Matheson, A. (1997) The Impact of Contracts on Public Management. In G. Davis, B. Sullivan and A. Yeatman (eds.) *The New Contractualism?* Melbourne, Macmillan.

Mattessich, R. (1993) On the Nature of Information and Knowledge and the Interpretation in the Economic Sciences, *Library Trends*, Spring 41, (4), 567 (27).

McKean, R. (1974) Property Rights within Government, and Devices to Increase Governmental Efficiency. In E. G. Furubotn and S. Pejovich (eds.), *The Economics of Property Rights*. Pensacola,FL , Ballinger.

Merlingen, M. (2006) Foucault and World Politics: Promises and Challenges of Extending Governmentality Theory to the European and Beyond, *Millennium* 35 (1), 181–196.

Middleton, S. (1998) *Disciplining Sexuality: Foucault, Life Histories and Education.* New York & London, Teachers College Press.

Miller, D. and Walzer, M. (1995) (eds.) *Pluralism, Justice, and Equality*, Oxford, Oxford University Press.

Miller, P., Rose, N. (1990) Governing Economic Life, *Economy and Society*, 19 (1): 1–31.

Ministry of Research, Science and Technology (MoRST), NZ (1998) *Building Tomorrow's Success: Guidelines for Thinking beyond Today. The Foresight Project*, MoRST, Wellington. See the Ministry's web site at: http://www.morst.govt.nz/foresight/front.html

Mirowski, P. (2003) *Machine Dreams: Economics Becomes a Cyborg Science.* Cambridge, Cambridge University Press.

Mirowski, P. (2009) Postface: Defining Neoliberalism. In Philip Mirowski and Dieter Plehwe, *The Road from Mont Pèlerin: The Making of the Neoliberal Thought Collective.* Cambridge, MA, Harvard University Press, 417–455.

Mirowsky, P. and Plehwe, D. (2009) *The Road from Mont Pèlerin: the Making of the Neoliberal Thought Collective*, Cambridge, MA, Harvard University Press.

Mishra, R. (1999) *Globalization and the Welfare State.* Cheltenham, Edward Elgar.

Mont Pèlerin Society (1947–): Inventory of the General Meeting Files (1947–1998). Retrieved from http://www.liberaalarchief.be/MPS2005.pdf

Mouffe, C. (1988) Radical Democracy: Modern or Postmodern? trans. P. Holdengraber in A. Ross (ed.) *Universal Abandon? The Politics of Postmodernism.* Minneapolis, University of Minnesota Press.

Müller, J-W. (2008) Fear and Freedom: On 'Cold War Liberalism,' *European Journal of Political Theory,* 7; 45–64.

Nadesan, M.H. (2008) *Governmentality, Biopower, and Everyday Life*, London, Routledge.

Nixon, J., Marks, A., Rowland, S. and Walker, M. (2001) Towards a New Academic Professionalism: A Manifesto of Hope. *British Journal of the Sociology of Education,* 22 (2), 227–244.

Nonaka, I. and Nishiguchi, T. (2001) *Knowledge Emergence: Social, Technical, and Evolutionary Dimensions of Knowledge Creation*, Oxford, Oxford University Press.

Nozick, R. (1974) *Anarchy, State and Utopia*, Oxford, Blackwell.

O'Connor, J. (1984) *Accumulation Crisis*. New York, Basil Blackwell.

OECD (1987) *Universities Under Scrutiny* by William Taylor, Paris, The Organisation.

OECD (1988) *New Technologies in the 1990s: A Socio-Economic Strategy*, Paris, The Organisation.

OECD (1991) Information Networks and New Information Technologies: Emerging Economic Opportunities and Implications for IT Policies in the 1990s (Final Analytical Report), Expert Group on Economic Implications of Information Technologies, Paris, The Organisation.

OECD (1996a) *Measuring What People Know: Human Capital: Accounting for the Knowledge Economy*, Paris, The Organisation.

OECD (1996b) *The Knowledge-based Economy*. Paris, The Organization.

OECD (1996c) *Employment and Growth in the Knowledge-based Economy*, OECD Documents, Paris, The Organisation.

Offe, C. (1984) *Contradictions of the Welfare State.* London, Hutchinson.

Oliver, W.H. (1989) The Labour Caucus and Economic Policy Formation, 1981–1984. In B. Easton, ed., *The Making of Rogernomics.* Auckland, Auckland University Press.

Olssen, M. (1999) *Michel Foucault: Materialism and Education.* Westport, CT & London, Bergin & Garvey.

Olssen, M. (2002a) *The Neo-Liberal Appropriation of Tertiary Education Policy in New Zealand: Accountability, Research and Academic Freedom*, State of the Art Monograph, No. 8, Wellington, New Zealand Association for Research in Education.

Olssen, M. (2002b) Terrorism, Globalisation and Democracy. On Reading Michael Peters Post 9/11, *Access: Critical Perspectives on Communication, Cultural and Policy Studies,* 21 (1): 75–90.

Olssen, M. (2002c) Citizenship, Difference and Education. In David Scott and Helen Lawson (Eds.) *Curriculum and Assessment*, (series: *International Perspectives on Curriculum*) July, 7–26, Westport, CT, Greenwood.

Olssen, M. (2002d) Michel Foucault as 'Thin' Communitarian: Difference, Community, Democracy, *Cultural Studies—Critical Methodologies,* 2 (4), November, 483—513.

Olssen, M. (2003a) Structuralism, Post-Structuralism, Neo-Liberalism: Assessing Foucault's Legacy, *Journal of Education Policy*, 18 (2), 189–202.

Olssen, M. (2003b) Foucault's Conception of Critique: Kant, Humanism and the Human Sciences, in Peters, M., Olssen, M., Lankshear, C. (eds.), *Futures of Critical Theory: Dreams of Difference*, lanham, MD, Rowman and Littlefield, 73—102.

Olssen, M. (2004) The School as the Microscope of Conduct: On Doing Foucauldian Research in Education, in J. Marshall (ed.), *Poststructuralism and Education*, Dordrecht, Kluewer.

Olssen, M. and Morris-Matthews, K. (1997) (eds.) *Education Policy in New Zealand: The 1990s and Beyond*, Palmerston North (NZ), Dunmore.

Olssen, M. and Peters, M.A. (2005) Neoliberalism, Higher Education and the Knowledge Economy: From the Free Market to Knowledge Capitalism, *Journal of Education Policy* 20, (3): 313–345.

Olssen, M., Codd, J., and O'Neill, A-M. (2004) *Education Policy: Globalization, Citizenship, Democracy.* London, Sage.

O'Malley, P. (1996) Risk and Responsibility. In Barry, A., Osborne, T. and Rose, N. (eds.), *Foucault and Political Reason: Liberalism, Neo-liberalism and Rationalities of Government*, 189–208. London, UCL Press.

O'Manique, J. (1992) Development, Human Rights and Law, *Human Rights Quarterly*, August 14, 3, 383–408.

Ong, A. (2006) *Neoliberalism as Exception: Mutations in Citizenship and Sovereignty.* Durham, NC, Duke University Press.

Osborne, T. (1993) On liberalism, Neo-liberalism and the 'Liberal Profession' of Medicine, *Economy and Society*, 22 (3), 345–356.

Pavlich, G. and Wickham, G. (2001) (Eds.) *Rethinking Law, Society and Governance: Foucault's Bequest*, Oxford, Hart.

Pearson, R. and Pike, G (1989) *The Graduate Labour Market in the 1990s.* IMS Report No. 167. Sussex, Institute of Manpower Studies.

Pearson, R., Seccombe, I., Pike, G., Holly, S. and Connor, H. (1991) *Doctoral Social Scientists and the Labour Market*, IMS Report No. 217. Sussex, Institute of Manpower Studies.

Perry, R.W. and Maurer. B. (2003) (Eds.), *Globalization under Construction: Governmentality, Law, and Identity*, Minneapolis, University of Minnesota Press.

Peters, M. A. (1989) Techno-Science, Rationality and the University: Lyotard on the 'Postmodern Condition,' *Educational Theory*, 39 (2): 93–105.

Peters, M. A. (1990) Postmodernism: The Critique of Reason and the Rise of the New Social Movements, *Sites*, 22 (Autumn): 142–160.

Peters, M. A. (1991) Re-reading Touraine: Postindustrialism and the Future of the University, *Sites*, 23 (Spring):63–83.

Peters, M. A. (1992a) Educational Myth-Making: An Interview with C. E. Beeby, University of Canterbury, unpublished paper.

Peters, M. A. (1992b) Starship Education: Enterprise Culture in New Zealand, *Access*, 11, 1: 1–12.

Peters, M. A. (1993) Postmodernity and Neo-liberalism: Restructuring Education in Aotearoa, *Delta* 47(1): 46–60.

Peters, M. A. (1994) Governmentalidade Neoliberal e Educacao. In T. Tadeu da Silva (ed.), *O Sujeito Educacao, Estudos Foucaulianos*, Rio de Janeiro, Editora Vozes.

Peters, M. A. (1995) (ed.) *Education and the Postmodern Condition*, Foreword by Jean-François Lyotard, Westport, CT and London, Bergin & Garvey.

Peters, M. A. (1996) *Poststructuralism, Politics and Education*, Westport, CT, and London, Bergin and Garvey.

Peters, M. A. (1997a) Introduction: The University in Crisis. In M. A. Peters (Ed.) *Cultural Politics and the University in Aotearoa/New Zealand*. Foreword by Bruce Jesson. Palmerston North, NZ, Dunmore Press: 15–50.

Peters, M. A. (1997b) Neoliberalism, Welfare Dependency and the Moral Construction of Poverty in New Zealand, *New Zealand Journal of Sociology*, 12 (1): 1–34.

Peters, M. A. (2000) *Orthos Logos, Recta Ratio*: Pope John Paul II, Nihilism and Postmodern Philosophy, *Journal for Christian Theological Research*, 5, http://home.apu .edu/~CTRF/jctr.html

Peters, M. A. (2001a) The New Zealand Education Experiment: From Participatory Democracy to Self-Management, ("Valfrihet pa de svagas bekostnad"), translated into Swedish by Leif Mathiasson, *Pedagogiska Magasinet*, No. 1, January: 36–41.

Peters, M. A. (2001b) Education, Enterprise Culture and the Entrepreneurial Self: A Foucauldian Perspective, *Journal of Educational Enquiry*, 2 (2).

Peters, M. A. (2001c) *Poststructuralism, Marxism and Neoliberalism*, Lanham, MD, Rowman & Littlefield.

Peters, M. A. (2001d) Foucault and Governmentality: Understanding The Neoliberal Paradigm of Education Policy, *The School Field*, XII (5/6): 59–80

Peters, M. A. (2001e) National Education Policy Constructions of the 'Knowledge Economy': Towards a Critique, *Journal of Educational Enquiry*, 2 (1), May, (http://www.education.unisa.edu.au/JEE/).

Peters, M. A. (2001f) Foucault, Neoliberalism and the Governance of Welfare, Chapter 4 of *Poststructuralism, Marxism, and Neoliberalism: Between Theory and Politics*, Lanham & Oxford, Rowman & Littlefield.

Peters, M. A. (2002a) Anti-Globalization and Guattari's *The Three Ecologies*, *Globalization*: (http://www.icaap.org/iuicode?193.2.1.2).

Peters, M. A. (2002b) Globalisation and the Knowledge Economy: Implications for Education Policy, *Common Ground* (http://MichaelPeters.Author-Site.com/).

Peters, M. A. (2002c) The University in the Knowledge Economy. In *Scholars and Entrepreneurs: The Universities in Crisis*, Simon Cooper, John Hinkson and Geoff Sharp (eds.), Melbourne, Arena Publications: 137–152.

Peters, M. A. (2002d) New Zealand as the 'Knowledge Society': Universities, the Foresight Project and the Tertiary White Paper, *Leading and Managing*, 6, 2: 16–32.

Peters, M. A. (2002e) Universities, Globalisation and the Knowledge Economy, *Southern Review*, 35 (2).

Peters, M. A. (2003a) *Building Knowledge Cultures: Education in an Age of Knowledge Capitalism*, Lanham, MD, Rowman & Littlefield.

Peters, M. A. (2003b) Educational Research, 'Games of Truth' and the Ethics of Subjectivity, Ethical Educational Research: Practices of the Self, Symposium: Michael A. Peters, Tina Besley, Clare Caddell, BERA.

Peters, M. A. (2003c) Why Foucault? New Directions in Anglo-American Educational Research," Invited keynote at the conference "After Foucault: Perspectives of the Analysis of Discourse and Power in Education," 29–31 October, The University of Dortmund. In Pongratz L. et al. (eds.) (2004) *Nach Foucault. Diskurs- und machtanalytische Perspectiven der Pädagogik*, Wiesbaden, VS Verlag Für Sozialwissenschaften.

Peters, M. A. (2003d) Truth-Telling as an Educational Practice of the Self: Foucault, Parrhesia and the Ethics of Subjectivity, *Oxford Review of Education*, 29 (2): 207–223.

Peters, M. A. (2005a) Foucault, Counselling and the Aesthetics of Existence, *The British Journal of Counselling and Guidance*, 33 (3): 383–396, special issue on Foucault and counselling, Tina Besley and Richard Edwards (eds.).

Peters, M. A. (2005b) The New Prudentialism in Education: Actuarial Rationality and the Entrepreneurial Self, in *Educational Theory*, 55 (2): 123–137, special issue on education and risk, Padraig Hogan and Paul Smeyers (eds.).

Peters, M. A. (2005c) Citizen-Consumers, Social Markets and the Reform of Public Services, *Policy Futures in Education*, 2 (3–4), 2004.

Peters, M. A. (2010) Three Forms of Knowledge Economy: Learning, Creativity, Openness, *British Journal of Educational Studies*, 58 (1): 67–88.

Peters, M. A. and Besley, T. (2008) Academic Entrepreneurship and the Creative Economy, *Thesis Eleven*, 95.

Peters, M. A. and Marshall, J. D. (1988) Social Policy and the Move to Community, and Social Policy and the Move to Community: Practical Suggestions for the delivery of Welfare Services. In *Future Directions*, 3(2), The Royal Commission on Social Policy, Wellington, Government Printer: 657–702.

Peters, M. A. and Marshall, J. D. (1996) *Individualism and Community: Education and Social Policy in the Postmodern Condition*, London, Falmer Press.

Peters, M. A. and Olssen, M. (1999) Compulsory Education in a Competition State. In J. Boston, P. Dalziel, and S. St John (eds.) *Redesigning New Zealand's Welfare State*, Auckland, Oxford University Press: 164–192.

Peters, M. A. and Roberts, P. (1999) *University Futures and the Politics of Reform*, Palmerston North, NZ, Dunmore Press.

Peters, M. A., Rodrigo Britez, R. and Bulut, E. (2010) Cybernetic Capitalism, Informationalism, and Cognitive Labor, *Geopolitics, History and International Relations*, 1 (2): 1–15.

Pieterse, J. N. (2000) (Ed.), *Global Futures: Shaping Globalization*, New York, Zed Books.

Pignatelli, F. (1993) Dangers, Possibilities: Ethico-Political Choices in the Work of Michel Foucault, at: http://www.ed.uiuc.edu/EPS/PES-Yearbook/93_docs/PIGNATEL.HTM

Polanyi, M. (1958) *Personal Knowledge: Towards a Post-Critical Philosophy*, London, Routledge & Kegan Paul.

Polanyi, M. (1967) *The Tacit Dimension*. London, Routledge and Kegan Paul.

Pollin, R. (2003) *Contours of Descent: U.S. Economic Fractures and the Landscape of Global Austerity*. New York, Verso.

Popper, K.(2008) *Popper, After the Open Society*, Shearmur and Turner (eds.), London, Routledge.

Poster, M. (1989) *The Mode of Information: Poststructuralism and the Social Context*. Cambridge, Polity Press.

PSA (1989) *Private Power or Public Interest? Widening the Debate on Privatisation*. Palmerston North (NZ), Dunmore Press.

Pusey, M. (1992) *Economic Rationalism in Canberra*, Cambridge, Cambridge University Press.

Raulet, G. (1983) Structuralism and Post-Structuralism: An Interview with Michel Foucault, *Telos*, 53:195–211.

Rawls, J. (1971) *A Theory of Justice*. Cambridge, Massachusetts, Belknap Press of Harvard University Press.

Rawls, J. (1993) *Political Liberalism*. The John Dewey Essays in Philosophy, 4. New York, Columbia University Press.

Rawls, J. (2001) *Justice as Fairness: A Restatement*. Cambridge, Massachusetts, Belknap Press.

Reinhart, C. A. and K. S. Rogoff (2008) The Aftermath of Financial Crises, at http://www.economics.harvard.edu/faculty/rogoff/files/Aftermath.pdf

Reisman, D. (1990) *The Political Economy of James Buchanan*. College Station, Texas A&M University Press.

Renwick, W. (1998) Fraser on Education. In Clark, Margaret (1998) ed. *Peter Fraser Master Politician*, Palmerston North, NZ., Dunmore Press

Report of the Change Team on Targeting Social Assistance (1991) Department of the Prime Minister and Cabinet, Parliament Buildings, Wellington.

Richardson, R. (NZ Minister of Finance) (1991) *Budget 1991*, Wellington, Government Printer.

Romer, P. M. (1986) Increasing Returns and Long-Run Growth, *Journal of Political Economy* 94(5), pp.1002–37.

Romer, P. M. (1990) Endogenous Technological Change, *Journal of Political Economy* 98(5), 71–102.

Romer, P. M. (1990) Endogenous Technological Change, *Journal of Political Economy* 98(5), pp. 71–102.

Romer, P. M. (1994) The Origins of Endogamous Growth, *The Journal of Economic Perspectives*, 8.

Rorty, R. (1993) Human Rights, Rationality, and Sentimentality. In Stephen Shute and Susan Hurley (Eds.) *On Human Rights*, The Oxford Amnesty Lectures 1993, New York, Basic Books: 111–134.

Rose, N. (1996) Governing 'advanced' liberal democracies. In A. Barry, T. Osborne, and N. Rose (Eds.), *Foucault and Political Reason*. Chicago, University of Chicago Press, pp. 37–64.

Rose, N. (1999) *Powers of Liberty*. Cambridge, Cambridge University Press.

Rose, N., O'Malley, P. and Valverde, M. (2006) Governmentality, *Annual Review of Law and Social Science*, December 2006, Vol. 2, Pages 83–104

Rosenberg, W. (1977) Full Employment: The Fulcrum of the Welfare State. In A.D. Trlin, Ed, *Social Welfare and New Zealand Society*. Methuen, Wellington, pp. 45–68.

Ruccio, D. and Amariglio, J. (2003) *Postmodern Moments in Modern Economics*. Princeton, Princeton University Press.

Sackett, D.L., Rosenberg, W.M.C., Muir Gray, J.A., Brian Haynes, R. and Scott Richardson, W. (1996) Evidence-Based medicine: what it is and what it isn't, *British Medical Journal*, Vol 312, No. 7023, pp. 71–72.

Sawyer, M. (1982) Introduction. In M. Sawyer (ed.) *Australia and the New Right*, Sydney, Allen and Unwin.

Schatzki, T., Knorr Cetiona, K., Von Savigny, E. (Eds.) (2001) *The Practice Turn in Contemporary Theory.* London & New York, Routledge.

Schultz, T. (1963) *The Economic Value of Education*, New York, University of Columbia Press.

Scissors, D. (2009) Deng Undone: The Costs of Halting Market Reform in China, *Foreign Affairs*, May/June: 24–39.

Scott, G. and P. Gorringe (1989) Reform of the Core Public Sector: The New Zealand Experience, *Australian Journal of Public Administration*, 48(1), pp. 81–92.

Scott, G. (1997) The New Institutional Economics and the Shaping of the State in New Zealand. In G. Davis, B. Sullivan and A. Yeatman (Eds.) *The New Contractualism?* Melbourne, Macmillan Education, pp. 154–163.

Scott, G., Bushnell, P. and Sallee, N. (1990) Reform of the core public sector: New Zealand experience. *Governance: An International Journal of Policy and Administration*, 3 (2), 138–167.

Sending, O. J. and Iver, B. Neumann (2006) Governance to Governmentality: Analysing States, NGOs, and Power, *International Studies Quarterly* 50 (3): 651–672.

Sexton, S. (1991) *New Zealand Schools: An Evaluation of Recent Reforms and Future Directions*. Wellington, New Zealand Business Roundtable.

Shearmur, J. (1998) Popper, Hayek, and the Poverty of Historicism Part I: A Largely Bibliographical Essay, *Philosophy of the Social Sciences*; 28; 434.

Shiller, Robert J. (2008) *The Subprime Solution: How Today's Global Financial Crisis Happened, and What to Do about It.* Princeton, Princeton University Press.

Shiller, R. J. (2000) *Irrational Exuberance*. Princeton, Princeton University Press.

Simkins, T. (2000) Education Reform and Managerialism: Comparing the Experience of Schools and Colleges. *Journal of Education Policy* 15 (3), 317–332.

Smith, L. (NZ Minister of Education) (1991) *Investing in People: Our Greatest Asset*, Wellington, Government Printer.

Smith, L. (NZ Minister of Education) (1992) Address to the 'Education for Enterprise' Conference, Parliament Buildings, Wellington, 12 February.

Solow, R. M. (1956) A Contribution to the Theory of Economic Growth, *Quarterly Journal of Economics*, 70, 65–94.

Solow, R. M. (1994) Perspectives on Growth Theory, *Journal of Economic Perspectives*, 8, 45–54.

Stehr, N. (1994) *Knowledge Societies*, London, Sage Publications.

Stewart, T. A. (1997) *Intellectual Capital: The New Wealth of Organizations*, London, Nicholas Brealey.

Stiglitz, J. (1999a) Knowledge as a Global Public Good, September at: http://www.world-bank.org/knowledge/chiefecon/index2.htm.

Stiglitz, J. (1999b) Public Policy for a Knowledge Economy, Remarks at the Department for Trade and Industry and Center for Economic Policy Research, London, Jan. 27 http://www.worldbank.org/html/extdr/extme/jssp012799a.htm.

Stiglitz, J. (1999c) On Liberty, The Right to Know, and Public Discourse: The Role of Transparency in Public Life, Oxford Amnesty Lecture, Oxford, U.K., January 27, http://www.worldbank.org/html/extdr/extme/jssp012799.htm.

Stiglitz, J. (2002) *Globalization and Its Discontents*, London, Allen Lane.

Streit, M. S. and Wohlgemuth, M. (1997) The Market Economy and the State: Hayekian and Ordoliberal Conceptions, at http://www.dundee.ac.uk/cepmlp/journal/html/vol4/Vol4–19.pdf.

Sutch, W. B. (1966) *The Quest for Security in New Zealand, 1840–1966*. London, Oxford University Press.

Sutch, W. B. (1971) *The Responsible Society in New Zealand*. Christchurch, Whitcombe and Tombs.

Tagma, H. M.(2006) Sovereignty, Governmentality and the State of Exception: 'Terrorism' and the Camp as the Constitutive Outside. Paper presented at the annual meeting of the International Studies Association, Town & Country Resort and Convention Center, San Diego, California, Mar 22, 2006 http://www.allacademic.com/meta/p100533_index.html.

Thurow, L. (1996) *The Future of Capitalism: How Today's Economic Forces Shape Tomorrow's World*. London, Nicholas Breasley.

Touraine, A. (1974) *The Post-Industrial Society: Tomorrow's Social History, Classes, Conflicts and Culture in the Programmed Society*, trans. L. Mayhew, London, Wildwood House.

Treasury, The (1984) *Economic Management*. Wellington, Government Printer.

Treasury, The (1987) *Government Management: Volume II—Education Issues*. Wellington, Government Printer.

Treasury, The (1996) *Briefing to the Incoming Government: 1996*. Wellington, New Zealand Treasury.

Trosa, S. (1994) *Next Steps: Moving On*. London, HMSO.

Turner, B. S. (1993) Outline of a Theory of Human Rights, *Sociology*, August, 27 (3), 489(24).

Turner, R. S. (2007) The 'Rebirth of Liberalism': The Origins of Neo-liberal Ideology, *Journal of Political Ideologies* (February), 12(1), 67–83.

Turner, S. (1994) *The Social Theory of Practices: Tradition, Tacit Knowledge, and Presuppositions*. Chicago, Chicago University Press.

Tweeten, L. and Zulauf, C. (1999) The Challenge of Postmodernism to Applied Economics, *American Journal of Agricultural Economics*, Dec, 81, 5, 1166.

Upton, S (1987) *The Withering of the State*. Wellington, Allen and Unwin.

Valverde, M. (1996) Despotism and Ethical Legal Governance. *Economy and Society*, 25(3), 357–372.

Van Horn, R. and Mirowski, P. (2005) The Road to a World Made Safe for Corporations: The Rise of the Chicago School of Economics. Retrieved from www.uri.edu/artsci/ecn/starkey/ECN342/Corporations_Chicago.pdf.

Vanberg, V. (2004) The Freiburg School: Walter Eucken and Ordoliberalism, Freiburg Discussion Papers on Constitutional Economics, at http://opus.zbw-kiel.de/volltexte/2004/2324/pdf/04_11bw.pdf.

Ventura, H.E., Miller, J.M. and Mathieu Deflem, M. (2005) Governmentality and the War on Terror: FBI Project Carnivore and the Diffusion of Disciplinary Power, *Critical Criminology* 13(1): 55–70.

Vernon, R. (1976) The 'Great Society' and the 'Open Society': Liberalism in Hayek and Popper, *Canadian Journal of Political Science*, 9 (2): 261–276.

von Mises, L. (1922) *Socialism: An Economic and Sociological Analysis*. Retrieved from http://mises.org/books/socialism/contents.aspx.

von Mises, L. (1927) *Liberalism (Liberalismus)*. Jena, Gustav Fischer Verlag.

Waldron, J. (1984) (ed.) *Theories of Rights*. New York, Oxford University Press.

Walsh, P. (1992) The Employment Contracts Act. In J. Boston and P. Daziel (Eds.), *The Decent Society? Essays in Response to National's Economic and Social Policies*, Auckland, Oxford University Press: 59–76.

Walters, W., and Haahr, J. H. (2006) *Governing Europe: Discourse, Governmentality and European Integration*. London, Routledge.

Walzer, M. (1983) *Spheres of Justice*, New York, Basic Books.

Walzer, M.(1995) Response, in Miller, D. and Walzer, M. (eds.), *Pluralism, Justice, and Equality*. Oxford, Oxford University Press: 281–298.

Ward, A. (1990) Review of *The Ideal Society and Its Enemies*, *New Zealand Journal of History*, 24(1): 73–78.

Watts, M. (2003) Development and Governmentality. *Singapore Journal of Tropical Geography*, Volume 24 (1): 1–144

Welch, Anthony (1997) *Class, Culture and the State in Australian Education: Reform or Crisis?* New York, Peter Lang.

Williamson, O. E. (1975) *Markets and Hierarchies*. New York, The Free Press.

Williamson, O. E. (1983) Organisational Innovation: The Transaction-Cost Approach. In J. Ronen, (Ed.) *Entrepreneurship*. Lexington, MA: Heath Lexington, 101–34.

Williamson, O. E. (1985) *The Economic Institutions of Capitalism: Firms, Markets, Relational Contracting*. New York, The Free Press.

Williamson, O. E. (1991) Comparative Economic Organization: The Analysis of Discrete Structural Alternatives. *Administrative Science Quarterly*, 36, 269–96.

Williamson, O. E. (1992) Markets, Hierarchies and the Modern Corporation: An Unfolding Perspective. *Journal of Economic Behaviour and Organisation*, 17, 335–52.

Williamson, O. E. (1994) Institutions and Economic Organization: The Governance Perspective. Paper prepared for the World Bank's Annual Conference on Development Economics, April 28–29, Washington DC.

Witt, U. (2002) Germany's 'Social Market Economy': Between Social Ethos and Rent Seeking, *The Independent Review*, IV (3): 365–375.

World Bank, The (1998) *World Development Report: Knowledge for Development*, Oxford, Oxford University Press.

Wylie, C. (1994) *Self-Managing Schools in New Zealand: The Fifth Year*. Wellington, New Zealand Council for Educational Research.

Young, I. M. (1990) *Justice and the Politics of Difference*. Princeton, Princeton University Press.

Zappia, C. (1999) The Economics of Information, Market Socialism and Hayek's Legacy. *History of Economic Ideas*. Vol. 1–2, (http://www.econ-pol.unisi.it/dipartimento/zappia.html).

Zechenter, E. M. (1997) In the Name of Culture: Cultural Relativism and the Abuse of the Individual. *Journal of Anthropological Research*, Fall, 53, 3, 319.

A.C. (Tina) Besley, Michael A. Peters,
Cameron McCarthy, Fazal Rizvi
General Editors

Global Studies in Education is a book series that addresses the implications of the powerful dynamics associated with globalization for re-conceptualizing educational theory, policy and practice. The general orientation of the series is inter-disciplinary. It welcomes conceptual, empirical and critical studies that explore the dynamics of the rapidly changing global processes, connectivities and imagination, and how these are reshaping issues of knowledge creation and management and economic and political institutions, leading to new social identities and cultural formations associated with education.

We are particularly interested in manuscripts that offer: a) new theoretical, and methodological, approaches to the study of globalization and its impact on education; b) ethnographic case studies or textual/discourse based analyses that examine the cultural identity experiences of youth and educators inside and outside of educational institutions; c) studies of education policy processes that address the impact and operation of global agencies and networks; d) analyses of the nature and scope of transnational flows of capital, people and ideas and how these are affecting educational processes; e) studies of shifts in knowledge and media formations, and how these point to new conceptions of educational processes; f) exploration of global economic, social and educational inequalities and social movements promoting ethical renewal.

For additional information about this series or for the submission of manuscripts, please contact one of the series editors:

A.C. (Tina) Besley: tbesley@illinois.edu
Cameron McCarthy: cmccart1@illinois.edu
Michael A. Peters: mpet001@illinois.edu
Fazal Rizvi: frizvi@unimelb.edu.au

Department of Educational Policy Studies
University of Illinois at Urbana-Champaign
1310 South Sixth Street
Champaign, IL 61820   USA

To order other books in this series, please contact our Customer Service Department:

(800) 770-LANG (within the U.S.)
(212) 647-7706 (outside the U.S.)
(212) 647-7707 FAX

Or browse online by series:
www.peterlang.com